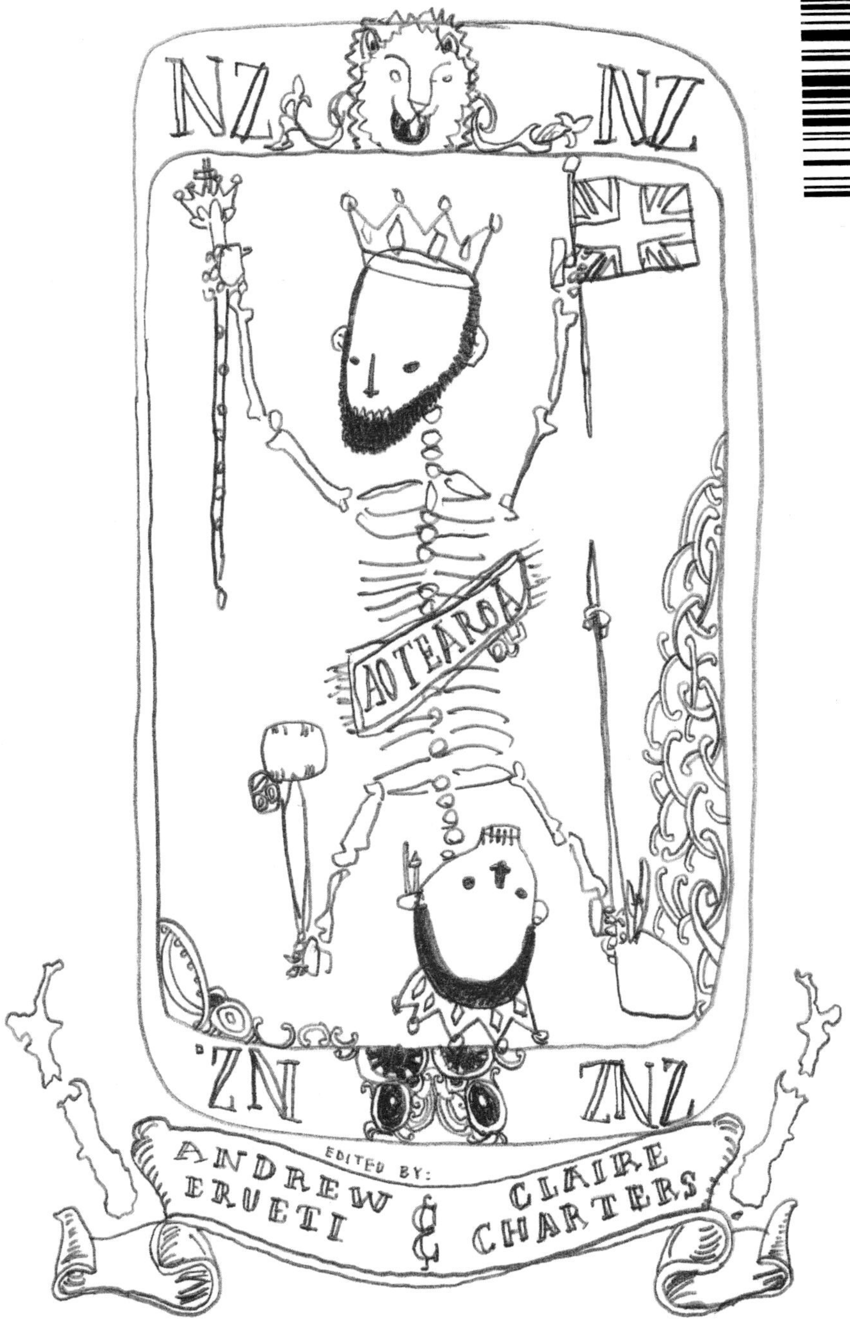
NZ
NZ
AOTEAROA
ZN
ZNZ
EDITED BY:
ANDREW ERUETI
&
CLAIRE CHARTERS

Māori Property Rights and the Foreshore and Seabed
The Last Frontier

Edited by
Claire Charters and Andrew Erueti

Victoria University Press

VICTORIA UNIVERSITY PRESS
Victoria University of Wellington
PO Box 600 Wellington

Copyright © the editors and contributors 2007

First published 2007

This book is copyright. Apart from any fair dealing for the purpose of private study, research, criticism or review, as permitted under the Copyright Act, no part may be reproduced by any process without the permission of the publishers.

National Library of New Zealand Cataloguing-in-Publication Data

Māori property rights and the foreshore and seabed : the last frontier / edited by Claire Charters and Andrew Erueti.
Includes index.
ISBN 978-0-86473-553-9
1. Seashore—Law and legislation—New Zealand. 2. Ocean bottom—Law and legislation—New Zealand. 3. Customary law —New Zealand. 4. Maori (New Zealand people)—Legal status, laws, etc. 5. Maori (New Zealand people)—Claims.
[1. Takutai moana. 2. Kaitiakitanga. 3. Ture whenua.]
I. Charters, Claire. II. Erueti, Andrew K.
346.93043—dc 22

Printed by Printlink, Wellington
Typeset by Ahi Text Solutions, Wellington

Contents

Preface	*The Honourable Edward Taihakurei Durie*	vii
Table of Cases		ix
Table of Statutes		xiii
Introduction	*Claire Charters and Andrew Erueti*	1

PART ONE – HISTORICAL PERSPECTIVE

Foreshore and Seabed in New Zealand Law: A Legal-Historical Introduction	*Richard Boast*	9
Wi Parata is Dead, Long Live *Wi Parata*	*David V Williams*	31

PART TWO – COMPARATIVE PERSPECTIVE

An Australian Comparison on Native Title to the Foreshore and Seabed	*Shaunnagh Dorsett*	59
Legal Rights and Legislative Wrongs: Māori Claims to the Foreshore and Seabed	*Kent McNeil*	83

PART THREE – SPECIFIC ISSUES

The Foreshore and Seabed Legislation: Resource- and Marine-Management Issues	*Catherine Iorns Magallanes*	119
Fiduciary Duties to Māori and the Foreshore and Seabed Act 2004: How Does it Compare and What Have Māori Lost?	*Claire Charters*	143

PART FOUR – INTERNATIONAL PERSPECTIVE

The Recognition of Indigenous Peoples' Rights to Traditional Lands: The Evaluation of States by International Treaty Bodies	*Andrew Erueti*	175

Contributors	206
Index	208

Preface

In this era of indigenous peoples' rights recognition, states around the globe are faced with reconciling the pre-existing, inherent rights of indigenous peoples with those held and asserted by the state. In New Zealand we have made significant progress but there remain many outstanding and controversial questions about the status of Māori and their Treaty and customary rights. This fact was brought into sharp focus by the Court of Appeal decision of *Ngati Apa*.

The decision was one of the most controversial in the modern cases on Māori rights. It drew a strong response from Māori and Pākehā New Zealanders as they struggled to come to terms with its full implications. Did the decision grant Māori tribes exclusive rights to the New Zealand coastline or was it merely an endorsement of their right to engage in long-practised traditional activities? It was quickly decided by government that Parliament would intervene and enact legislation to administer Māori customary claims to foreshore. However, the speed with which the legislation was enacted left little time for meaningful debate and reflection.

Now that the dust has settled it is time to reflect more fully on these matters. This collection of essays does not aim to be an exhaustive treatment of the legal issues raised by *Ngati Apa* and the Foreshore and Seabed Act 2004 (the FSA). It does, however, address many of the most salient. Topics covered include the historical origins of *Ngati Apa*, how the FSA compares with schemes created in other countries with indigenous inhabitants, and how the FSA compares with international human rights law and environmental law. They are essays written by leading academics on topics within their area of expertise. The general tenor is that New Zealand in its haste has enacted legislation that undermines the rights of Māori tribes. In short, the view is that the reconciliation process has tipped too far in favour of the rights of the state and non-Māori.

These essays will contribute towards a deeper understanding of the foreshore debate. They should also stimulate further discussion about the on-going process of reconciliation in New Zealand. While the foreshore may be the last land frontier in the extinguishment of native title, there are other challenging issues ahead of us. *Ngati Apa* should provide a valuable lesson for the future.

The Honourable Edward Taihakurei Durie

Table of Cases

Amodu Tijani v Secretary, Southern Nigeria (1921)	45 n 51, 85 n 13
Apirana Mahuika et al v New Zealand (15 November 2000)	197 nn
Assets v Mere Roihi (1905)	10 n 6
Attorney-General for Canada v Hallet and Carey Ltd (1952)	103 n 88
Attorney-General v Emerson (1891)	9 n 3
Attorney-General v Ngati Apa (2003)	1, 2, 3, 4, 5, 6, 9, 10, 21, 23, 27 n 75, 29, 31, 42, 45, 47–49, 50–51, 57, 60 n 4, 68, 80, 83, 84, 85–89, 90, 93, 94, 97, 102, 103, 115, 116, 117, 118, 122, 126, 128, 138, 143, 170, 171, 175, 186, 196
Bernard Ominayak, Chief of the Lubicon Lake Band v Canada (1990)	197 n 97
Blueberry River Indian Band v Canada (Department of Indian Affairs and Northern Development) (1995)	151, 152 nn, 158, 159, 164, 171
Boardman v Phipps (1967)	144 n 4
Brader v Ministry of Transport (1981)	103 n 88
Bulun Bulun v R & T Textiles Pty Ltd (1998)	66 n 24
Cherokee Nation v Georgia (1831)	148 n 20, 156
Colet v R (1981)	103 n 88
Colonial Sugar Refining Co v Melbourne Harbour Trust Commissioners (1927)	103 n 88
Confederated Salish and Kootenai Tribes v Namen (1982)	16 n 28
County of Oneida v Oneida Indian Nation (1985)	156 n 72
Cramer v United States (1923)	156 n 68
De Rose v South Australia (2002)	76
Delgamuukw v British Columbia (1997)	61, 62 n 9, 63, 64, 74, 85–6, 88 n 30, 91 n 36, 98 n 62, 109, 110, 111, 112, 113–14, 155 n 60, 180–1, 182, 183, 184 n 47, 185 n 49, 191 n 72
Everton v Attorney-General (2000)	167 n 104
Fairford First Nation v Canada (Attorney-General) (1999)	152
Faulkner v Tauranga District Council (1996)	13 n 15
Fejo v Northern Territory (1998)	69 n 36, 105
Fleetwing Farms Ltd v Marlborough District Council (1997)	123 n 16, 124 n 25
Frame v Smith (1987)	145
Gann v Free Fishers of Whitstable (1865)	9 n 3
Gotobed v Pridmore (1970)	115 n 143
Graham v Attorney-General (1966)	103 n 88
Guerin v The Queen (1984)	86 n 13, 150, 151, 153, 154, 157, 159, 162, 164, 167, 171

Haida Nation v British Columbia (Minister of Forests) (2004)	63nn, 79, 148, 149n26, 153, 154nn, 158, 170, 171, 172, 174
Heath v Deane (1905)	106n102
Hohepa Wi Neera v Bishop of Wellington (1902)	38n24, 51
Hopu and Bessert v France (1997)	197
Hospital Products Ltd v United States Surgical Corporation (1984)	145n5
Inupiat Community of the Arctic Slope v United States (1982)	66n25
Joint Tribal Council of Passamaquoddy Tribe v Morton (1975)	156n71
Kai Tohu o Puketapu Hapu Incorporated v Attorney-General and Te Atiawa Iwi Authority (1999)	168
Kauwaeranga (1870)	15, 97n32
Keech v Sandford (1726)	144n4
Keepa v Inspector of Fisheries (1965)	23, 28
Kitchooalik and Tucktoo, Re (1972)	107n105
LAC Minerals Ltd v International Corona Resources (1989)	145
Lake Omapere (1929)	19
Lane v Pueblo of Santa Rosa (1918)	156n68
Lundon and Whitaker Claims Act 1871, Re (1872)	45
Mabo v Queensland (No 1) (1988)	95, 96
Mabo v Queensland (No 2) (1992)	11, 12, 18, 63, 64, 65, 68, 75n63, 83n3, 85n13, 87n24, 88n27, 103, 105, 108, 111, 115, 116, 157, 160, 162, 163, 164, 178n10, 179n12, 184
Manchester Band of Pomo Indians v United States (1973)	156n68
Manu Kapua v Para Haimona (1913)	45n51
Maya Indigenous Communities of the Toledo District v Belize (2004)	189n62, 190, 191, 192, 193, 199, 204
Mayagna (Sumo) Awas Tingni Community v Nicaragua (2001)	189, 190, 191, 192, 193, 199, 204
Members of the Yorta Yorta Aboriginal Community v Victoria (2002)	63, 64n17, 65, 66, 71, 72n52, 76, 77, 83n3, 87n, 104–5, 108, 115, 116, 179nn
Milroy v Attorney-General (2003)	168nn
Mitchell v MNR (2001)	100n70, 114n139
Moffat v Kazana (1969)	115n143
Montana v United States (1981)	16n28
Morton v Ruiz (1974)	156n71
Native Village of Eyak v Evans (2004)	86n19
Native Village of Eyak v Trawler Diane Marie Inc (1998)	66n25, 86n19
Nevada v United States (1983)	156n70
New South Wales v Commonwealth (1975)	67n26
New Windsor Corporation v Mellor (1975)	106n102
New Zealand Air Line Pilots Association v Attorney-General (1997)	103n86
New Zealand Maori Council v Attorney-General & Ors (2000)	167n106
New Zealand Maori Council v Attorney-General (1987)	161, 165, 169

New Zealand Maori Council v Attorney-General (1996)	166, 167, 169
Ngai Tahu Maori Trust Board v Director-General of Conservation (1993)	164, 165, 169
Ngakororo (1942)	24, 25nn
Nireaha Tamaki v Baker (1901)	10n5, 13n15, 19, 24, 34, 38, 39, 45n51, 48, 51, 84
Osoyoos Indian Band v Oliver (Town of) (2001)	151, 152, 159, 172
Parumoana (1883)	15
Pascoe Ltd v DFC Overseas Investments Ltd (1994)	144n4
Puyullap Indian Tribe v Port of Tacoma (1883)	16–17n27, 17n29
Pyramid Land Paiute Tribe of Nations v Morton (1973)	156n68
Quilter v Attorney-General (1998)	103n86
R v Adams (1996)	61, 112n129, 155,
R v Bernard (2000)	182n27
R v Bernard (2003)	182n34
R v Bernard (2005)	62n9, 98n62, 112, 113n133, 182, 183
R v Côté (1996)	62n8, 110n119,
R v Gladstone (1996)	76n66, 78n74, 81n82, 108, 109, 111, 155
R v Kruger (1985)	151
R v Marshall (2001)	182n27
R v Marshall (2003)	182n34
R v Marshall (2004)	111, 112, 114n136, 149n26
R v Marshall (2005)	62, 64, 98n62, 112nn, 113n133, 182, 183
R v Powley (2003)	88n30, 114n138
R v Sappier; R v Gray (2007)	101, 102nn, 113n131
R v Sparrow (1990)	63n11, 100n70, 151, 153, 155, 158, 160, 162
R v Symonds (1847)	35, 37, 38, 50, 89n31, 116n148
R v Van der Peet (1996)	62n7, 76n66, 81n82, 83n2, 88n29, 98, 99nn, 100nn, 101nn, 102, 107, 108n111, 109, 110, 111, 114, 155, 185n49
Rama v Millar (1996)	144n4
Reg v Keyn (1876)	67, 68
Saanichtan Marina Ltd v Claxton (1989)	63n11
Sampson v Hoddinott (1857)	115n143
Sandra Lovelace v Canada (1981)	197n94
Scales v Key (1840)	106
Sellers v Maritime Safety Inspector (1999)	103n86
Semiahmoo Indian Band v Canada (1998)	151, 152n40, 158, 171
Seminole Nation v United States (1942)	156n70
Simpson v Gowers (1981)	115n143
Sims v Craig Bell & Bond (1991)	144n4

Swan v Sinclair (1924)	115n143
Tamihana Korokai v Solicitor-General (1912)	17, 20, 23, 40
Te Runanga o Muriwhenua v Attorney-General (1990)	45n51, 148n22, 161, 162, 164, 165, 169
Te Runanga o Ngai Tahu v Attorney-General & Ors (2003)	167n107, 169
Te Runanga o Te Ika Whenua v Attorney-General (1994)	21, 45n51, 148n22, 163, 164nn, 165, 166, 169, 171
Te Runanga o Wharekauri Rekohu Inc v Attorney-General (1993)	148n22, 161n83, 162, 163nn, 165, 168, 169, 171
Te Teira Te Paea v Te Roera Tareha (1902)	10n6
Te Waka Hi Ika o Te Arawa v Treaty of Waitangi Fisheries Commission (2000)	165, 166
Te Weehi v Regional Fisheries Officer (1986)	12, 23, 29
Tehidy Minerals Ltd v Norman (1971)	115n143
The Bed of the Wanganui River, Re (1955)	22
The Bed of the Wanganui River, Re (1962)	21, 22, 28, 40n35
The Lardil People v State of Queensland (2004)	60, 70, 71nn, 72, 73, 78, 86n16
The Ninety-Mile Beach, In re (1963)	5, 9, 15, 23, 25, 26, 27, 28n77, 29, 45, 47, 48, 49, 85, 116
The Ninety-Mile Beach, Re (1957)	25n70, 26n72
The Wik Peoples v Queensland (1996)	68, 69, 77n71, 78n72
Tucktoo and Kitchooalik, Re (1972)	107n105
United States v Aam (1989)	16–17n28
United States v Creek Nation (1935)	156n68
United States v Kagama (1886)	156
Waipapakura v Hempton (1914)	24, 45
Wallis v Solicitor-General (1903)	38, 45n51, 84n5
Ward v Ward (1852)	115n143
Ward v Western Australia (1998)	78n
Watene & Ors v The Minister in Charge of the Treaty of Waitangi (2001)	168n110
Western Australia v Commonwealth (1995)	59, 68, 96
Western Australia v Ward (2000)	76n75
Western Australia v Ward (2002)	64, 65, 66, 71, 72, 76n64, 77n71, 78, 79, 87n24, 179n15, 185, 193
Wewaykum Indian Band v Canada (2002)	152, 153, 154, 158, 171
Wi Parata v Bishop of Wellington (1877)	4, 19, 31, 32, 34, 37, 38, 39, 40, 44, 45, 46, 48, 51, 57, 58, 84, 116
Williams v Phillips (1957)	115n143
Wyld v Silver (1963)	107
Yarmirr v Northern Territory (1998)	60, 60n, 66, 67, 67n, 68, 69, 69n, 70, 71, 72, 73, 86n, 87n, 149, 160
Yateley Common, Re (1977)	106

Table of Statutes

Aquaculture Reform Act 2004	11
Biosecurity Amendment Act 2004	12 n 10, 127 n 39
Coal Mines Act 1925	21 n 54
Coal Mines Act 1979	21 n 54
Coal Mines Amendment Act 1903	21
Conservation Amendment Act 2004	2 n 10, 127 n 39
Constitution Act 1982 (Canada)	61, 98, 110, 112, 114, 148, 155
Constitution Act 1986	55
Crown Grants Act 1866	47
English Laws Act 1858	34, 50
English Laws Act 1908	34 n 9
Fisheries (Kaimoana Customary Fishing) Regulations 1998	127 n 40
Fisheries (South Island Customary Fishing) Regulations 1999	127 n 40
Fisheries Act 1983	46
Fisheries Act 1988 (NT) (Australia)	73 n 59
Fisheries Act 1994 (Qld) (Australia)	74 n 60
Fisheries Act 1996	123 n 15, 127 n 15
Fisheries Amendment Act (No 3) 2004	12 n 10, 127 n 39
Foreshore and Seabed Act 2004	1, 2, 3, 4, 5, 6, 11, 29, 32, 44, 57, 59, 60, 61, 74, 77, 78, 79n, 78, 81, 82, 83, 84, 89, 90, 91, 92, 93, 94, 95, 96, 97, 102, 103, 115, 117, 133, 135 n 83, 136, 137 n 96, 139 n n 107, 108; 141 n 111, 143, 144, 146, 147, 148, 158, 159, 160, 161, 169, 170, 171, 172, 173, 174, 175, 176, 186, 187, 188, 195, 196, 205
Foreshore and Seabed Endowment Revesting Act 1991	48, 85
Geothermal Energy Act 1953	11
Harbour Act 1855	84–5
Harbours Act 1866	47
Harbours Act 1878	84–5
Horowhenua Lake Act 1925	20 n 52
Imperial Laws Application Act 1988	34 n 9
Lake Waikaremoana Act 1971	20
Land (Titles and Traditional Usages) Act 1993 (WA) (Australia)	59 n 2, 96
Land Claims Ordinance 1841	33
Land Titles Protection Act 1902	38 n 25, 58
Limitation Act 1950	46
Local Government Act 2002	135
Maori Affairs Amendment Act 1967	54

Maori Commercial Aquaculture Claims Settlement Act 2004	11, 44
Maori Fisheries Act 1989	167n108
Maori Fisheries Act 2004	44, 87n21,
Maori Land Claims Adjustment and Laws Amendment Act 1904	38n25
Marine Farming Act 1971	11, 122
Native Land Act 1902	19
Native Land Act 1909	38
Native Land Amendment and Native Land Claims Adjustment Act 1922	20n49
Native Land Amendment and Native Land Claims Adjustment Act 1926	20n51
Native Land Claims Adjustment Act 1921	20n52
Native Lands Act 1862	36
Native Lands Act 1867	14
Native Rights Act 1865	37, 51, 88n27,
Native Title Act 1993 (Cth) (NTA) (Australia)	5, 63–6, 67, 72, 73, 77, 79, 81, 87n24, 88n27, 104, 105, 115, 116, 174, 179, 194–5, 196, 198, 205
Native Title Amendment Act 1998 (Cth)	104n92
New Zealand Bill of Rights Act 1990	3, 96n58
New Zealand Settlements Act 1863	36
Poukawa Native Reserve Act 1903	20n52
Racial Discrimination Act 1975 (Cth) (Australia)	59, 96
Reserves and Other Lands Disposal Act 1914	20n52
Reserves and Other Lands Disposal Act 1956	20n52
Reserves and Other Lands Disposal and Public Bodies Empowering Act 1907	20n52
Resource Management (Foreshore and Seabed) Amendment Act 2004	6, 32, 119n1, 134n80, 137
Resource Management Act 1991	21n54, 22, 93, 119, 120, 121, 122, 123, 124, 128, 129, 130, 131, 132, 133, 134, 135, 136, 137, 138, 139, 140
Resource Management Amendment Act 1993	123n15
State-Owned Enterprises Act 1986	161n83
Supreme Court Act 2003	31n2
Te Ture Whenua Maori Act (No 3) 2004	12n10, 127n39
Te Ture Whenua Maori Act 1993	2, 39n27, 45, 46n56, 47, 88n27, 159n80, 171
Territorial Sea Act 1965	21
Territorial Sea Act 1977	21
Territorial Sea and Fishing Zone Act 1965	85
Territorial Sea, Contiguous Zone and Exclusive Economic Zone Act 1977	85
Treaty of Waitangi (Fisheries Claims) Settlement Act 1992	46n57, 87n21, 92

Introduction

Claire Charters and Andrew Erueti

The title of this book, *Māori Property Rights and the Foreshore and Seabed: The Last Frontier*, encapsulates that the foreshore and seabed is the most recent and final frontier on which the indigenous peoples of New Zealand and the colonising government have clashed over customary land rights. It reflects that the New Zealand Government has now confiscated, as it did on other 'frontiers', any remaining robust property interests Māori had in New Zealand's outer boundaries.

We hope this book will enrich ongoing discourse on the foreshore and seabed. The catalyst for this book is our concern that there has been insufficient examination of the issues raised by the *Attorney-General v Ngati Apa* (*Ngati Apa*) decision and the Government's response to it.[1] There simply wasn't the time for this analysis in the fast-evolving and highly politically charged seventeen months between *Ngati Apa* and the enactment of the Foreshore and Seabed Act 2004 (the FSA). This point has been made many times, not least by the Waitangi Tribunal[2] and the United Nations Committee on the Elimination of Racial Discrimination (CERD Committee).[3] Further, the discussion that did take place was often reactive. The Government drove the debate on the foreshore and seabed post-*Ngati Apa*; it set the agenda. Commentators were forced to respond to the various Government policy proposals rather than step back and take a more considered view of the decision and its implications.

The passage of the FSA does not mean the time for analysis of legal issues arising from *Ngati Apa* is over. On the contrary, it is as important as ever, and not just because certain legal issues have not yet been adequately debated. The foreshore and seabed question continues to influence New Zealand political

---

1. *Attorney-General v Ngati Apa* [2003] 3 NZLR 143 (CA).
2. Waitangi Tribunal *Report on the Crown's Foreshore and Seabed Policy: Wai 1071* (Legislation Direct, Wellington, 2004).
3. United Nations Committee on the Elimination of All Forms of Racial Discrimination, 'Decision 1(66): New Zealand Foreshore and Seabed Act 2004' (11 March 2005) CERD/C/66/NZL/Dec.1. For a close analysis of the arguments made, process leading to, and substance of the CERD Committee's FSA Decision, see Claire Charters and Andrew Erueti 'Report from the inside: the CERD Committee's Review of the Foreshore and Seabed Act 2004' (2005) 36 VUWLR 257.

and social life in very real ways. For example, it prompted a reassessment of the relationship between Māori and non-Māori in New Zealand; it led to the establishment of the Māori Party, which went on to win four seats in Parliament in September 2005; and the implementation of the FSA will be monitored closely by United Nations human rights mechanisms following critical comment of the FSA by a United Nations human rights treaty body.[4] We expect that there will be continuing calls for the FSA's repeal and that the issue will be discussed for decades to come.

We hope that all the chapters in this book have broad appeal for people interested in the foreshore and seabed issue, even if the focus is on 'the law'. It is not, however, designed for lawyers, judges and students of law alone. In any event, it is impossible to distinguish the law from broader public policy and governance issues.

One way or another, each chapter in this book comments on the process leading up to the enactment of the FSA and particular aspects of the FSA. To assist the reader, and especially those who are new to the subject, we provide a short overview of both here.

In June 2003, the Court of Appeal in *Ngati Apa* held that the Māori Land Court had jurisdiction to determine (i) whether specific areas of the foreshore and seabed had the status of Māori customary land and (ii) whether land so designated could be converted into Māori freehold titles under Te Ture Whenua Maori Act 1993. In finding that Māori customary title in the foreshore and seabed had survived the assertion of Crown sovereignty and had not been extinguished by general legislation, the *Ngati Apa* decision also opened the door to claims to the High Court under the doctrine of aboriginal rights. The Government responded almost immediately with a public declaration that it would legislate to vest the foreshore and seabed in the Crown,[5] and released its first foreshore and seabed policy in August 2003 (the August Policy).[6] That policy introduced the principles guiding the Government's response to *Ngati Apa*, from which the Government did not deviate, including public access, regulation, protection and certainty. The policy proposed the vesting of the foreshore and seabed in either the public domain or the Crown, the removal of the Māori Land Court's jurisdiction to grant freehold titles in the foreshore and seabed, and new procedures for the recognition of Māori customary rights. The ensuing consultation with New Zealand on that policy resulted in a clear

---

4. United Nations Committee on the Elimination of All Forms of Racial Discrimination, 'Decision 1(66): New Zealand Foreshore and Seabed Act 2004' (11 March 2005) CERD/C/66/NZL/Dec.1.
5. As reported by Audrey Young 'Quick Move Blocks Maori Bid to Claim Rights Over Seabed' (24 June 2003) *New Zealand Herald*.
6. Department of Prime Minister and Cabinet *The Foreshore and Seabed of New Zealand: Protecting Public Access and Customary Rights* (Government Proposals for Consultation, New Zealand Government, Wellington, 2003).

message from Māori and many non-Māori: rejection of the Government's proposals. Nonetheless, the Government's subsequent December 2003 policy did not differ significantly from the August Policy, and was criticised by the Waitangi Tribunal for, among other things, breaching the Treaty of Waitangi and human rights.[7]

The Foreshore and Seabed Bill (the FS Bill) was introduced into Parliament on 6 May 2004. For the most part, it mirrored the Government's August policy with one major exception: the High Court would have the jurisdiction to grant territorial customary rights orders (TCROs). In effect, a TCRO is a declaration that, but for the vesting of ownership of the foreshore and seabed in the Crown, claimants would have been able to prove aboriginal title in the foreshore and seabed. The Attorney-General also reported on the FS Bill's compliance with the New Zealand Bill of Rights Act 1990 on 6 May 2004, finding no abrogation. The Fisheries and Other Sea-Related Legislation Select Committee, which received just short of 4000 submissions on the FS Bill, was unable to agree to any amendments and reported back to Parliament along party lines. However, substantial amendments to the FS Bill were made by Supplementary Order Paper during the Committee of the Whole House phase, only days before the FS Bill was eventually passed. They included further limitations on claimants' potential ability to prove a TCRO.

As passed in November 2004, the FSA:
- vests foreshore and seabed not held in private freehold title in the Crown;
- removes the Māori Land Court's original jurisdiction over the foreshore and seabed as accepted by the *Ngati Apa* decision, and also removes the High Court's inherent common law jurisdiction on aboriginal rights in relation to foreshore and seabed interests;
- enables groups (both Māori and non-Māori) to claim customary rights orders (CROs); and
- enables Māori groups to claim TCROs, which, if successful, require the establishment of either a foreshore or seabed reserve, or negotiations for redress (although there is no obligation on the Crown to provide redress).

As mentioned above, the story does not end there. In March 2005, the CERD Committee found the FSA to contain elements that discriminated against Māori. Not long after this the United Nations Special Rapporteur on the Situation of Human Rights and Fundamental Freedoms of Indigenous People, the United Nations watchdog on indigenous rights, criticised the FSA and recommended that it be repealed or significantly amended.[8] The current Māori

---

7. Waitangi Tribunal Report, above n 2.
8. *See* ECOSOC, The Special Rapporteur, *Report of the Special Rapporteur on the Situation of the Human Rights and Fundamental Freedoms of Indigenous Peoples, Mission to New Zealand*, U.N. Doc. E/

Party Members of Parliament campaigned on an anti-FSA platform, and soon after the September 2005 general election began working towards repeal of the FSA.[9] And in December 2006, Tariana Turia, co-leader of the Māori Party, introduced a Private Member's Bill which seeks to repeal the FSA.[10]

The seven chapters of this book deal with discrete and specialised subjects, some from renowned academics, such as leading international expert on Canadian aboriginal rights law, Professor Kent McNeil. It deliberately does not provide comprehensive coverage of all foreshore and seabed legal issues – that is an ongoing broader project for New Zealand as a whole. Nor does it set out to describe the process leading to the FSA or the FSA itself (apart from the above brief introduction); that is done elsewhere.[11] It starts with historical analyses, continues with comparative perspectives, moves on to specific issues relating to resource management and Crown fiduciary duties to Māori, and finishes with an international legal perspective.

Though it was not our particular intention, most of the chapters in this book are critical of the Government's handling of the foreshore and seabed issue and the FSA, albeit to varying degrees. The central theme is that the FSA has diminished the rights available to Māori in the foreshore and seabed, and that this could have been avoided. The chapters first saw the light of day in their early incarnations as conference papers presented at Victoria University of Wellington on 10 December 2004. The discussions that took place on that day were enriched by all the participants' contributions, which included iwi representatives, Governmental officials and a cast of international academics.

David V Williams and Richard Boast place the *Ngati Apa* decision and the FSA in their historical context. Professor Williams highlights the similarity between the Government's response to *Ngati Apa* in the FSA and the New Zealand Supreme Court's 1877 decision in *Wi Parata v Bishop of Wellington*:[12] both deny the legal justiciability of Māori customary rights claims, characterising them instead as rights that exist 'by grace and favour of the Crown'.[13] His approach is holistic in that he places New Zealand's historical and modern approaches to Māori customary rights in their broader political context. He notes, also, the parallels between the Government's assimilation

---

CN.4/2006/78/Add. 3 (Mar. 13, 2006), para 92 (*prepared by* Rodolfo Stavenhagen).

9. NZPA 'Maori Party Starts to Talk Detail on Foreshore Bill' (28 November 2005), *New Zealand Herald*.
10. Foreshore and Seabed Act (Repeal) Bill (No 86-1).
11. For example, R Boast 'Māori Proprietary Claims to the Foreshore and Seabed after *Ngati Apa*' (2004) 21 NZULR 1; B Arthur, P McHugh and C Owen *Foreshore and Seabed Act, the RMA and Aquaculture* (New Zealand Law Society, Wellington, 2005); T Bennion, M Birdling and R Paton *Making Sense of the Foreshore and Seabed* (The Maori Law Review, Wellington, 2004): and Claire Charters and Andrew Erueti, above n 3.
12. *Wi Parata v Bishop of Wellington* (1877) 3 NZ Jur (NS) (SC) 72.
13. See *Wi Parata v Bishop of Wellington* (1877) above n 12.

policies that dominated between 1840 and the 1970s and the 'one law for all' arguments made by politicians in the midst of the foreshore and seabed policy debate.[14] Richard Boast outlines efforts made by Māori tribes to obtain due recognition of their rights in the foreshore and seabed, and other water bodies (including inland lakes and river beds), through the New Zealand courts since the nineteenth century. He also details the reasons why the Government could not have reasonably staked its claim to ownership of the foreshore on the basis of the now-discredited legal decision of *Ninety Mile Beach* – illustrating that the *Ngati Apa* decision should have been of no surprise to the Government.[15] He notes that issues similar to those raised by *Ngati Apa* could arise in relation to Māori claims to river beds.

Kent McNeil and Shaunnagh Dorsett assess the FSA against comparative law on common law aboriginal title in Australia and Canada. Their contributions are important because they provide alternative perspectives to that offered by Dr Paul McHugh on how New Zealand's common law aboriginal rights law could have developed after *Ngati Apa* in the light of Australian and Canadian law.[16] Ms Dorsett and Professor McNeil are recognised experts in Australian native title law and Canadian aboriginal rights law respectively. Dr McHugh appeared to have a monopoly on the Government's and the Waitangi Tribunal's thinking on common law aboriginal rights. He heavily influenced the content of the FSA: his predictions of what the common law would offer as a result of *Ngati Apa*, based on his assessment of comparative law, formed the basis of the TCRO and CRO sections in the FSA. He argued that it was unlikely, in the light of recent Australian native title law, that Māori tribes would have been able to acquire an aboriginal right to exclusive titles in the foreshore.

Professor McNeil and Ms Dorsett illustrate that Dr McHugh's interpretation of comparative jurisprudence is not the only one available. Ms Dorsett suggests that Australian jurisprudence has been restricted by judicial interpretations of the Australian Native Title Act 1993 concluding, contrary to Dr McHugh, that Australian jurisprudence might be peculiar to Australia and of limited authority in New Zealand. The upshot of this argument is that the common law in New Zealand, unlike that in Australia, might indeed have been able to recognise Māori exclusive titles in the foreshore and seabed. Finally, her

---

14. Dr Don Brash 'Nationhood' (Orewa Rotary Club, 27 January 2004). He described endeavours to provide redress to Māori for historical breaches of the Treaty of Waitangi as an entrenched 'treaty grievance industry'; stated Māori partly lost their land historically because of deficient Māori leadership; and criticised special measures for Māori in the health sector despite serious disparities in health statistics between Māori and non-Māori.
15. *In re the Ninety-Mile Beach* [1963] NZLR 461 (CA).
16. Dr Paul Gerard McHugh *Brief of Evidence to the Waitangi Tribunal, 13 January 2004, in the Matter of the Treaty of Waitangi Act 1975 and of Applications for an Urgent Inquiry into the Foreshore and Seabed Issues, Wai 1071*; Paul McHugh 'Aboriginal Title in New Zealand: A Retrospective and Prospect' (2004) 2 NZJPIL 139.

comparative analysis points to issues in the FSA that might be problematic in the future.

Professor McNeil concludes that the Court of Appeal's decision in *Ngati Apa* was perfectly consistent with the common law. However, he criticises the FSA on the basis that it is discriminatory and adopts: '[T]wo of the most doctrinally flawed and heavily criticised aspects of the law on indigenous land rights in Canada and Australia, namely the integral to the distinctive culture test and the requirement of substantial maintenance of the connection with the land in accordance with traditional laws and customs.'[17]

He concludes by making the point that the FSA's stated objective of preserving the foreshore and seabed is a misrepresentation of its real goal of converting land not already owned by the Crown, or held in freehold, to Crown land.[18]

Catherine Iorns' chapter considers the FSA from an environmental law perspective. She outlines the existing resource management regime, its provision for Māori interests and, in particular, the issue that gave rise to the *Ngati Apa* claim – a dispute between iwi and local government over marine farming in the foreshore and seabed. She then describes the evolution of the resource management provisions in the Resource Management (Foreshore and Seabed) Amendment Act 2004 and assesses whether specific provisions are consistent with environmental principles and the Treaty of Waitangi.

Claire Charters' chapter compares the FSA sections on the Crown's fiduciary duties to Māori to Canadian law on governmental fiduciary duties to First Nations. It finds the FSA legislative override of fiduciary duties comparatively draconian. It also illustrates that Māori were likely to have been able to hold the Crown to fiduciary standards when dealing with Māori interests in the foreshore and seabed but for the FSA, and suggests that Māori should receive redress for the loss of that opportunity.

Andrew Erueti places *Ngati Apa* in an international context by comparing state methods of recognising indigenous property rights with the methods used by international human rights treaty bodies.[19] He argues that the focus on 'tradition' in indigenous peoples' land claims, and the legal formalism inherent in domestic aboriginal rights litigation, has resulted in the development of strict evidential standards that indigenous peoples often struggle to meet. This approach was adopted in the FSA. He also notes that experience shows that international human rights treaty bodies serve an important function in monitoring state practice and, in particular, in encouraging states to adopt less-restrictive approaches to the recognition of indigenous peoples' rights in

---

17. See Kent McNeil's chapter in this book, 97.
18. FSA 2004, s 3.
19. *Ngati Apa*, above n 1.

traditional lands.

A number of people and institutions have made this book possible. Not least is Matthew Palmer who, as the former Dean of the Victoria University of Wellington Law Faculty, was supportive of this project. The Law Faculty also generously contributed funds for both the conference and the production of this book, for which we are appreciative. Our extra-special thanks go to Karen Jackson, whose research and editorial assistance was unfailingly superb. Jane May also helped edit a couple of chapters, and her work was equally impressive. We gratefully acknowledge David Bloch for his collegiality when he was in New Zealand in early 2004, and for inspiring the title of this book.[20] We wish to thank Fergus Barrowman at Victoria University Press, and John Huria, for steering the book towards publication. And, we appreciate and thank Wayne Youle for his excellent artwork.

Finally, we would like to thank all the authors in this book for their contributions, and the insightful observations made by all those who participated in our conference. It has been a fun and interesting project largely because of their enthusiasm and professionalism.

---

20. It is borrowed from his article 'Aboriginal Rights and Judicial Wrongs: Colonizing the Last Frontier' (2004) 29 Am Indian L Rev 1.

Foreshore and Seabed in New Zealand Law: A Legal-Historical Introduction

Richard Boast*

I   Introduction

This chapter addresses the legal, historical – and legal-historical – context of the decision of the Court of Appeal in *Attorney-General v Ngati Apa* (*Ngati Apa*).[1] The decision did not come out of a clear sky. The legal uncertainty of the Crown's title to the foreshore – not so much the seabed – had been known for many years. Looking back, it now all seems so unwise for Crown title to such an important and contestable asset to have been allowed to rest for over forty years on nothing but a single and clearly flawed decision of the Court of Appeal in *In Re Ninety-Mile Beach* (*Ninety-Mile Beach*).[2]

At common law the foreshore, the beds of navigable rivers and the territorial seabed were in a special position as lands presumed, in the absence of evidence to the contrary, to belong to the Crown.[3] In a jurisdiction such as New Zealand, however, the issue is whether a prerogative interest of that kind in English common law can translate directly into a proprietary title to the

---

*   Barrister at Law, Reader in Law, Victoria University of Wellington. For earlier discussions of the material covered here see R P Boast '*In re Ninety-Mile Beach* Revisited: the Native Land Court and the Foreshore in New Zealand Legal History' (1993) 23 VUWLR 145, and R P Boast *The Foreshore* (Waitangi Tribunal Rangahaua Whanui Series Theme Q, GP Publications, Wellington, 1996).
1.   *Attorney-General v Ngati Apa* [2003] 3 NZLR 643 (CA).
2.   *Re the Ninety-Mile Beach* [1963] NZLR 461 (CA).
3.   See K McNeil *Common Law Aboriginal Title* (Clarendon Press, Oxford, 1989) 103–105; *Halsbury's Laws of England* (4 ed, Butterworths, London, 1973) vol 8(1) Compulsory Acquisition of Land, 1418; *Gann v Free Fishers of Whitstable* (1865) 11 HLC 192. In *Attorney-General v Emerson* [1891] AC 649, 653 (HL), Lord Herschell stated that 'it is beyond dispute that the Crown is prima facie entitled to every part of the foreshore between high and low water mark, and that a subject can only establish a title to any part of the foreshore, either by proving an express grant from the Crown, or by giving evidence from which such a grant, though not capable of being produced, will be proved.'

benefit of the Crown in right of New Zealand. A key obstacle to any such direct translation is of course the common law of native title, and the absolute requirement that native title to any land be extinguished before it is available to be Crown granted.

Legal commentators have a particular interest in the common law of native title, but in fact this is a body of common law that has long been of marginal practical importance in New Zealand. This is not because New Zealand law on indigenous customary lands is undeveloped – far from it. Beginning in 1862 New Zealand built up a complex statutory edifice relating to Māori land, so complex, indeed, that by 1891 lawyers could be found testifying to a royal commission that the law had become unworkably confused and intricate.[4] Nor is it the case that the New Zealand courts were uninvolved in the development of the law. One can open any volume of the New Zealand Law Reports at random for the years 1870–1920 and find cases at all levels of the court hierarchy, the Privy Council included, dealing with native lands. But these cases are of a particular kind, deriving from a legal structure New Zealand assembled on its own and for itself, and relate to the manifold confusions and complexities ushered in by the Native Lands Acts of 1862 and 1865. While, of course, there are Privy Council appeals from New Zealand which deal with native title in the strict sense,[5] such decisions also revolved around such questions as to whether confiscated lands returned on statutory tenures to named individuals were subject to trusts in favour of customary owners or whether the protective mechanisms of the Native Lands Acts were circumvented by a bona fide purchaser taking a Torrens title under the Land Transfer Acts.[6] At the Supreme Court and Court of Appeal level there is a vast amount of case law on such questions as the effects of the memorial of title provisions of the Native Lands Act 1873, completely overwhelming the case law on common law native title.

Ngati Apa exemplifies perfectly these particular, and peculiar, characteristics of New Zealand law relating to indigenous lands. The case was not strictly speaking about aboriginal or native title at all. It was about the extent of the jurisdiction of the Māori Land Court (which has been in continuous existence since 1865). *Ngati Apa* did not even originate in the ordinary courts but in an application for investigation of title in the Māori Land Court. To the greater public the issue has been debated in terms of ownership – who

---

4. Rees–Carroll Commission 'Report of the Commission Appointed to Inquire into the State of the Native Land Laws' [1891] AJHR G1. The Commission's words are often cited:
  [S]o complete has the confusion become in law and practice that lawyers of high standing and extensive practice have testified on oath that if the Legislature had desired to create a state of confusion and anarchy in Native-land titles it could not have hoped to be more successful than it has been.
5. For instance *Nireaha Tamaki v Baker* [1901] AC 561 (PC).
6. *Te Teira Te Paea v Te Roera Tareha* [1902] AC 56 (PC); *Assets v Mere Roihi* [1905] AC 176 (PC).

'owns' the foreshore and seabed. But legally, the issue is not that, but one of jurisdiction: can the Māori Land Court grant titles to the foreshore and seabed *in the same way* as it can (or rather, did) for other areas? This is something the Government has long been vigilant to ensure it could not do.

Professor McNeil is famous for his analysis of 'common law native title' – that in a colony of settlement aboriginal or native title in fact equates to a Crown-granted freehold.[7] His analysis was considered, and to some extent applied, in Toohey J's remarkable, if unorthodox, judgment in *Mabo v Queensland (No 2)(Mabo (No 2))*.[8] That native title is equivalent to a Crown-granted freehold is, however, not at all a startling proposition in New Zealand. That was the very outcome achieved by the Native Lands Acts of 1862 and 1865, which set up a statutory mechanism which allowed Māori to convert land held under customary tenure to a freehold grant. To fully contextualise the foreshore and seabed issue it is necessary, first and foremost, to begin with the first Native Lands Acts, and the functions, powers and jurisdiction of the Native (now Māori) Land Court.

The importance of title to the foreshore and seabed needs no explanation. As in many other countries New Zealand is witnessing a marked upsurge in the value and importance of the coast. Once perceived as infinite, the coast has suddenly become scarce and valuable to an unprecedented degree. This has come about partly because of changes in attitude (not so long ago New Zealanders tended to see estuaries and mudflats as unsightly, fit for pollution, rubbish dumps and reclamation),[9] an increase in population, and the emergence of new technologies which have facilitated marine farming in particular. This chapter attempts to demonstrate that controversy over title to the foreshore is nothing new, but it is significant that the issue has flared into a major national controversy only recently, culminating in the enactment of a new statute dealing specifically with title to the foreshore and seabed, this being the Foreshore and Seabed Act 2004 (FSA). The FSA has many links with earlier statutes, such as the Geothermal Energy Act 1953, which vested key natural resources in the Crown once their value had become apparent. Underscoring the importance of the coast even further, 2004 also saw major legal changes relating to the legislative regime for aquaculture. The old Marine Farming Act 1971 was repealed, two new acts were passed (the Aquaculture Reform Act 2004 and the Maori Commercial Aquaculture Claims Settlement Act 2004)

---

7. See K McNeil, above n 3, especially 207–208, where the core of the argument is summarised.
8. See Toohey J's judgment, *Mabo v Queensland (No 2)* (1992) 107 ALR 1 161–167 (HCA).
9. The change in perception is one New Zealanders share with people in other developed countries, and derives in part from a new consciousness arising from Rachel Carson's famous book *The Edge of the Sea* (2 ed, Mariner Books, Boston, 1998).

and at the same time there were substantial amendments to four key statutes.[10] The importance of the coast and coastal waters is shown also by the number of Waitangi Tribunal reports that deal with various issues touching on coastal fisheries, marine pollution, and title to coastal lagoons.[11] More recently there is the Waitangi Tribunal's Foreshore and Seabed Report (2004), which arose directly from a challenge to the Government's foreshore and seabed policies before the Waitangi Tribunal.[12] In addition, the Government's aquaculture policies have been considered separately by the Waitangi Tribunal and resulted in a report in 2002.[13]

II The Native Land Court and the Foreshore in the Nineteenth Century

Although New Zealand law to some extent 'rediscovered' native title following the *Te Weehi v Regional Fisheries Officer* (*Te Weehi*) decision in 1986,[14] the core principles of native title have been a part of the basic structure and the wiring of New Zealand common law from the very start. It has always been assumed that Māori title needs to be extinguished prior to Crown grant. In *Mabo (No 2)* Brennan J had to allow a category of extinguishment of native title by inconsistent grant in Australia (had he not done so, who knows how many freehold grants in Australia would be burdened by unextinguished native title), but in New Zealand it has never been the practice to extinguish native title *merely* by Crown grant. Independent extinguishment, by purchase usually, has always been a prerequisite, in contrast to Australia. Indeed in recent cases the New Zealand courts have explicitly rejected inconsistent grant as a valid

---

10. Implemented by four separate amending Acts, these being Te Ture Whenua Maori Act (No 3) 2004; Biosecurity Amendment Act 2004; the Conservation Amendment Act 2004; and the Fisheries Amendment Act (No 3) 2004.
11. Waitangi Tribunal *Motunui-Waitara Report: Wai 6* (Waitangi Tribunal Department of Justice, Wellington, 1983); Waitangi Tribunal *Finding of the Waitangi Tribunal on the Manukau Claim: Wai 8* (Government Printer, Wellington, 1985); Waitangi Tribunal *Mangonui Sewerage Report: Wai 17* (Waitangi Tribunal, Department of Justice, Wellington, 1988); Waitangi Tribunal *Muriwhenua Fishing Report: Wai 22* (Waitangi Tribunal, Department of Justice, Wellington, 1988); Waitangi Tribunal *Ngai Tahu Sea Fisheries Report: Wai 27* (Waitangi Tribunal, Department of Justice, Wellington, 1992); Waitangi Tribunal *Te Whanganui-a-Orotu Report: Wai 55* (Waitangi Tribunal, Department of Justice, Wellington, 1995). For a discussion see Stephanie Milroy 'The Fisheries Reports' and Nicola Wheen and Jacinta Ruru 'The Environmental Reports' in J Hayward and N R Wheen (eds) *The Waitangi Tribunal: Te Roopu Whakamana i te Tiriti o Waitangi* (Bridget Williams Books, Wellington, 2004) 83–96; 97–112.
12. Waitangi Tribunal *Report on the Crown's Foreshore and Seabed Policy: Wai 1071* (Legislation Direct, Wellington, 2004).
13. Waitangi Tribunal *Ahu Moana: The Aquaculture and Marine Farming Report: Wai 953* (Legislation Direct, Wellington, 2002).
14. *Te Weehi v Regional Fisheries Officer* [1986] 1 NZLR 680 (HC).

means of extinguishment and have insisted that any such grant would be burdened by the surviving native title, if any.[15]

Crown pre-emption, a standard feature of imperial constitutional law, was recognised in the Treaty of Waitangi itself, and soon received statutory recognition in local ordinances and statutes. Until 1862 the main method of extinguishment was by pre-emptive Crown purchase, with which the Crown gained title in dominium to about three-fifths of the country before 1862, including nearly all of the South Island. By 1862 Māori still held under customary title most of the North Island, which is where the bulk of the Māori population was actually concentrated. In 1862, however, New Zealand enacted its first Native Lands Act, followed by the much more comprehensive Native Lands Act of 1865. Nothing would be the same again.

This is not the place for a comprehensive analysis of the effects of the Native Lands Acts, still less of the elaborate historiography of the Native Land Court.[16] (The latest word on both, and one very worth reading, is the Waitangi Tribunal's Turanga–Gisborne report; the effects of the Native Land Court on the lands in and around Gisborne being one of the key issues in that particular inquiry.[17]) The Native Lands Acts actually waived Crown pre-emption and instead allowed Māori to take a claim for an 'investigation of title' to the Native Land Court. If the applicants made out their claim, the applicants were granted a certificate of title to the block – which might be very substantial, hundreds of thousands of acres even – after which they could then receive a Crown grant. This created a category of land with no exact equivalent elsewhere in the British colonies, today known as Māori freehold land, which accounts for about 5 per cent of the entire country.

Investigations of title were never a contest between Māori and the Crown. The Crown may have sometimes influenced the Native Land Court from behind the scenes, although this happened only rarely. In fact, claims that the Native Land Court was some kind of passive agency of the state are well off the mark – the state did not usually contest cases in the Native Land Court. The Native Land Court principally adjudicated on contests among Māori

---

15. See *Faulkner v Tauranga District Council* [1996] 1 NZLR 357, 363 (HC) Blanchard J, following *Nireaha Tamaki v Baker*, above n 5. Here Blanchard J states that 'the Executive cannot ... extinguish customary title by granting the land to someone other than the customary owners'; if it does so 'the grantee's interest is taken subject to the customary title.'

16. See R Boast, A Erueti, D McPhail and N Smith *Maori Land Law* (2 ed, LexisNexis, Wellington, 2004) 65–119; D Williams *'Te Kooti tango whenua': The Native Land Court 1864–1909* (Huia, Wellington, 1999); P Spiller, J Finn and R Boast *A New Zealand Legal History* (2 ed, Brookers, Wellington, 2001) 123–185. On the origins of the Native Lands Acts the best discussion is now D Loveridge *The Origins of the Native Lands Acts and the Native Land Court in New Zealand* (report prepared for the Crown Law Office, 2000).

17. Waitangi Tribunal *Turanga Tangata Turanga Whenua: The Report on the Turanganui a Kiwa Claims: Wai 814* (Legislation Direct, Wellington, 2004) vol 2, 395–537.

inter se. The Court operated on the working assumption that all land to which Crown title had not been extinguished by the Crown by earlier pre-emptive purchase or by statute *must* belong to *some* Māori descent group: the question for examination was, which group? Cases in the Native Land Court could be very contested. But the working assumptions were that all land belonged to Māori in the first place, there was no vacant land, and there was no sense at all that only cultivations and habitations were claimable. Remote, vast regions were routinely vested by the Court in applicants, who were then free to sell their lands to whoever they liked: to private purchasers, or, more usually, the Government. This has obvious implications for the foreshore and seabed. If the Native Land Court did indeed have a jurisdiction to deal with these lands, should the same presumption still apply?

Section 4 of Native Lands Act 1867 allowed the government to suspend the operation of the Court in any district or districts. From 1873 to 1877 Sir Donald McLean, the Native Minister in the Fox–Vogel Government, prohibited the Court from sitting in the Taupō district, an area where the Government was particularly concerned to prevent private alienations and where some Court decisions had caused tribal tensions. This should be seen perhaps as one means by which the Government could reimpose a *de facto* pre-emptive regime, but it also shows that the Native Land Court largely ran its own independent course which did not always suit the convenience of the government of the day.[18]

In the late 1860s and early 1870s there was a forerunner of present-day controversies. The matter of control of the foreshore and seabed became intensely politicised and a matter of great concern to the Government of the day. In particular, there was concern over control over the foreshore at Shortland (Thames), valuable because of the gold thought to be present in the sands.[19] This issue, and the real risk of violence between miners and local Māori, led to a round of official investigations and reports in 1869.[20] In an effort to stop the Native Land Court from issuing titles to land below the high water mark in 1872, the Government issued a proclamation suspending the Court's operations 'within the Province of Auckland, being all that portion of the said Province situate below high water mark.'[21] At the next foreshore

---

18. See Kathryn Rose *The Bait and the Hook: Crown Purchasing in Taupo and the Central Bay of Plenty in the 1870s*, Technical Witness Evidence, *Turanga Tangata Turanga Whenua: The Report on the Turanganui a Kiwa Claims: Wai 814* (Legislation Direct, Wellington, 2004) 8–9.
19. For the historical background see generally Paul Monin's outstanding *This is My Place: Hauraki Contested 1769–1875* (Bridget Williams Books, Wellington, 2001).
20. See James Mackay 'Report by Mr Mackay on the Thames Gold Fields' [1869] AJHR A17; Native Lands Bill Committee '*Report of the Select Committee on the Evidence Adduced before the Native Lands Bill Committee*' [1869] AJHR F6A; Thames Sea Beach Bill Committee '*Report of the Select Committee on the Thames Sea Beach Bill*' [1869] AJHR F7.
21. 'A Proclamation' 28 (29 May 1872) *New Zealand Gazette* Wellington 347.

case at Thames, involving a block known as Kapanga Moana No 2, Crown counsel intervened in the hearing and produced the proclamation, bringing the case to a halt.[22] This might well show that the Government saw the Court as an executive agency, which it could freely tamper with at its convenience. Or it might be argued, more plausibly, that if the Native Land Court was as pliant an instrument of the executive as some seem to believe, there would have been no need to interfere: it was precisely because the Native Land Court was a reasonably independent-minded judicial body that governments from time to time felt the need to scale down its operations for reasons of policy.

The situation in the Firth of Thames was concerned with title to the foreshore, not with fisheries matters. But, historically, it is the latter issue that has dominated. In the key early decision of *Kauwaeranga*,[23] decided in 1870, Chief Judge Fenton repudiated the previous Native Land Court practice of granting titles to parcels below the high water mark, and instead granted to the applicants a still-substantial right of fishery instead. Fenton stated that he could not 'contemplate without uneasiness the evil consequences which might ensue from judicially declaring that the soil of the foreshore of the colony will be vested absolutely in the natives, if they can prove certain acts of ownership.' That was particularly so 'when I consider how readily they may prove such, and how impossible it is to contradict them if they only agree amongst themselves.' The approach taken in *Kauwaeranga* was followed in a decision given by Chief Judge Macdonald and Judge Puckey, in *Parumoana*, dealing with certain areas of mudflats at Porirua belonging to Ngāti Toa.[24] The Native Land Court held that 'the present applicants are entitled not to the land but to a right [of] fishery.' This right, an incorporeal hereditament, remained in existence until 1960, when following the decision of the Supreme Court in *Ninety-Mile Beach*, Ngāti Toa received legal advice from their solicitors that the original grant had been made without jurisdiction and must be deemed to have lapsed.

III Water Bodies and Crown Law Office Policy

By the early twentieth century the Crown Law Office was becoming concerned about whether water bodies – inland lakes, river beds, the foreshore – could be investigated by the Native Land Court or whether they were, in some sense or

---

22. See *Kapanga Moana No 2* (1872) 2 Coromandel Minute Book 315–316.
23. *Kauwaeranga* (1870) 4 Hauraki Minute Book 236, reprinted and annotated by Alex Frame 'Kauwaeranga Judgment – Introduction' (1984) 14 VUWLR 224.
24. *Parumoana* (1883) 1 Wellington Minute Book 315. (The area is sometimes spelled 'Parimoana'. It means 'adjoining the sea'.) The Court found that 'the present applicants are entitled not to the land but to a right of fishery – the collection of Pipis [a shellfish] being taken by the judgement referred to [i.e., *Kauwaeranga*] as "fishery" and so this court finds.'

other, exceptional lands which belonged to the Crown in dominium from the point of the acquisition of sovereignty. It is here, above all, that the foreshore and seabed issue sits in New Zealand law. A linked question was that of coastal fisheries, and in particular the effect of investigations of title to coastal blocks on customary fishing rights at sea. Crown Law's stance is exemplified very clearly in the position taken by Sir John Salmond with respect to the lakebed cases which were fought out in the early part of the twentieth century.

In general the Crown has been very reluctant to concede that Māori can have title to the beds of large navigable lakes (such as Taupō, Rotorua, Waikaremoana, Wairarapa and so on). This was a particular stance of Sir John Salmond and of the Crown Law Office. In an opinion written in 1914 (relating to the Rotorua lakes) Salmond argued that it 'is quite out of the question to allow freehold titles to be obtained by the Natives' to navigable waterways, including lakebeds: 'Such titles would enable the Natives to exclude the whole of the European population from all rights of fishing, navigation and other uses now enjoyed by them.'[25]

It must be said, however, that there is very little support for the notion that the Crown has any kind of prerogative title to lakebeds at common law. According to *Halsbury's Laws of England* the 'soil of lakes and pools, even when they are so large that they might be termed inland seas, does not of common right belong to the Crown.'[26] Professor McNeil's authoritative text on the law of native title states that only the foreshore and related waters are deemed to belong to the Crown: 'Unlike other lands in the realm, the foreshore and the beds of tidal rivers and coastal waters are presumed to be owned by the Crown by prerogative right.'[27]

There is no common law presumption of Crown ownership of lakebeds. Salmond's views may have been affected by United States law. In the United States the position is that ordinarily title to navigable waterways, including lakebeds, vests in the various States except on those rare occasions where the courts are prepared to find that Congress intended to grant the bed of a navigable watercourse to a tribe when creating a reservation.[28] The ordinary presumption

---

25. J Salmond, Solicitor-General, to the Attorney-General 'Opinions Relating to Lands Department 1913–15' (1 August 1914) Letter, in Alex Frame *Salmond: Southern Jurist* (Victoria University Press, Wellington, 1995) 119. It has to be said that it is important to keep separate Salmond's opinions written in his official capacity, where naturally he was putting the legal position of the government foremost, and what he may have believed as a jurist and scholar.
26. *Halsbury's Laws of England* (4 ed, Butterworths, London, 1973) vol 49 Water, 219, cited in B White *Inland Waterways* (Waitangi Tribunal Rangahaua Whanui Series Theme Q, GP Publications, Wellington, 1998) 3.
27. K McNeil, above n 3, 103.
28. The general rule is set out in *Montana v United States* (1981) 450 US 544, a decision of the United States Supreme Court. The presumption of state ownership has however been found to have been rebutted in a sequence of Ninth Circuit Court of Appeals decisions, these being *Confederated Salish and Kootenai*

of state title in American law is rebutted in those circumstances where a grant to an Indian tribe 'includes within its boundaries a navigable water' where the tribe is known to be 'dependent on the fishery resource in that water for its survival.'[29] The approach of American law on the point is probably influenced by the scale and importance of the great freshwater lakes and of the rivers of North America; it is safe to say that original Indian title to Lake Michigan or the bed of the Mississippi River was not an appealing prospect to the Government of the United States. The existence of very large inland water bodies in New Zealand, such as Lake Taupō, far bigger than anything to be found in England, would presumably have influenced Salmond's thinking on the matter as well. (It has to be wondered, however, quite what the public interest in 'navigation' in lakes such as Lake Waikaremoana or Lake Taupō might be. Neither lake could be described as a major commercial artery, and both were at that time 'navigated' only by a few canoes and rowboats).

The leading New Zealand case is the decision of the Court of Appeal in *Tamihana Korokai v Solicitor General* (*Tamihana Korokai*).[30] This case, which arose out of the Rotorua lakes title investigation case in the Native Land Court, held that the Native Land Court had jurisdiction to investigate titles to the bed of navigable lakes. It probably follows from this that lakebeds have no particular status in New Zealand common law and that they are simply Māori customary land until investigated by the Court and Crown granted. However, the Crown Law Office, led by Sir John Salmond and despite *Tamihana Korokai*, remained very reluctant to concede that lakebeds merely had the status of ordinary Māori customary land. In its legal argument before the Native Land Court in the *Rotorua Lakes* case, the Crown, represented by Salmond, tried to limit the application of the decision in *Tamihana Korokai*:[31]

> In *Tamihana Korokai v Solicitor-General* an attempt was made to get the Supreme Court to decide as a matter of law the legal position of the inland lakes and waters of this country. Unsuccessful. The Court decided merely that the Native customary title might exist in respect of such waters but that the question whether it does exist is a matter for the Native Land Court. A question of fact or mixed law and fact such that the Native Land Court could alone determine it on the facts of each particular case. Hence these proceedings.

Essentially the Crown's stance, even after the decision in *Tamihana Korokai*,

---

Tribes v Namen (1982) 665 F 2d 951 (9th Cir), *Puyullap Indian Tribe v Port of Tacoma* (1883) 717 F 2d 1251 (9th Cir) and *United States v Aam* (1989) 887 F 2d 190 (9th Cir).
29. *Puyullap Indian Tribe v Port of Tacoma*, above n 28, 1258.
30. *Tamihana Korokai v Solicitor-General* (1912) 32 NZLR 321 (CA).
31. Crown Law Office *Crown Legal Argument in Rotorua Lakes Case (Rotorua Lakes)* (Archives file, National Archives, Wellington CL 174/2) [presumably this was written by Salmond, although it is not clear from the document].

was that while Māori could be said to have title to *small* non-navigable lakes or waterways, Māori could not own, as a matter of law, *large* lakes such as Rotorua, Taupō or Waikaremoana. In the *Rotorua Lakes* case the Crown argued, probably correctly, that freehold grants bounded by the lakeshore did not extend to the centre of the lake on the *ad medium aquae* rule.[32] The lake, therefore, could only be either Crown land or Māori customary (uninvestigated) land.

A basic plank of Salmond's argument was that he did not accept that Māori had native or aboriginal title to the whole of the country as at the formal acquisition of sovereignty in 1840. The Crown argued in the *Rotorua Lakes* case that 'native title is not universal':[33]

> It is not true that the whole of New Zealand, whether land or water, is necessarily the subject of Native title except so far as such title has been extinguished by cession, forfeiture or otherwise. It is not true therefore that Rotorua must be awarded to the Natives unless the Crown succeeds in proving cession or forfeiture.

Salmond argued that 'the burden of proving native title is therefore on the claimant', a proposition which, however true it might have been then, is certainly at odds with the modern presumption against extinguishment as stated in *Mabo (No 2)* and other cases. Salmond goes on to argue that there could be no native title to navigable waters:[34]

> It is admitted that some waters can be the subject of Native title and that freehold orders can be made in respect thereof. The question in issue relates only to navigable waters whether rivers or lakes. Un-navigable waters are merely appurtenant to the adjoining land and go with it in title. It does not follow, however, that because some water is the subject of Native title all water is. Navigability is of course a question of degree. Water may be navigable for a canoe but not for a battleship ... In the meantime it is sufficient to say that contention of the Crown is limited to navigable waters.

With respect to navigable water bodies, Salmond contended, there was no

---

32. *Rotorua Lakes*, above n 31: 'No existing freehold title to Lake Rotorua. This is common ground. The boundary of the freehold titles is the edge of the lakes. The presumption as to ad medium filum is merely a presumption and is easily capable of rebuttal. *Taupiri Coal Mines Company v. Mueller.* It may be doubted indeed how far it applies to a lake at all owing to the irregularity in its shape and the impossibility of saying what the *medium filum* is. In any case, it is rebutted where the grant of freehold consists of or is based upon a freehold order. The freehold title cannot extend further than the land investigated by the Court. *Non constat* [I do not dispute] that if the Lake is owned by the Natives at all it is owned by the same Natives as those who own the adjoining land. It may be taken as admitted therefore that the Lake is either Native customary land or Crown land free from Native ownership.'
33. *Rotorua Lakes*, above n 31.
34. *Rotorua Lakes*, above n 31.

Māori customary *proprietary* title but 'merely rights of fishery and navigation.'

The Crown has assented to the Māori Land Court's jurisdiction over lakebeds with much reluctance, and in the *Lake Omapere*[35] case (decided by Judge Acheson of the Native Land Court in 1929) continued to argue that there was no Māori title to lakebeds in New Zealand law. This, however, was once again rejected, Judge Acheson stating that to any Māori the possibility that 'he did not possess the beds of his own lakes' could only be a 'grim joke.'[36] In *Lake Omapere* Judge Acheson found that: Māori customary law recognised the ownership of lakebeds;[37] that the Ngā Puhi people owned and occupied the lake in 1840;[38] that native title had to be legally extinguished before it could be 'disregarded by New Zealand Courts';[39] that title to Lake Omapere never had been extinguished in accordance with the law;[40] that the New Zealand legislature had 'by inference' recognised Māori ownership of lakes;[41] that the Native Land Court was bound to take 'judicial notice' of the Treaty of Waitangi[42] ('the emphatic comments of the Judicial Committee of the Privy Council in *Nireaha Tamaki v Baker* make it improbable that the view-point of *Wi Parata v Bishop of Wellington* as to the Treaty of Waitangi will ever be taken again'[43]); that the words of article 2 of the Treaty – referring to the English text – were 'ample to include by description a lake or a lakebed';[44] that the parties to the Treaty of Waitangi certainly did contemplate that Māori would be entitled to the lakebed;[45] that it was never contemplated by the Treaty of Waitangi partners that the Crown would ever claim the lake or its bed;[46] that the lake had continued in customary use and management since 1840;[47] and that it was undoubtedly customary land within the meaning of the Native Land Act 1902.[48] As will be seen, Acheson held similar views about the foreshore and estuarine waters as well. This decision deserves to be better-known – that it is not is yet another illustration of the ongoing scandal that decisions of the Māori Land Court and Māori Appellate Court never

---

35. *Lake Omapere* (1929) Bay of Islands MB 253.
36. *Lake Omapere* above n 35, 278.
37. *Lake Omapere* above n 35.
38. *Lake Omapere* above n 35, 262; 10.
39. *Lake Omapere* above n 35, 263; 11.
40. *Lake Omapere* above n 35, 265; 13.
41. *Lake Omapere* above n 35, 266; 14.
42. *Lake Omapere* above n 35.
43. *Lake Omapere* above n 35, 270; 18.
44. *Lake Omapere* above n 35, 271; 19.
45. *Lake Omapere* above n 35, 272; 20.
46. *Lake Omapere* above n 35, 273; 21. Here Judge Acheson notes that the Crown had no prerogative right to lakes or lakebeds, following the House of Lords decision in *Bristow v Cormican* [1878] 3 App Cas 641 (HL).
47. *Lake Omapere* above n 35, 276; 14.
48. *Lake Omapere* above n 35, 277; 25.

have been, and are still not, officially reported.

The decision in *Tamihana Korokai*, as noted, arose out of the litigation relating to title to the Rotorua lakes. That particular issue was in the end resolved with a special statutory settlement in 1922.[49] This has in fact been the typical means of resolution of legal issues relating to lakebeds. In 1936 the Crown Law Office proposed that special legislation be enacted to simply vest the beds of all navigable lakes in the Crown,[50] as had already been done in the case of the beds of navigable rivers. But rather than take this approach the preferred strategy has been to deal with lakebed claims on a case-by-case basis. Rather than concede the Māori title to inland water bodies the Crown has preferred to negotiate ad hoc special deals and then give them formal effect in statute, Lake Waikaremoana being no exception. The precedent set in *Rotorua Lakes* was repeated in the case of Lake Taupō in 1926,[51] and there have been a number of other similar statutory arrangements, including the Lake Waikaremoana Act 1971.[52] The Crown's complete abandonment of any sense that lakes are a special juridical space of some sort is exemplified by recent decisions to vest the entire bed of Lake Taupō in Ngāti Tūwharetoa, and by the Te Arawa Māori Trust Board's acceptance in December 2003 of the Crown's offer to settle the Rotorua lakes issue by re-vesting the lakebeds in the Board.[53]

The long struggle over lakebeds reveals with great clarity the stance of the Crown Law Office on the law of water bodies, the Government's position on the foreshore being very similar: these are, in Salmond's view, exceptional lands over which the ordinary powers of the Māori Land Court cannot be

---

49. Native Land Amendment and Native Land Claims Adjustment Act 1922, s 27. This provision relates to the 'Arawa District lakes' and vests the bed of 14 lakes in the Crown 'freed and discharged from the Native customary title, *if any*' (emphasis added). This legislation also provided for the recognition and protection of customary fishing rights and set up the Arawa District Maori Trust Board which received income from the Crown and from fishing licences. For a discussion, see Geoff Park *Effective Exclusion?* (Waitangi Tribunal publication for the indigenous flora and fauna claim (Wai 262), Waitangi Tribunal, Wellington, 2001) 197.
50. Crown Law Office Opinion 'Solicitor General to Attorney General and Minister of Native Affairs' (15 February 1935) (Archives file, National Archives, Wellington, CL 200/15), cited in White, above n 26, 163.
51. Native Land Amendment and Native Land Claims Adjustment Act 1926, s 14(1) (this stated that – in language more or less the same as that used in the case of the legislation relating to the Rotorua lakes – that the beds of the lake and of the Waikato River down to the Huka Falls 'are hereby declared to be the property of the Crown, freed and discharged from the Native customary title (if any).' See generally Park, above n 49, 198–199.
52. There is, for instance, legislation relating to Lake Poukawa (Poukawa Native Reserve Act 1903), the Wairarapa lakes (Reserves and Other Lands Disposal and Public Bodies Empowering Act 1907, s 53; Reserves and Other Lands Disposal Act 1914, s 57, and Native Land Claims Adjustment Act 1921, s 12), and Lake Horowhenua (Horowhenua Lake Act 1925; Reserves and Other Lands Disposal Act 1956, s 18).
53. For details of the Te Arawa Lakes settlement, see Office of Treaty Settlements 'Te Arawa Lakes Settlement Summary' http://www.ots.govt.nz (last accessed 24 March 2006).

allowed to operate. In the case of lakebeds the Crown simply failed to get its way in the ordinary courts, and although tempted to take the plunge and simply expropriate lakebeds, did not actually do so. Instead it preferred a policy of case-by-case statutory settlements. With river beds, a different approach was tried, with the result that ownership of river beds is a mixture of statute and common law. Section 14 of the Coal Mines Amendment Act 1903 (CMAA) vested the beds of all 'navigable' rivers in the Crown.[54]

The Court of Appeal has taken different views over the legal effects of the 1903 legislation. In *Te Runanga o Te Ika Whenua v Attorney-General* (*Te Runanga o Te Ika Whenua*)[55] Cooke P doubted whether the provisions of the CMAA were by themselves sufficient to extinguish Māori customary title to river beds:[56]

> In their *Te Ika Whenua-Energy Assets Report* in 1993 and *Mohaka River Report* in 1992 the Waitangi Tribunal have adopted the concept of the river as being taonga. One expression of the concept is "a whole and indivisible entity, not separated into beds, banks and waters". The vesting of the beds of navigable rivers in the Crown may not be sufficiently explicit to override or dispose of that concept, although it is odd that the concept seems not to have been put forward in quite that way in the line of cases concerning the Wanganui River, of which the last is the decision of this Court in *Re the Bed of the Wanganui River.*

However, in *Ngati Apa* Keith and Anderson JJ stated that the language of section 14 of the CMAA was sufficient to extinguish Māori customary title to river beds. Indeed they contrasted this with the language used in the Territorial Sea Acts of 1965 and 1977, wording which was not sufficient to vest full dominium to that area in the Crown. To them the key phrase was 'absolute property of the Crown.' In their view:[57]

> There is a crucial difference between that provision [section 14 of the CMAA] and those of 1965 and 1977. The latter do not include the "absolute property" phrase. That phrase recognises the coexistence of the radical title of the Crown and other (beneficial) property; in the particular case of the 1903 Act the Crown had both and was the "absolute owner", to use the statutory language.

---

54. This was enacted in response to *Mueller v Taupiri Coal Mines Ltd* (1900) 20 NZLR 89 (CA). In *Mueller* the Court of Appeal had held that in the circumstances of a military grant bounded by a public navigable river the presumption that the grantee acquired a title *ad medium filum aquae* (to the mid-line) was rebutted, but this was subject to a powerful dissent from Stout CJ. Section 14 of the 1902 Act became section 206 of the Coal Mines Act 1925 and section 261 of the Coal Mines Act 1979. Although the provision is now repealed, its effect is preserved by section 354 of the Resource Management Act 1991.
55. *Te Runanga o Te Ika Whenua v Attorney-General* [1994] 2 NZLR 20 (CA).
56. *Te Runanga o Te Ika Whenua* above n 55, 25 Cooke P.
57. *Ngati Apa*, above n 1, para 161 Keith and Anderson JJ.

Section 14 of the CMAA does not, however, state that the Crown has 'absolute property' of river beds. Rather the provision states that the beds of navigable rivers are 'vested' in the Crown and that only *minerals* 'within' the bed are the 'absolute property' of the Crown. The CMAA arguably vests only a beneficial title to minerals, not river beds, as is clear from its historical context. The CMAA was a response to some contemporaneous legal questions relating to the ownership of coal lying beneath the bed of the Waikato River. I would argue that while the CMAA does extinguish customary title, if any, to minerals in the subsoil of river beds, the legislation is still insufficiently 'clear and plain' to extinguish a customary title to the beds as such and that the Crown's title remains burdened by Māori title.

Historically, the main cases relating to Māori property rights in river beds have been fought out over the Whanganui River, in a lengthy series of inquiries, Native Land Court cases and litigation in the ordinary courts, culminating in the decision of the Court of Appeal in *Re the Bed of the Wanganui River* in 1962.[58] In this case it was held that there was no separate tribal title to the river bed, and that investigation of title by the Native Land Court of the riparian blocks extinguished the customary title *ad medium filum aquae*. This case was argued on the basis that the statutory vesting of 'navigable' riverbeds would be ignored for the purposes of debate with a view to determining whether the 1903 legislation was confiscatory and whether compensation was payable. The basic legal position today is that 'navigable' river beds are owned by the Crown, and non-navigable river beds forming the boundaries of Māori freehold land blocks (as with other titles bounded by rivers) are owned by the owners of the block *ad medium filum aquae*. The beds of non-navigable rivers and streams otherwise have no particular status and belong to the owner of the relevant titles, although of course rights to take and discharge water are no longer governed by the common law but are controlled by statute, the operative provisions currently found in the Resource Management Act 1991.

The Wanganui River decision of the Court of Appeal indicates very clearly the concept of a 'downstream' consequence of investigation of title by the Native Land Court. Essentially the notion grew that once a title was issued by

---

58. *Re the Bed of the Wanganui River* [1962] NZLR 600 (CA). See now Waitangi Tribunal *The Whanganui River Report: Wai 167* (GP Publications, Wellington, 1999). See also Waitangi Tribunal *Mohaka River Report: Wai 119* (Waitangi Tribunal, Department of Justice, Wellington, 1992); Waitangi Tribunal *Ika Whenua Rivers Report: Wai 212* (GP publications, Wellington, 1998). For the legal history of the Whanganui River litigation, see generally J P Ferguson *Maori Claims Relating to Rivers and Lakes* (LLM Research Paper, Victoria University of Wellington, 1989). See also *R v Morison* [1950] NZLR 247 (SC); Sir Harold Johnston 'Report of the Royal Commission on Claims Made in respect of the Wanganui River' [1950] 27 AJHR G 2; *Re the Bed of the Wanganui River* [1955] NZLR 419 (CA); David Young *Woven by Water: Histories from the Whanganui River* (Huia Publishers, Wellington, 1998).

the Native Land Court, the whole of Māori property rights with respect to that area were comprised wholly within the title leaving no scope for anything cognisable at common law. This, as will be seen, was extended by the Court of Appeal to the foreshore in 1961. An equivalent doctrine developed with regard to Māori fishing rights at sea, exemplified clearly in *Keepa v Inspector of Fisheries*.[59] Here the Court held that the grant of a native land freehold order to a coastal property extinguished customary fishing rights in respect of the adjacent seacoast. The rejection of this approach by Williamson J in *Te Weehi v Regional Fisheries Officer*[60] was a decisive turning-point and a significant step along the path which led ultimately to the *Ngati Apa* decision in 2003.

IV *The Background to* re Ninety-Mile Beach

In the twentieth century there was a series of legally inconclusive investigations to Te Whanganui-a-Orotū, the huge area of estuarine marshes and salt flats which stretched north and west of the town of Napier.[61] (This convoluted and intricate issue had the added novelty that as a result of the Napier earthquake of 1931 the entire area was raised above sea level and converted into the flat plain which stretches north of the modern city.) The inquiries into Te Whanganui-a-Orotū tended to be based on the assumption that the Crown did own the foreshore; therefore the real question for investigation was whether the lagoon ought to be classed as an estuarine lagoon or as a lake. If it was a lake, then following the decision in *Tamihana Korokai* title could indeed be investigated by the Native Land Court; however, if it was a tidal body then it could not be. (In terms of the principles of the Treaty of Waitangi, of course, the Waitangi Tribunal decided in 1995 that this was irrelevant).[62]

Over the years the lagoon was the subject of varying arguments. The issue over ownership of the Napier lagoon as estuary or foreshore was clouded by the question of whether or not the harbour, and all of the islands in it, were included within the boundaries of the Ahuriri purchase of 1851. In

---

59. *Keepa v Inspector of Fisheries* [1965] NZLR 322 (SC). The decision in *Keepa v Inspector of Fisheries* followed F B Adams J's decision in *Inspector of Fisheries v Weepu* [1956] NZLR 920 (HC), a case about whitebait fisheries in the Arahura River. The High Court here insisted that customary fishing rights could not be severed from land ownership.
60. *Te Weehi v Regional Fisheries Officer*, above n 14.
61. There were two judicial inquiries into Te Whanganui-a-Orotū, in 1920 and 1934. (The judge hearing the latter, Judge Harvey of the Native Land Court, did not report until 1948.) For a full narrative see Waitangi Tribunal *Te Whanganui-a-Orotu Report: Wai 55* (Waitangi Tribunal, Department of Justice, Wellington, 1995).
62. See Waitangi Tribunal *Te Whanganui-a-Orotu Report: Wai 55,* above n 61, 209: '[W]e do not see why the presence of substantial quantities of salt water within Te Whanganui-a-Orotu and the influence of the tide should alter the position in Treaty terms. Indeed, the word 'moana' denotes a lake as well as the sea. To the claimants and other petitioners it was (like Lake Omapere) Maori customary land.'

1916 Salmond's opinion was that although the harbour was not included in the Ahuriri purchase it belonged to the Crown in any event by prerogative right.[63] The harbour 'is tidal water and the limits of Native customary title are the high water mark.' In 1934, however, the Crown Law Office was no longer confident that the claim to title to the lagoon by prerogative right was sustainable.[64] The Crown Solicitor's views were startlingly prescient:

> With all respect to the late Solicitor-General's opinion, I doubt if *Waipapakura v Hempton* (1914), 33 NZLR 1065, goes as far as he suggests; once the law has recognised the assertability of Native rights in the demesne law of the Crown, which no doubt it has done – *Nireaha Tamaki v Baker*, [1901] AC 561 – it is difficult to find a good ground for excluding any land over which the Crown has imperium, dominium, and mesne ownership, whether the covering water be river, lake, or sea, whether tidal or not, and whether the land be above, within or below the foreshore strip. But I trust such important issues will not be raised on the present reference.

One may say that in recent years the chickens so clearly perceived by the Crown Solicitor as long ago as 1934 have well and truly come home to roost.

There was another, also somewhat inconclusive, investigation of Awapuni Lagoon at Gisborne.[65] But the most significant developments took place in Northland, in the Tai Tokerau division of the Native Land Court. The key factor here was the presence of a remarkable judge, Frank Acheson, Tai Tokerau judge during the period 1924–1943, who we have already encountered earlier with respect to his remarkable Lake Omapere decision.[66] Judge Acheson carried out a long courtroom battle over Māori foreshore claims with Sir Vincent Meredith, Crown solicitor at Auckland. Judge Acheson made grants below high water mark and Meredith appealed the decisions to the Māori Appellate Court. Of these cases the most significant was one over the Ngakororo mudflats on the Hokianga harbour, decided by Judge Acheson in 1941 and dealt with by the Appellate Court in 1944.[67]

In *Ngakororo* the Māori Appellate Court was unable to see any difference in principle between investigating title to the foreshore and conducting an

---

63. J Salmond, Solicitor General, to the Under-Secretary of Lands and Survey (28 August 1916) Letter (Archives file, National Archives, Wellington, L&S 1, 29057).
64. Crown Solicitor, Crown Law Office, to the Under-Secretary of Lands and Survey (15 March 1934) Letter (Archives file, National Archives, Wellington, L&S 1, 29057).
65. *Awapuni Lagoon* (1928) 56 Gisborne Minute Book 284. For a full analysis of this somewhat intractable affair, see R P Boast *The Foreshore* (Waitangi Tribunal Rangahaua Whanui Series Theme Q, GP Publications, Wellington, 1996) 52–56.
66. On Acheson see John Acheson and R P Boast 'Acheson, Frank Oswald Victor 1887–1948: Clerk, Land Purchase Officer, Land Court Judge, Writer' in *Dictionary of New Zealand Biography* (Allen & Unwin; Department of Internal Affairs, Wellington, 1998) vol 4, 1–3.
67. *Ngakororo* (1942) 12 Auckland Native Appellate Court Minute Book 137.

investigation of title to any other piece of land:[68]

> The Native Land Court's decision as to whether these mud flats are papatupu land must rest upon findings of fact. Just as in the investigation of title to customary land, it is necessary for the claimants to establish their right, and this is done by showing that the land has descended to them from a tribal ancestor and has been in the continual occupation of the claimants and their predecessors prior to 1840 and down to the date of investigation.

In terms of what was needed to be proved, it was stressed that the standard was a relatively strict one. Māori use of the *locus in quo* had to be differentiated from that of the general public. The area claimed needed to be carefully defined; there had to be 'reliable' evidence 'to suggest the continuous and exclusive use of this land by the claimants and their predecessors from time immemorial', and the mudflats had to be shown to exist 'in 1840 in much the same condition as they appear today.'[69]

The *Ninety-Mile Beach* case in the Court of Appeal also began, of course, in the Māori Land Court, which conducted a full investigation of title and heard a great deal of evidence relating to customary use of the beach.[70] The hearing took place in 1957 at Kaitaia before Chief Judge Morison. The case commenced with applications for investigation of title lodged by a Mr Tepania of the Te Rarawa people claiming that the 'land is customary land having been at one time completely under the control and jurisdiction of a Maori, [namely] Tohe' – Tohe having been a founding ancestor of the Te Rarawa people many centuries ago. A key issue raised in the application was control and management of toheroa and an order was sought vesting the beach in trustees. The case was brought by a Mr Dragicevich, a local solicitor based in Kaitaia, and was opposed by Sir Vincent Meredith, the formidable Crown solicitor at Auckland (which was not necessarily a mismatch: Dragicevich was obviously a very good lawyer who argued the High Court appeal himself and appeared in the Court of Appeal as junior counsel).

Evidence was given by kaumātua and by some members of the Pākehā community at Ahipara (the coastal community at the southern end of the beach). The claim was proved in the Māori Land Court in the same way as title to a mainland block: by proof of descent from a particular ancestor, of exclusive use, of resource harvesting, and of control through the mechanisms of Māori customary law. Chief Judge Morison stated that the evidence had clearly demonstrated the following:[71]

---

68. *Ngakororo*, above n 67.
69. *Ngakororo*, above n 67.
70. *Re the Ninety-Mile Beach* (1957) 85 Northern Minute Book 126–127.
71. *Re the Ninety-Mile Beach*, above n 70, 126–7.

A. That the Northern portion [of the beach] was within the territory occupied by Te Aupouri and the Southern portion was within the territory occupied by Te Rarawa.
B. That the members of these tribes had their kaingas and their burial grounds scattered inland from the beach at intervals along the whole distance.
C. That the two tribes occupied their respective portions to the exclusion of other tribes.
D. That the land itself was a major source of food supply for these tribes in that from it the Maoris obtained shell fish [etc.]
E. That the Maoris caught various fish in the sea off the beach …
F. That for various reasons from time to time rahuis [prohibitions] were imposed upon various parts of the beach and the sea itself.
G. That the beach was generally used by members of these tribes.

The case does show that as far as the Māori Land Court is concerned the foreshore and seabed is not 'special' in any way (as lakes are not): title is a matter of fact, to be proved by the elements of exclusivity, actual use and management by customary law. Chief Judge Morison applied standard Māori Land Court practice. He reviewed the evidence he had heard and the reasons given by the Crown for opposing the application, and concluded that the claim had been made out:[72]

> The Court is of opinion that these tribes were the owners of the territories over which they were able to exercise exclusive dominion or control. The two parts of this land were immediately before the Treaty of Waitangi within the territories over which Te Aupouri and Te Rarawa respectively exercised exclusive dominion and control and the Court therefore determines that they were owned and occupied by these tribes respectively, according to their customs and usages.

As is well-known, the decision of the Māori Land Court in *Ninety-Mile Beach* was appealed by way of case stated, first to the Supreme Court (High Court) and then to the Court of Appeal. The Court of Appeal's decision was based on certain assumptions about native title which were questionable even at the time and certainly could not withstand scrutiny by a modern court. But in some ways the decision also hammered the first nails into the coffin of the Crown's position. In the Court of Appeal the Crown took the position that it 'owned' the foreshore by prerogative right in New Zealand just as it did in England (this being something of a simplification of the position at common law in any event). The Solicitor-General argued that: '[O]n the assumption of sovereignty by Her Majesty Queen Victoria, the foreshore of the lands of New

---

72. *Re the Ninety-Mile Beach*, above n 70.

Zealand ... became and has ever since remained vested in the Crown, and that the Maori Land Court ... has not and never did have jurisdiction to investigate title to land below high-water mark.'[73]

But the Court of Appeal did not agree. Although Māori lost in the *Ninety-Mile Beach* case it was not on the grounds that common law Crown prerogative title to the foreshore applied in New Zealand. North J remarked that while this argument had 'an attractive simplicity', it was nevertheless 'not well founded.'[74] Gresson J stated that although it *might* have been argued before 1862 – when the first Native Lands Act was enacted – that 'Native title over the foreshore had been extinguished by operation of the Common Law', this was in his view doubtful before 1862 and impossible to maintain afterwards. He stated: 'I doubt the validity of these submissions even prior to 1862, and the acceptance of either contention would involve a serious infringement of the spirit of the Treaty of Waitangi and would in effect amount to depriving the Maoris of their customary rights over the foreshore by a side wind rather than by an express enactment.'[75]

Having reached this point, the Court of Appeal found an alternative basis for the extinguishment of native title. This was, once again, by reference to the supposed 'downstream' effect of the Native Land Court process on appurtenant rights, an analysis which was more or less the same as in its decision relating to the Whanganui River and which closely paralleled the various Supreme Court fisheries decisions discussed above.

First, the Court of Appeal made the assumption that at some point or other the Native Land Court *must* have investigated the title to the various blocks of land along the coast adjoining the beach – an assumption which was, as it happens, completely wrong. According to North J:[76]

> The case stated by the Maori Land Court does not supply any information whether the whole of the land extending along the length of the Ninety Mile Beach above high-water mark has been investigated, but as the first Maori Land Court was constituted rather more than 100 years ago and it was recorded more than 50 years ago that the Native customary title to land in New Zealand had for the most part been extinguished, it would seem to me that the probabilities are all that it has.

---

73. *Re the Ninety-Mile Beach*, above n 2, 467.
74. *Re the Ninety-Mile Beach*, above n 2, 468.
75. *Re the Ninety-Mile Beach*, above n 2, 477–478. Of course the particular consequences attributed to the Native Lands Acts by the Court of Appeal in 1962 are not tenable and are now only of historical interest as a result of the decision in *Ngati Apa*, above n 1.
76. The Court of Appeal was overlooking the possibility that title to the lands inland of the beach may have been investigated by pre-emptive Crown purchase before the establishment of the Native Land Court – which was in fact the case: see R P Boast '*In re Ninety-Mile Beach* Revisited: The Native Land Court and the Foreshore in New Zealand Legal History' (1993) 23 VUWLR 145.

Having convinced itself, erroneously, that the Native Land Court must have sat everywhere, the Court of Appeal next turns to the consequences of such an investigation, revealing the clear parallels with the analysis applied in *Re the Bed of the Wanganui River*:[77]

> I am of opinion that once an application for investigation of title to land having the sea as one of its boundaries was terminated, the Maori customary title was then wholly extinguished. If the Court made a freehold order or its equivalent fixing the boundary as low water mark and the Crown accepted that recommendation, then without doubt the individuals in whose favour the order was made or their successors gained a title to low water mark. If on the other hand, the Court thought it right to fix the boundary at high water mark, then the ownership of the land between high water mark and low water mark likewise *remained* with the Crown, freed and discharged from the obligations which the Crown had undertaken when legislation was enacted giving effect to the promise contained within the Treaty of Waitangi.

One hardly knows where to begin in unpacking the flaws and non-sequiturs in this key passage. One may as well begin with the observation that few today would see the Native Lands Acts, of all things, as a statutory confirmation of the 'promise contained within the Treaty of Waitangi.' The giveaway is, of course, the word 'remained', which indicates that the Court of Appeal, despite its rejection of the Crown claim to foreshore ownership by prerogative right, nevertheless still sees the Crown as having some kind of title to the foreshore which goes much further than mere imperium. Unless Māori receive a title to the foreshore within the four walls of the Māori Land Court process, that process of itself extinguishes Māori title to the foreshore (the 'downstream' reasoning seen in the Whanganui River decisions and in *Keepa*). There is also, as mentioned, the peculiarity that the Court's reasoning has little applicability to Ninety-Mile Beach itself: the Court did not actually seem to be aware of the legal history of the beach, although there was clear evidence of this on the record.

It is clear from Crown Law opinions and memoranda that the Government's own legal advisers had become increasingly concerned about the Crown's uncertain title to the foreshore and seabed. Crown Law strongly advocated taking steps to ensure that the Māori Land Court had no jurisdiction over the area. Certainly Crown Law hoped that the ordinary courts would be a safer forum for the Crown, which indeed turned out to be the case, but the issue was in real doubt until the release of the Court of Appeal's decision in 1962.

---

77. *Re the Ninety-Mile Beach*, above n 2, 473 (emphasis added).

The Government's win in the *Ninety-Mile Beach* case seemed to obviate the need for any statutory clarification of title to the foreshore, and nothing was done to put the matter beyond doubt by vesting title to the foreshore in the Crown. Taking this step in the wake of *Ngati Apa* was, however, certain to cause a very strong Māori reaction.

The linking of title to the foreshore with title to the adjoining coastline, such an important aspect of the reasoning in the *Ninety-Mile Beach* case, has in one key respect been retained by the new FSA. That Act, while vesting title to the foreshore and seabed in the Crown, also makes provision for two types of orders which the courts can make to recognise Māori property rights in the foreshore and seabed, these being territorial customary rights orders (TCROs) and customary rights orders. Among the requirements that an applicant for a TCRO must demonstrate to the High Court is that of 'continuous title to contiguous land.'[78] This is going to prove a significant stumbling block for many groups, while privileging those such as Ngāti Porou or Te Whānau-a-Apanui who have been able to retain possession of much of their coastal land. If that seems unfair the rejoinder is perhaps that the FSA is a statutory recasting of the law of native title, which is a rule of property law and not a means of redress of historical grievances for which other processes are now available.

V Native Title, the Māori Land Court, and the Foreshore and Seabed: A Retrospect

There are many strands to the weave which came together in *Ngati Apa*, and this chapter has chosen to highlight one in particular, this being the interconnection between the Native Land Court title process and supposedly appurtenant rights to river beds, fisheries, and the foreshore. This line of analysis was dismantled first with regard to coastal fisheries in *Te Weehi*, an important decision, which seems to have been enhanced, rather than lessened, by the passing of time. Next to fall was the foreshore, to which the Government has responded with its recently enacted FSA, which takes the step of vesting the foreshore and seabed in the Crown.[79] What remains to be re-examined, as it happens, is the common law status of river beds. Whether the nation is ready for a rerun of the foreshore and seabed crisis is certainly debatable. Currently

---

78. FSA, s 32(2)(b). See also FSA s 32(6) for the definitions of 'contiguous land' and 'continuous title.'
79. FSA, s 13(1), which provides that 'the full legal and beneficial ownership of the public foreshore and seabed is vested in the Crown, so that the public foreshore and seabed is held by the Crown as its absolute property.' The phrase 'absolute property' has been stated by the Court of Appeal to be a clear indication of a parliamentary intention to vest full dominium in the Crown and an intention to extinguish the Native or customary title: see *Ngati Apa*, above n 1, para 161 Keith and Anderson JJ.

the issue of ownership and title to the Whanganui River is being dealt with by a negotiated settlement which no doubt will be implemented in statute, an example of the usually successful, pragmatic and case-by-case method of resolution of these matters which has been the true New Zealand tradition for most of the twentieth century.

Wi Parata is Dead, Long Live *Wi Parata*

David V Williams*

I Introduction

The title of this chapter is intended to pun the sense of the constitutional legitimacy and continuity that flows from the proclamation made on the death of a monarch. In the first language of English monarchs for 400 years the proclamation was '[f]eu le Roi, vive le Roi', and since Tudor times the words have been in English: '[t]he King is dead, long live the King.' The idea is an old one. The death of an Egyptian pharaoh was accompanied, a Google search informs me, by a formal announcement to the effect that '[t]he falcon is flown to heaven and [his successor] is arisen in his place.'[1] The thrust of this chapter is that there is a striking continuity between the views of Richmond J and Prendergast CJ in the 1877 Supreme Court decision of *Wi Parata v Bishop of Wellington* (*Wi Parata*),[2] on the non-justiciability of matters pertaining to Māori customary rights, and the response of almost all contemporary parliamentarians to the foreshore and seabed jurisdiction decision of the Court of Appeal in *Attorney-General v Ngati Apa* (*Ngati Apa*).[3]

---

*   Professor of Law, University of Auckland, Aotearoa New Zealand
1.   A www.google.co.nz search for 'the king is dead, long live the king' reveals numerous internet sites dedicated to Elvis Presley, Megadeth and Enigma lyrics, the replacement of one Australian rugby coach with another, the death of Louis XIV ('Le Roi est mort! Vive le Roi!') and assorted other contexts in addition to the proclamation of English monarchical succession which is my interest. I am informed that the Anglo-Norman *feu* is derived not from *focum*, meaning 'fire', but from *fatutus* meaning 'deceased': British Society for the Turin Shroud <http://www.shroud.com/bsts4805.htm> (last accessed 15 October 2004). For the words of the proclamation on the death of a pharaoh see Tour Egypt! <http://www.touregypt.net> (last accessed 6 October 2004).
2.   *Wi Parata v Bishop of Wellington* (1877) 3 NZ Jur (NS) (SC) 72. (From 1841 to 1980 the Supreme Court was the name of the first instance superior court that is now known as the High Court. Since the Supreme Court Act 2003 came into force, the court so named is now the final appellate court of the New Zealand legal system – two appellate tiers above the erstwhile Supreme Court prior to 1980).
3.   *Attorney-General v Ngati Apa & others* [2003] 3 NZLR 643 (CA). Though usually referred to as the *Ngati Apa* case, there were eight iwi with customary interests in the northern regions of the South

It is important to provide the historical context for the controversies that led to the enactment of the Foreshore and Seabed Act 2004 (the FSA) and the Resource Management (Foreshore and Seabed) Amendment Act 2004. The New Zealand Centre for Public Law conference where this chapter was first presented was entitled 'Foreshore and Seabed: the New Frontier'. It will become apparent, though, that in my view we are dealing with an old frontier rather than a new one. This chapter considers some aspects of the application of *Wi Parata* reasoning in governmental policy during the late nineteenth and early twentieth centuries. It also considers the wider context of the policies of amalgamation or assimilation in that era. These were aimed at eradicating Māori cultural and social norms or, as it would have then been put, 'civilising the Natives'. It notes that policies of integration in the mid-twentieth century had a similar tendency. It then concludes that the thrust of government policy in 2003 and 2004 is in many respects still consistent with *Wi Parata* reasoning.

There are a number of frequently quoted aphorisms about the relevance of history, some being less complimentary of history than others. A few of them are as follows:[4]

- History is the sum total of the things they're not telling us. – Don DeLillo
- Until the lions have their own historians, tales of the hunting will always glorify the hunter. – African Proverb
- The past is a foreign country; they do things differently there. – L P Hartley
- An account mostly false, of events unimportant, which are brought about by rulers mostly knaves, and soldiers mostly fools. – Ambrose Bierce
- History repeats itself. That's one of the things that's wrong with history. – Clarence Darrow
- History is nothing but a pack of tricks that we play upon the dead. – Voltaire
- We learn from history that we do not learn from history. – George Friedrich Wilhelm Hegel
- History is a nightmare from which we are trying to awaken. – James Joyce
- Those who cannot remember the past are condemned to repeat it. – George Santayana

My own favourite, however, is that of the famous American writer Samuel Clemens, otherwise known as Mark Twain, who observed that '[h]istory does

---

Island who combined to initiate this litigation.

4. These are non-authenticated quotations derived from searching 'history' in 'The Progressive Review: Free Thoughts, Sam Smith's Favorite Quotes' <http://prorev.com/quotes2.htm> (last accessed 7 February 2005).

not repeat itself, but it does rhyme a lot.'⁵

II Radical Title, Aboriginal Title and Māori Customary Rights

When the colonial state of New Zealand was established, it was plain as a matter of imperial policy that New Zealand was to be a settlement colony and that European settlers needed land. Land and immigration policy were therefore crucial to imperial and colonial officials. On the other hand, the cultural and spiritual relationships and inter-connections between land and people were central to the precepts of the indigenous systems of customary law, now collectively known as 'tikanga Māori'. The notion of sharing resources with incomers, under arrangements that involved an ongoing commitment to mutually beneficial and reciprocal outcomes, was entirely possible under tikanga Māori. In many parts of the country there had been a number of European sealers, whalers, traders and missionaries who had lived under customary law regimes in the fifty years of contact before 1840. However, the notion of permanent alienation of land, or even of 'ownership' of land as such, was not imaginable. Hohepa, formerly the Māori Language Commissioner, wrote about 'whenua' – the Māori word for land – in this way:⁶

> For Maori, whenua has an added meaning, being the human placenta or afterbirth. Through various birth ceremonies the placenta is returned to the land, and that results in each Maori person having personal, spiritual, symbolic and sacred links to the land where their whenua (placenta) is part of the whenua (land). The words 'nooku teenei whenua' (This is my land) is given a much stronger meaning because of the above extensions. Having ancestral and birth connections the above is also translated as 'I belong to this land, so do my ancestors, and when I die I join them so I too will be totally part of this land'.

The paradigms of land tenure written by the Colonial Office in instructions to governors as implemented by the Land Claims Ordinance 1841 were very different. That Ordinance declared 'all unappropriated lands within the said Colony of New Zealand, subject however to the rightful and necessary occupation and use thereof by the aboriginal inhabitants of the said Colony, are and remain Crown or Domain Lands of Her Majesty.' This was an assertion of the radical title of the Crown to all land.

There are many instances of Māori challenging the notion of the Crown's

---

5. See John Petrie's collection of Mark Twain quotes <http://www.arches.uga.edu/~jpetrie/clemens.html> (last accessed 7 February 2005).
6. P Hohepa and D V Williams *The Taking into account of Te Ao Maori in relation to the Reform of the Law of Succession* (Law Commission, Wellington, 1996) 10. See T A Royal (ed) *The Woven Universe: Selected Writings of Rev Maori Marsden* (Te Wānanga-a-Raukawa, Ōtaki, 2003).

radical title, not least in the *Wi Parata* and *Nireaha Tamaki v Baker* (*Nireaha Tamaki*) litigation that I will mention shortly.[7] In modern times the Waitangi Tribunal has pointed out the adverse consequences of the doctrine for Māori, and Chief Judge Durie (in extra-judicial remarks) has queried the basis for 'some legal magic from England' being applied in the circumstances of the colony of New Zealand.[8] Durie points to the fact that by section 1 of the English Laws Act 1858: 'The laws of England as existing on the 14th day of January 1840, shall, so far as applicable to the circumstances of the said Colony of New Zealand, be deemed and taken to have been in force therein on and after that day.'[9]

To what extent, queries Durie in the 1990s, ought English doctrines of law give way to tikanga Māori conceptions on the ground that a number of common law presumptions and the doctrines of tenure are inapplicable to the circumstances of New Zealand? In asking such questions Durie assumes that the answers should be governed by the 'circumstances of New Zealand' as they are now understood. For colonial officials in the 1840s, however, the immediate need was to develop policies that would provide land for the incoming settlers.

Operating on nineteenth-century common law assumptions, the officials pondered whether, prior to the issuance of Crown grants to land, Māori customary rights had first to be extinguished in respect of *all* land desired by the Government and settlers, or only in respect of land actually occupied and cultivated in 1840 by Māori tribes. There had been some inconsistent views on waste lands and on the nature and extent of Māori land rights expressed within the Colonial Office and in the imperial and colonial legislatures. Some of these ambiguities were expressed in the Normanby Instructions of 1839, in the Russell Instructions of 1840, and in letters and despatches prepared by Colonial Office officials. Then there were vigorous debates in the New South Wales legislature in 1840, and in the imperial legislature in regard to hearings of a House of Commons select committee that reported in 1844.[10]

In 1846 Earl Grey attempted to clarify the matter when he issued a new set of Instructions to the incoming governor, George Grey (not a relative). They were avowedly based on the views of Dr Arnold, Oxford historian, sometime

---

7. *Nireaha Tamaki v Baker* [1901] AC 561 (PC).
8. Waitangi Tribunal *Muriwhenua Land Report* (Wellington, 1997) 135–179; E T Durie 'Native Title Re-established' (International Bar Association Conference, Melbourne, 1994); E T Durie 'Will the Settlers Settle? Cultural Conciliation and Law' (1996) 8 OLR 449, 461–462.
9. The 1858 Act was re-enacted as the English Laws Act 1908. This was repealed and replaced by the Imperial Laws Application Act 1988 that is now in force.
10. See A H McLintock, *Crown Colony Government in New Zealand* (Government Printer, Wellington, 1958); Peter Adams *Fatal Necessity. British Intervention in New Zealand 1830–1847* (Oxford University Press, Auckland, 1977); Mark Hickford 'Making "Territorial Rights of the Natives": Britain and New Zealand, 1830–1847' (D Phil thesis, University of Oxford, 1999).

Headmaster of Rugby School and follower of the theories of John Locke: '[So] much does the right of property go along with labour, that civilized nations have never scrupled to take possession of countries inhabited only by tribes of savages – countries which have been hunted over but never subdued or cultivated.'[11]

Earl Grey (then known as Lord Howick) had been the primary author of the House of Commons committee report in 1844. That report argued for the settlement of waste lands in the colony without undue deference to the 'injudicious proceedings' of the Treaty of Waitangi. Now as Secretary of State for the Colonies he strongly dissented from the notion that aboriginal inhabitants are the proprietors of every part of the soil of any country. For him, civilised (that is, European) men had a right to step in and take possession of vacant territory: '[All] lands not actually occupied in the sense in which alone occupation can give a right of possession ought to have been considered as the property of the Crown.' The Governor was expressly empowered to depart from the strict application of these principles if it would be impracticable to enforce that policy.[12]

Governor FitzRoy in 1843 was faced with a virtually bankrupt colonial administration. As he had no money to enter into land-purchase transactions and yet settlers were clamouring to buy land from Māori, he decided that he would waive Crown pre-emption and thus permit settlers to engage in direct purchasing of land from Māori. Consistent with the 1846 Royal Instructions the new Governor refused to follow through with the procedures established by FitzRoy in relation to pre-emption waiver certificates. Instead, Grey initiated a test case in the Supreme Court to justify his refusal to award Crown grants over land to persons whose claims were based on those certificates. In *R v Symonds* in 1847 the judges of the Supreme Court asserted the paramount importance of the Crown's pre-emptive monopoly right to purchase lands from Māori.[13] Nevertheless, relying on Supreme Court judgments of Marshall CJ and the commentaries of Kent and Story in the United States of America, they took a more liberal view of the scope of aboriginal title than Earl Grey had:[14]

> Whatever may be the opinion of jurists as to the strength or weakness of the Native title, whatsoever may have been the past vague notions of the Natives of this country, whatever may be their present clearer and still growing conception

---

11. Earl Grey to Grey, 23 December 1846, *British Parliamentary Papers: Colonies New Zealand* (Irish University Press, Shannon, 1969) vol 5, 523–525.
12. Earl Grey to Grey, above n 11. See David V Williams' *Te Kooti tango whenua': The Native Land Court 1864–1909* (Huia Publishers, Wellington, 1999) 108–114.
13. *R v Symonds* (1847) NZPCC 387 (HC).
14. *R v Symonds*, above n 13, 390 (HC) Chapman J. See D V Williams '*Queen v Symonds* Reconsidered' (1989) 19 VUWLR 385.

of their own dominion over land, it cannot be too solemnly asserted that it is entitled to be respected, that it cannot be extinguished (at least in times of peace) otherwise than by the free consent of the Native occupiers. But for their protection, and for the sake of humanity, the Government is bound to maintain, and the Courts to assert, the Queen's exclusive right to extinguish it.

Bearing in mind the strongly expressed opposition by Māori rangatira to the waste-lands doctrine (at a time when Māori comprised the overwhelming majority of the population), the Governor decided that he should follow the Court's views on the doctrine of Crown pre-emption and aboriginal title.[15] He thus availed himself of the permission from Earl Grey to depart from the strict application of Lockean waste-lands principles if it would be impracticable to enforce that policy. Thereafter, Crown pre-emption was relied on by successive governors and governments until 1862. Crown pre-emption enabled government land-purchase agents to enter into transactions described as land-purchase deeds over very large blocks of land. These deeds purported to extinguish Māori customary title to the majority of the land in the country, especially in those regions where the Māori population was low and settler pressures for access to good pastoral land or to mining opportunities were great.

An increasing reluctance by Māori tribes to sell land, and the outbreak of war between Crown and Māori forces in several areas of the North Island, led to a change of policy. The Native Lands Act 1862 waived Crown pre-emption once again and replaced it with a Native Land Court system. This court over the next sixty years investigated the customary title rights to all land blocks not dealt with either in the earlier deeds or under the confiscation proclamations of the New Zealand Settlements Act 1863. After the Court's title investigation, customary title was extinguished and a form of individualised freehold title was then issued to named Māori 'owners'. As was desired and anticipated by the governments responsible for the Native Land Acts, most Māori freehold title land was alienated into the hands of the Crown or settlers within a short period after title investigations.[16]

III *Customary Rights Rejected*

By 1890 the settler population had grown rapidly. It was considerably larger than the indigenous population, which steadily diminished until the end of the century. Albeit with considerable difficulty at times, imperial armed might,

---

15. See also Mark Hickford 'Settling Some Very Important Principles of Colonial Law: Three "Forgotten" Cases of the 1840s' (2004) 35 VUWLR 1.
16. *'Te Kooti tango whenua': The Native Land Court 1864–1909*, above n 12, 58–62.

colonial militia and Māori kupapa forces had broken the military resistance of those Māori tribes who fought to retain their autonomy and independence during the period of warfare from 1860 to 1872.[17] These political and military facts are sometimes put forward as an explanation for the decision in *Wi Parata*. This was a judgment that refused to allow an inquiry into whether Māori customary rights had been properly extinguished as to do so would unsettle property rights based on a Crown grant.

In *Wi Parata* the Court significantly reinterpreted the reasoning of *R v Symonds*. The radical title of the Crown to all lands was emphasised. The Court now took the view not only that it had no jurisdiction to avoid a Crown grant of land, but also that it should not in any way go behind a Crown grant to inquire into the extinguishment or otherwise of any prior customary rights. In the judgment of Prendergast CJ and Richmond J, delivered by the Chief Justice, the 1841 Ordinance was said to 'express the well-known legal incidents of a settlement planted by a civilised Power in the midst of uncivilised tribes.' The Treaty of Waitangi was dismissed 'as a simple nullity.' No body politic existed capable of making a cession of sovereignty, nor could the thing itself exist. So far as the proprietary rights of the natives are concerned, the so-called treaty merely affirms the rights and obligations which, *jure gentium*, vested in and devolved upon the Crown.[18]

Nor did an explicit provision in the Native Rights Act 1865 make a difference. That Act speaks, the judges wrote, 'of the "Ancient Custom and Usage of the Maori people", as if some such body of customary law did in reality exist. But a phrase in a statute cannot call what is non-existent into being.' Rather, 'in the case of primitive barbarians, the supreme executive Government must acquit itself, as best it may, of its obligation to respect native proprietary rights, and of necessity must be the sole arbiter of its own justice.'[19]

It has been argued by McHugh that this was the only reasoning 'intellectually available to the common law thought of that time.'[20] This seems an odd statement to make and more especially so as the 1847 *Symonds* approach had been affirmed by a bench of the Court of Appeal just five years earlier, in 1872, in *Re Lundon and Whitaker Claims Act 1871*.[21] Be that as it may, when faced with what was in effect a challenge to the Crown's right to radical title by Ngāti Toa in 1877, the Supreme Court resiled from the

---

17. See J Belich *Making Peoples: A History of the New Zealanders From Polynesian Settlement to the End of the Nineteenth Century* (Penguin, Auckland, 1996).
18. *Wi Parata v Bishop of Wellington*, above n 2, 78.
19. *Wi Parata v Bishop of Wellington*, above n 2, 77–80.
20. P G McHugh 'Tales of Constitutional Origin and Crown Sovereignty in New Zealand' (2002) 52 UTLJ 69, 78–79.
21. *Re Lundon and Whitaker Claims Act 1871* (1872) 2 NZCA 41, 49 (CA).

fuller recognition of aboriginal rights expressed in the *Symonds* judgments. The *Wi Parata* approach thus replaced legal obligations to respect indigenous customary rights with unenforceable and non-justiciable moral obligations on the executive branch of government to deal with those rights as they saw fit. The proclamation of British sovereignty and the concomitant radical title of the Crown to all land was supported by the Court's refusal to permit the impeaching of Crown grants.

A number of aspects of the *Wi Parata* judgment attracted criticism from the Privy Council in later cases. In *Nireaha Tamaki* and again in *Wallis v Solicitor-General* (*Wallis*), the Judicial Committee pointed to the incontrovertible statutory recognition of the existence of customary Māori rights and the capacity of Māori tribes to enter into legal transactions.[22] In an extraordinary outburst of anger, the judges in Wellington publicly lambasted the Privy Council after the *Wallis* opinion in 1903, not only for its insinuation that the colonial judges were beholden to the executive but also for their Lordships' palpable ignorance, as the colonial bench viewed it, of laws and practices concerning native land issues. Consistently with the reasoning of *Wi Parata*, Stout CJ's protest included the assertion that '[a]ll lands of the Colony belonged to the Crown, and it was for the Crown under Letters Patent to grant to the parties to the Treaty such lands as the Crown had agreed to grant.'[23]

The colonial judiciary, therefore, refused to distance themselves from *Wi Parata* and rejected the admonitions of the final appellate court for the Empire.[24] The judges did not need to worry about further adverse findings from the Privy Council, however, because the legislature had no compunction to rapidly enact statutes reversing inconvenient Privy Council decisions. More than that, ongoing litigation by Nireaha Tamaki was explicitly discontinued and further proceedings by him or on his behalf were statutorily barred.[25]

It was the understandings of the colonial chief justices, Prendergast and Stout, in preference to the views of the Privy Council, that Parliament codified into the Native Land Act 1909. This Act was drafted by Salmond, perhaps New Zealand's most famous jurist, a long-serving Solicitor-General and later a Supreme Court judge.[26] Sections 84 to 87 of the 1909 Act made crystal clear

---

22. *Nireaha Tamaki v Baker*, above n 7; *Wallis v Solicitor-General* [1903] AC 173 (PC).
23. 'Protest of Bench and Bar, 25 April 1903' Appendix to *New Zealand Privy Council Cases, 1840–1932*, 732.
24. *Hohepa Wi Neera v Bishop of Wellington* (1902) 21 NZLR 655 (CA).
25. Land Titles Protection Act 1902; Maori Land Claims Adjustment and Laws Amendment Act 1904, s 4.
26. A Frame *Salmond: Southern Jurist* (Victoria University Press, Wellington, 1995). See also A Frame 'Salmond, John William. 1862 – 1924. Lawyer, university professor, law draftsman, solicitor general, judge' *Dictionary of New Zealand Biography*, Vol 3 (Auckland University Press, Auckland, 1996) 456–458 or Dictionary of New Zealand Biography <http://www.dnzb.govt.nz/dnzb> (last accessed 7 February 2005).

the non-justiciability of any Māori claims that their customary title rights had not been properly extinguished.[27] Salmond's personal explanation to Ngata, an eminent Māori member of Parliament, of those privative clauses in his Bill was as follows:[28]

> The intention is that when a dispute arises between Natives and the Crown as to the right to customary land, the dispute shall be settled by Parliament and not otherwise. The Native race will have nothing to fear from the decision of that tribunal, and to allow the matter to be fought out in the Law Courts would not, I think, be either in the public interest or in the interests of the Natives themselves.

His official explanatory memorandum accompanying the Bill made it clear that, in his view, customary title only existed on the basis of the radical rights of the Crown:[29]

> Customary land, since it has never been Crown-granted, belongs to the Crown. It is in a wide sense of the term Crown land, subject, however, to the right of those Natives who by virtue of Maori custom have a claim to it to obtain a Crown grant (or a certificate of title under the Land Transfer Act in lieu of a grant) on the ascertainment of their customary titles by the Native Land Court. This right of the Natives to their customary lands was recognised by the Treaty of Waitangi in 1840. In its origin it was merely a moral claim, dependent on the good will of the Crown, and not recognisable or enforceable at law.

Salmond went on to argue that whether or not legislative recognition of Māori custom had created a legal right enforceable against the Crown 'was left an open question by the Privy Council in *Nireaha Tamaki v Baker*.' On the other hand, he explained, 'it is settled' by *Wi Parata* that once a Crown grant has been issued then 'the validity of the title so obtained cannot be questioned on the ground that the antecedent Native title to that land had not been lawfully extinguished.'[30] Hence a definition in section 2 of the 1909 Act stated that '[c]ustomary land' means 'land (vested in the Crown) held by Natives under

---

27. These sections were re-enacted in the 1931 and 1953 statutory consolidations of Salmond's code, and they remained in force until the passage of Te Ture Whenua Maori Act/Maori Land Act 1993.
28. *Salmond: Southern Jurist*, above n 26, 114 (citing Salmond to Ngata, 22 December 1909, Crown Law Office, Wellington, Case File 84).
29. J Salmond 'Memorandum: Notes on the History of Native-Land Legislation'. Native Land Bill, 1909 Bills Books, No. 87-3, 1.
30. Salmond 'Memorandum', above n 29. Much of this memorandum was published with the 1931 consolidation *The Public Acts of New Zealand (Reprint) 1908–1931, vol VI*, 87–94. The words quoted above were omitted there, but are in H Bassett, R Steel, and D V Williams *The Maori Land Legislation Manual* (Crown Forestry Rental Trust, Wellington, 1994) App C, 95–96.

the customs and usages of the Maori people.'[31] This definition remained in force in the 1931 and 1953 consolidations of Māori affairs legislation.

By 1911 the area of dry land not yet investigated by the Native Land Court, with the consequent extinguishment of customary title, was tiny.[32] Just when the Government thought that all customary land issues had been well taken care of, however, Māori customary claims to the land comprised in the beds of inland lakes provided a thorny problem for Crown policy. The Court of Appeal affirmed the right of plaintiffs from Te Arawa tribes to have the Native Land Court investigate their title to the bed of Lake Rotorua in *Tamihana Korokai v Solicitor-General*.[33] In arguments to the court and in internal memoranda, Salmond as Solicitor-General expressed indignation that the judges had failed to understand the nature of the Crown's right to prevent customary title issues becoming justiciable issues. The Government then worked hard to ensure that this and other lakebed issues would not come to a hearing before the Native Land Court. In direct negotiations, the Government persuaded Māori tribes to accept the Crown's assertion of ownership in return for various forms of compensation, sometimes including a proportion of the fishing-licence revenues for fishing in those lakes.[34] For Salmond, 'it could never have been the intention of the Legislature to recognise and give legal effect to any Native claim to the exclusive ownership of the great navigable waters of the Dominion.'[35]

IV *The Legacy of Assimilation Policies*

The particularities of the *Wi Parata* doctrines need to be seen against the backdrop of general governmental policies towards Māori cultural knowledge and land tenure systems. Successive government policies of racial amalgamation, assimilation, and integration from 1840 right through to the early 1970s assumed by and large that 'civilisation' was a one-way process.[36] Māori learned from the Pākehā; Pākehā had little or nothing to learn from Māori. For reasons thought by governments at the time to be beneficial for Māori, much of our history since 1840 has included the denigration of

---

31. A full list of statutory definitions of land in the Native Land Acts 1862 to 1909 is set out in *'Te Kooti tango whenua': The Native Land Court 1864–1909,* above n 12, App 3, 255–259.
32. *'Te Kooti tango whenua': The Native Land Court 1864–1909,* above n 12, 59.
33. *Tamihana Korokai v Solicitor-General* (1912) 32 NZLR 321 (CA).
34. *Salmond: Southern Jurist,* above n 26, 115–28.
35. *Salmond: Southern Jurist,* above n 26, 127. See also *In Re the Bed of the Wanganui River* [1962] NZLR 600 (CA); E J Haughey 'Maori Claims to Lakes, River Beds and the Foreshore' (1966) 2 NZULR 29.
36. David Williams *Crown Policy Affecting Maori Knowledge Systems and Cultural Practices* (Waitangi Tribunal Publication, Wellington, 2001).

Māori language and of Māori tribal and cultural knowledge systems. These were considered to be relics of a bygone superstitious past and irrelevant to a modern people in the contemporary world. The collectivism of Māori societies had to be replaced by individualised rights as a necessary ingredient of Crown policy to promote 'progress'. This policy was most apparent in the eradication of 'beastly communism' by the workings of the Native Land Court.[37] Assimilation and individualisation were also the underlying premises of Crown policies towards Māori on the whole gamut of state interventions such as in health, education, housing and criminal justice.

Moreover, this was not just the policy of some distant past when imperial notions of British political, economic, cultural and military supremacy predominated in the thinking of a colonial society that thought of itself as a 'Better Britain in the South Seas.'[38] Sir Apirana Ngata represented the Young Maori Party in Parliament continuously from 1905 until 1943 and was Minister of Native Affairs in two administrations from 1928 to 1930 and from 1931 to 1934. He, like many of his generation of Māori leaders (especially members of Te Aute College Old Boys' Association), was a long-time advocate of the Government's English-language-only policy in the education of Māori children. This education, he thought, would prepare coming generations of Māori for the new world, dominated by Pākehā ways, that they must now live in. But he changed his mind in 1945 when he saw the startling statistics of inability to speak Māori among Māori new entrants to primary schools. He wrote a letter that helped to persuade a Māori Language Committee to recommend that ways must now be found to teach the Māori language in primary schools. He concluded, '[l]astly there [is] something in the sentiment of preserving a culture which belonged to the country. With that goes the assertion that New Zealand would be all the richer for a bilingual and bicultural people.'[39]

Decision makers ignored these remarks and the Committee's recommendations. They preferred to remember Ngata's 1930s views that English should be the only medium of education, rather than pay attention to his late in life alarm call for action to foster the indigenous language and culture of Māori. Bird, a long-serving Senior Inspector of Native Schools, sternly countered Ngata's letter with this remark: 'And finally if the result [of education policies] has been to make Maori lose his language, don't forget that in its place he has the finest language in the world and that the retention

---

37. '*Te Kooti tango whenua*': *The Native Land Court 1864–1909*, above n 12, 63–100.
38. James Belich *Paradise Reforged: A History of the New Zealanders, From the 1880s to the Year 2000* (Allen Lane/Penguin, Auckland, 2001) Part I.
39. *MS-papers-0148-028A, Maori Purposes Fund Board 1945–50* (Alexander Turnbull Library, Wellington, fol 1); *Crown Policy Affecting Maori Knowledge Systems and Cultural Practices*, above n 36, 145.

of Maori is after all largely a matter of sentiment.'[40]

There are scores of documents stored in the archives that I have read expressing similar views. Countless Crown ministers and government officials embraced such views right through until the end of the 1960s. It was not until the 1970s that they were displaced in official discourse by notions of bicultural development. Then, in the 1980s, the invention and development of the 'principles of the Treaty of Waitangi' became the focus of governmental attention. There can be no doubt that the policies, known in the post-World War Two period as 'integration', were deliberate impositions on Māori for their own good as perceived by the governments of the time. The Hunn Report 1960 was the most eloquent statement of the need for a forced march to make Māori become 'modern' people.[41] Some among the current generation of Māori leaders speak of those assimilation and integration policies as a form of 'cultural genocide'. That is not surprising. What is more surprising is how little rancour is generally expressed by Māori and how rarely such sentiments are publicly aired. What is disturbing, on the other hand, is how angry and defensive many Pākehā become when these issues are broached and how unwilling they are to look in any detail at the historical record of the impact of Crown policies on Māori.

V Aboriginal Title Reappears Again (But Not For Long?)

A RESPONSES TO THE COURT OF APPEAL DECISION

Anger and defensiveness were particularly evident in many of the responses, sometimes of an hysterical and scaremongering nature, to the *Ngati Apa* decision of the Court of Appeal in June 2003. A full bench of the Court held that the Māori Land Court did have jurisdiction to inquire into customary entitlements to foreshore and seabed lands. The Court of Appeal media release stressed that the decision 'is a preliminary one about the ability of the iwi to bring their claims. The validity and extent of the customary claims in issue have yet to be decided by the Māori Land Court. The impact of other legislation controlling the management and use of the resources of maritime areas also remains to be considered.'[42]

The Court's decision in *Ngati Apa* was a modest procedural victory for seven iwi from the north of the South Island. They had resorted to litigation after years of unresolved difficulties over procedures to obtain permission to engage

---

40. MS-papers-0148-028A, *Maori Purposes Fund Board 1945–50*, above n 39, fol 4; *Crown Policy Affecting Maori Knowledge Systems and Cultural Practices*, above n 36, 146.
41. J K Hunn 'Report on Department of Maori Affairs with Statistical Supplement' [1961] II AJHR G20; *Crown Policy Affecting Maori Knowledge Systems and Cultural Practices*, above n 36, 77–81.
42. New Zealand Court of Appeal 'Media Release: Seabed Case' (19 June 2003) Press Release.

in commercial aquaculture activities on the foreshore and seabed lands of the Marlborough Sounds. The decision did not define their customary rights, if any. It merely enabled the plaintiffs to adduce evidence to the Māori Land Court by holding that, regardless of explicit parliamentary assertions of Crown ownership, there had been no statutory extinguishment of customary rights or aboriginal title rights. Nevertheless, the Court ruling created a storm of controversy. The fierce debates on talkback radio, letters to editors, opposition political party rallies and the like went on about public access to beaches being threatened by Māori claims to exclusive rights. This rhetoric had little or no connection to the narrow findings of the Court of Appeal or to the actual practical claims of the plaintiffs.

The normal means to resolve ambiguities in the law, following the due process that is supposed to be a fundamental feature of the common law heritage, is to allow a court to hear evidence and to make a ruling based on that evidence. The Government immediately decided that it could not and would not wait. The received political wisdom was that the Pākehā (non-Māori) majority of the population was deeply incensed by the 'judicial activism' of the Court of Appeal. Therefore, the Government would introduce legislation to assert Crown ownership over the foreshore and seabed areas.[43] This then provoked a howl of anguish from Māori interests, including the Government's own Māori members of Parliament.

What followed was a proposal to create a new concept of 'public domain' and to recognise customary rights if, and only if, those rights stopped well short of ownership rights.[44] It was decided that the Māori Land Court must be deprived of its jurisdiction to hear evidence from iwi of their claims to customary entitlements in accordance with tikanga Māori, and the High Court must be deprived of its jurisdiction to apply the doctrine of aboriginal title to similar effect. No court judgment about the property rights, if any, that might flow from any proven customary rights would be allowed to proceed to the issuance of a title. The Government also flatly rejected the recommendations of the Waitangi Tribunal, after an urgent hearing, which called for a 'longer conversation' between the Crown and Māori on these matters and suggested a number of practical alternative options for the Government's consideration.[45]

To ensure a parliamentary majority for the Foreshore and Seabed Bill when it was introduced in 2004, even the 'public domain' concept was dropped and 'full legal and beneficial ownership of the Crown' over the contested

---

43. 'Seabed owned by the Crown says PM' (23 June 2003) *New Zealand Herald* <http://www.nzherald.co.nz> (last accessed 17 February 2005).
44. Department of the Prime Minister and Cabinet *The Foreshore and Seabed of New Zealand: Protecting Public Access and Customary Rights: Government Proposals for Consultation* (Wellington, 2003).
45. Waitangi Tribunal *Report on the Crown's Foreshore and Seabed Policy: Wai 1071* (Legislation Direct, Wellington, 2004).

lands, with existing customary entitlements extinguished, was reasserted. The Bill was significantly amended in the House after the Select Committee's inconclusive consideration of its provisions. As eventually enacted in the FSA, after fierce debates (and in spite of mammoth Māori protest actions), customary entitlements were replaced by a complex regime of court proceedings that purport to permit recognition of the customary rights of Māori in relation to specific foreshore and seabed lands. However those rights are now defined only in terms of the statute's boundaries and prerequisites, and without reference to the actual indicia of tikanga Māori entitlements. If Māori litigants might otherwise have been entitled to a property right equivalent to a freehold title based on common law aboriginal title, then they must now negotiate with the Government for such 'redress' as the Government thinks fit to offer to them.[46] The FSA is now law and its details are the subject of the other chapters presented in this book.

Grandstanding and posturing associated with the FSA continued to be a focus of national politics in the general election of 2005. Yet the Government made an offer in 2004 to vest in Māori interests a proportion of the marine aquaculture commercial licences – the practical issue for Marlborough iwi that started the whole controversy over the foreshore and seabed lands. With minimal political fuss the Māori Commercial Aquaculture Claims Settlement Act 2004 now provides for 20 per cent of new space in aquaculture management areas to be allocated to a trustee company established under the Maori Fisheries Act 2004. The pity is that this modest but practical settlement has been achieved only after huge social and cultural chasms had been created in our communities by the Government's handling of the foreshore and seabed customary rights debacle. Judicial due process was cast aside for the uncertain merits of a political and legal outcome imposed on Māori rather than negotiated with them. It is not surprising that a United Nations body (the UN Committee on the Elimination of Racial Discrimination) has criticised the actions of the New Zealand Government that ran roughshod over the legal rights recognised in court proceedings without the courtesy of engaging in a 'longer conversation' with the indigenous people of Aotearoa/New Zealand.[47] My focus now is on the fate of the legal reasoning in the *Wi Parata* doctrines.

---

46. See Tom Bennion, Malcolm Birdling and Rebecca Paton *Making Sense of the Foreshore and Seabed, A Special Edition of the Maori Law Review* (The Maori Law Review, Wellington, 2004); Tom Bennion, 'Lands Under the Sea: Foreshore and Seabed' in M Belgrave, M Kawharu and D Williams (eds) *Waitangi Revisited: Perspectives on the Treaty of Waitangi* (Oxford University Press, Melbourne, 2004) 233–247.
47. United Nations Committee on the Elimination of All Forms of Racial Discrimination 'Decision 1(66): New Zealand Foreshore and Seabed Act 2004' (11 March 2005) CERD/C/66/NZL/Dec.1.

B Te Ture Whenua Maori Act 1993

It is apparent that the Government was unprepared for the unanimous decision of the five-judge bench of the Court of Appeal in the *Ngati Apa* case. Crown advisers apparently assumed the indisputable correctness of the 1963 Court of Appeal decision in *In Re Ninety-Mile Beach*.[48] In fact, however, *In Re Ninety-Mile Beach* had long been the subject of sustained academic criticism.[49] That decision had been based on the reasoning of cases such as *Wi Parata*, and *Waipapakura v Hempton*[50] and the arguments of Solicitors-General who followed in the footsteps of Salmond. Modern critics suggested that line of cases was inconsistent with the reasoning in a number of more recent Court of Appeal decisions as well as of the Privy Council decisions in the past, noted above.[51] The Government's position, however, was, 'there had never been any intention' that Te Ture Whenua Maori Act 1993 (TTWMA) should apply to land that was foreshore and seabed.[52]

A Maori Affairs Bill was on the Order Paper of the House every year from 1978 to 1993. The 1978 Bill was initially intended to be a new consolidation of the legislation that dated back to Salmond's codification in 1909 and had been amended many times since the previous consolidation in 1953. In February 1983 the Minister of Māori Affairs, Ben Couch, received a paper from the New Zealand Māori Council on a new philosophical approach for the Bill based on the Treaty of Waitangi.[53] By 1988 it was clear that one of the features of a redrafted Bill would be the repeal of sections 155 to 158 (which were the re-enactments of Salmond's adoption of the *Wi Parata* doctrine in sections 84 to 87 of the 1909 Act). This delighted Paul McHugh, who trumpeted the possible implications for new applications of the doctrine of aboriginal title in a manner that would be 'simple and for the Government frightening.'[54] The

---

48. *In Re Ninety-Mile Beach* [1963] NZLR 461 (CA).
49. K Roberts-Wray *Commonwealth and Colonial Law* (Stevens, London, 1966) 626–635; F M Brookfield 'The New Zealand Constitution: The Search for Legitimacy' in I H Kawharu (ed) *Waitangi. Maori and Pakeha Perspectives of the Treaty of Waitangi* (Oxford University Press, Auckland, 1989) 10–12; R P Boast '*In Re the Ninety-Mile Beach* Revisited' (1993) 23 VUWLR 145; P G McHugh *The Maori Magna Carta: New Zealand Law and the Treaty of Waitangi* (Oxford University Press, Auckland, 1991) 117–26. See *Ngati Apa*, above n 3, para 87 Elias CJ.
50. *Waipapakura v Hempton* (1914) 33 NZLR 1065 (SC).
51. Recent Court of Appeal decisions cited included *Te Runanga o Muriwhenua v Attorney-General* [1990] 2 NZLR 641 and *Te Runanganui o Te Ika Whenua Inc v Attorney-General* [1994] 2 NZLR 20. Relevant Privy Council cases on appeals from New Zealand include the *Nireaha Tamaki* and *Wallis* cases, above n 7 and 22, and *Manu Kapua v Para Haimona* [1913] AC 761. The advice of the Privy Council in a Nigerian appeal, *Amodu Tijani v Secretary, Southern Nigeria* [1921] 2 AC 399, was crucial to the reasoning of the judges in *Ngati Apa*, above n 3.
52. Department of the Prime Minister and Cabinet, above n 44, 9.
53. New Zealand Māori Council *Kaupapa: Te Wahanga Tuatahi* (Wellington, 1983).
54. P G McHugh 'The Role of Law in Maori Claims' [1990] NZLJ 16, 18–19. See also R P Boast 'Treaty rights or aboriginal rights?' [1990] NZLJ 32.

risk-minimisation approach of the Crown eventually adopted in TTWMA was to go ahead with the repeal of the previous sections 155 to 158 but to insert two new sections at the end of the new Act. By sections 360 and 361, the Limitation Act 1950 was amended to apply a limitation period to any actions to recover land that is claimed to be Māori customary land. No action could be brought for the recovery of customary land after the expiration of twelve years from the date on which the cause of action accrued. This would prevent historical customary rights land claims being relitigated. On the other hand, the Crown was now left unprotected by the *Wi Parata* and previous Native Land Act doctrines in respect of any *new* claims that might arise based on tikanga Māori customary rights and on common law aboriginal title doctrines.

Another innovation in TTWMA was the repeal of Salmond's definition of 'customary land.' As noted above, Salmond had defined Māori customary land as land that 'belongs to the Crown' subject only to a 'moral claim' that Māori could not enforce in the courts.[55] The new definition acknowledged an entirely different conceptual framework: '[l]and that is held in accordance with tikanga Maori shall have the status of Maori customary land.'[56] This was the provision that was invoked by the eight iwi of the South Island in the Marlborough Sounds litigation in relation to foreshore and seabed lands.

I had thought it likely that in 1993, when Te Ture Whenua Maori Bill was passing through Parliament with very little debate, that the Government was willing to go along with the radical change in the definition of customary land because it was taken for granted that there was very little (if any) such land left to be investigated. Customary rights to dry land and the beds of inland waters had been extinguished already. The then recent Sealords settlement on commercial and customary fisheries provided for a statutory regime for commercial and non-commercial customary food gathering rights. Any Māori fishing rights thought to have been protected by section 88(2) of the Fisheries Act 1983 were extinguished and rendered non-justiciable under that statutory regime.[57] There was thus thought to be no land or sea resource of practical significance left for tikanga Māori to apply to. However, at the conference when this chapter was presented as a paper, the Minister of Māori Affairs in 1993, Hon Douglas Kidd, publicly stated that at the time he had made a positive and deliberate commitment to a new definition of customary land that might cover foreshore areas. He made this decision after receiving advice from a number of younger Māori law practitioners. He also stated

---

55. See Part III Customary Rights Rejected of this chapter.
56. Te Ture Whenua Maori Act 1993, s 129(2)(a). For a list of some 17 statutes now in force that explicitly mention 'tikanga' see A Frame *Grey & Iwikau: A Journey Into Custom* (Victoria University Press, Wellington, 2002) 90 (footnote 102).
57. Treaty of Waitangi (Fisheries Claims) Settlement Act 1992, ss 9–11.

that, from the time when he was a young law clerk employed by the law firm in which D G B Morison had been a partner, he had always believed the *In Re Ninety-Mile Beach* case to be wrongly decided.[58] Chief Judge Morison, it should be noted, was the Chief Judge of the Māori Land Court whose Case Stated on questions of law commenced the *Re Ninety-Mile Beach* proceedings. The outcome of that case in the Court of Appeal in 1963 was that, by virtue of the Crown Grants Act 1866 and the Harbours Act 1866, the title to all land between the high and low water marks remained vested in the Crown and the Māori Land Court had no jurisdiction to investigate customary title claims over that foreshore land.[59]

The former Minister's statement about *In Re Ninety-Mile Beach* tends to undermine the Government's suggestions that the success of the Marlborough Sounds iwi in the *Ngati Apa* case arose from an unintended consequence of the new provisions in TTWMA. The Solicitor-General's submissions to the Waitangi Tribunal stated that '[w]hen a case comes along like the Marlborough Sounds case, overturning long-held assumptions, difficult issues arise for Government.'[60] When the Foreshore and Seabed Bill was passed in November 2004 the Deputy Prime Minister, Michael Cullen, claimed that it had been necessary to remedy the problems caused by the Court of Appeal and 'to align the law to Parliament's original intention which was that Te Ture Whenua Maori Act 1993 should apply to dry land only.'[61] He did not state how he had ascertained 'Parliament's original intention', but it transpires that his understanding is different from the recollections of the Minister actually responsible for the passage of the Bill at the time.

C   IN RE THE NINETY-MILE BEACH OVERRULED

I turn now to the Court of Appeal decision in *Ngati Apa*. It was the unanimous decision of the full bench of the Court that *In Re Ninety-Mile Beach* was wrongly decided and that it should be overruled. Tipping J, perhaps one of the more conservative figures on the Court of Appeal, began his judgment with these words:[62]

When the common law of England came to New Zealand its arrival did not

---

58. Hon D Kidd, Victoria University of Wellington, 10 December 2004. (In a private communication Mr Kidd indicated that he and the Opposition spokesperson, Koro Wetere, agreed to steer this much delayed Bill through the House quickly and without seeking to emphasise the innovations in the legislation. The young Māori practitioners who advised the Minister were Annette Sykes, Joe Williams and Whaimutu Dewes).
59. *In Re the Ninety-Mile Beach*, above n 48.
60. *Report on the Crown's Foreshore and Seabed Policy*, above n 45, 87.
61. M Cullen 'Certainty restored to foreshore and seabed' (18 November 2004) Press Release, New Zealand Government Website <http://www.beehive.govt.nz> (last accessed 9 February 2005).
62. *Ngati Apa*, above n 3, paras 183 and 185 Tipping J.

> extinguish Maori customary title. Rather, such title was integrated into what then became the common law of New Zealand. Upon acquisition of sovereignty the Crown did not therefore acquire wholly unfettered title to all the land in New Zealand.
>
> ...
>
> It follows that as Maori customary land is an ingredient of the common law of New Zealand, title to it must be lawfully extinguished before it can be regarded as ceasing to exist.
>
> ...
>
> Undoubtedly Parliament is capable of effecting such extinguishment but, again in view of the importance of the subject matter, Parliament would need to make its intention crystal clear. In other words Parliament's purpose would need to be demonstrated by express words or at least by necessary implication.

Tipping J went on to stress, 'I have deliberately referred to the common law of New Zealand in this context to distinguish it from the common law of England which of course lacked any ingredient involving Maori customary title or land.'[63] Despite parliamentary enactments explicitly vesting foreshore and seabed lands in the Crown – the Foreshore and Seabed Endowment Revesting Act 1991 and statutes on the territorial sea and exclusive economic zone, along with many more statutes empowering harbour boards – the Court held that none of them had unambiguously and conclusively extinguished Māori customary title. One judge, Gault P, expressed 'real reservations about the ability of the appellants to establish that which they claim' in terms of an ownership interest under TTWMA.[64] He agreed, however, that the appeal should be allowed so as to permit a Māori Land Court hearing to investigate the facts and assess the evidence.

The Court's emphasis on New Zealand common law is strongly apparent in the judgment of the Chief Justice. The first instance High Court decision of Ellis J in favour of the Crown was in error, she held, and had to be reversed. Elias CJ wrote:[65]

> I agree with Keith and Anderson JJ and Tipping J that *In Re the Ninety-Mile Beach* was wrong in law and should not be followed. *In Re the Ninety-Mile Beach* followed the discredited authority of *Wi Parata v Bishop of Wellington*, which was rejected by the Privy Council in *Nireaha Tamaki v Baker*. This is not a modern revision, based on developing insights since 1963. The reasoning the Court

---

63. *Ngati Apa*, above n 3, para 212 Tipping J.
64. *Ngati Apa*, above n 3, para 106 Gault P.
65. *Ngati Apa*, above n 3, para 13 Elias CJ.

applied in *In Re the Ninety-Mile Beach* was contrary to other and higher authority and indeed was described at the time as 'revolutionary'.

Further on she stated:[66]

> The applicable common law principle in the circumstances of New Zealand is that rights of property are respected on assumption of sovereignty. They can be extinguished only by consent or in accordance with statutory authority. They continue to exist until extinguishment in accordance with law is established. Any presumption of the common law inconsistent with the recognition of customary property is displaced by the circumstances of New Zealand (see Roberts-Wray, at 635) ... The common law as received in New Zealand was modified by recognising Maori customary property interests. If any such custom is shown to give interests in foreshore and seabed, there is no room for a contrary presumption derived from English common law. The common law of New Zealand is different.

D NOT A MODERN REVISION?

With respect, the Chief Justice's suggestion that the Court's emphasis on New Zealand common law is 'not a modern revision, based on developing insights since 1963' is difficult to justify. A technique of English common law judges through the centuries has been to assert the timelessness of the common law. As McHugh has put it, '[s]ince the common law's past is designed to solve contemporary problems, presentism necessarily underlies its method.'[67] In relation to the 1980s Court of Appeal decisions on the principles of the Treaty, McHugh observed, '[t]he Court of Appeal was using the Treaty of Waitangi less as a means for describing the past than as a means of living in the common law's eternal present. It used the Treaty as a source for timeless 'Treaty principles' by which contemporary Crown conduct was to be measured.'[68]

The historical record does not support the Chief Justice in her assertion that '[f]rom the beginning of Crown colony government, it was accepted that the entire country was owned by Māori according to their customs and that until sold land continued to belong to them.'[69] On the contrary, as noted above, for the first seven years of the Crown colony it was assumed by many in the Colonial Office, in the New South Wales legislature and in the House of Commons that most of the country was 'waste land' vested in the Crown. Māori customary and Treaty rights applied, on this analysis, only to land

---

66. *Ngati Apa*, above n 3, paras 85–86 Elias CJ.
67. 'Tales of Constitutional Origin and Crown Sovereignty in New Zealand', above n 20, 74.
68. 'Tales of Constitutional Origin and Crown Sovereignty in New Zealand', above n 20, 92.
69. *Ngati Apa*, above n 3, para 37 Elias CJ.

actually occupied and cultivated by Māori – sometimes described as being limited to 'the pā and the kūmara patch'. Only after the *Symonds* case in 1847 was it finally accepted that *all* land in the country should be treated as being subject to Māori customary rights.

The strength of the Chief Justice's judgment for present-day purposes, for lawyers at least, need not be impaired by any factual historical inaccuracy. It is, in any case, a legal fiction (without any supporting historical facts) to assert that the common law applied to the whole country in 1840 or in 1847. The legal fiction was enacted in the declaratory English Laws Act 1858. The common law was 'received' in New Zealand as from 14 January 1840 when Hobson was in Sydney and he was sworn in as Lieutenant Governor of the New Zealand Dependency of New South Wales.[70] In reality, tikanga Māori prevailed as the only law in the country in January 1840 (before the Treaty of Waitangi) and continued operating as the only legal system in some areas, especially in the interior of the North Island, for many decades to come. Belich has written compellingly of the distinct difference between British claims of 'nominal sovereignty' and 'actual control.'[71]

It is another legal fiction that the New Zealand common law as laid down authoritatively by a court in 2003 is the 'correct' view of the law and that earlier cases were 'wrong' and should be overruled because 'common law as received in New Zealand was modified by recognising Māori customary property interests' from the outset of colonial rule. This is an ill-disguised version of the declaratory theory of the common law. Judges prefer to speak in that way and it might be calculated that to do so shields them from accusations of judicial activism. As noted below, our politicians are not fooled by the fiction.

Likewise, the joint judgment of Keith and Anderson JJ takes a significantly new approach to the reception of English common law but without admitting that it is a new approach. Under English law, they point out 'without prejudice to public (or common) rights especially of navigation (including anchoring), that the Crown could grant and did grant to subjects the soil below low water mark including areas outside ports and harbours. Those rights could also arise by prescription or usage.'[72] They cite a number of English cases and authorities, and then write: 'Accordingly, under the law of England which became part of the law of New Zealand in 1840 "so far as applicable to the circumstances of New Zealand", private individuals could have property in sea areas including the seabed. The "circumstances" qualification is well and

---

70. David V Williams 'The Foundation of Colonial Rule in New Zealand' (1988) 13 NZULR 54. (The English Laws Act has been re-enacted in the Imperial Laws Application Act 1988.)
71. *Making Peoples: A History of the New Zealanders From Polynesian Settlement to the End of the Nineteenth Century*, above n 17, 180–181.
72. *Ngati Apa*, above n 3, para 133 Keith and Anderson JJ.

relevantly demonstrated by the judgment of Stout CJ in *Baldick v Jackson*.⁷³

The 'circumstances' qualification had not been invoked in a number of earlier New Zealand cases discussed in the judgments, nor indeed in the judgment of Ellis J at first instance. On the contrary, those decisions had either assumed or explicitly stated that Crown prerogative ownership of the foreshore and seabed was entirely appropriate to the circumstances of New Zealand. The Court of Appeal, quite rightly in my view, is now distancing itself from those assumptions. Yet it is odd that the highly exceptional 1910 judgment of Stout CJ in *Baldick v Jackson* is treated in 2003 as if it is a perfectly ordinary application of the local circumstances caveat in Blackstone's views on the application of the birthright of Englishmen in new colonies. Elsewhere I have argued that that case was a very rare exception to the normal assumption of Stout CJ and the colonial bench on the plenary reception of all English law as New Zealand law.⁷⁴ In the 1910 case the Chief Justice did indeed hold that a statute from the reign of Edward II in the fourteenth century based on a royal prerogative deeming whales to be 'royal fish' was not applicable to the circumstances of New Zealand. However, the same Chief Justice in 1911 happily accepted the norm of plenary reception when he found that the royal prerogative to 'royal metals' derived from a 1568 English case was applicable.⁷⁵ In any case, on the matters here in question, about the relevance of Māori customary land rights in the circumstances of the colony, the dismissive views of Stout CJ himself were made abundantly clear in the 1903 Protest of the Bench and Bar as noted above. *Baldick v Jackson* apart, Stout CJ adopted a position that was quite at odds with the views on the 'circumstances' qualification now expressed by Anderson and Keith JJ. This was most explicit in *Hohepa Wi Neera v Bishop of Wellington* in 1902 when Stout CJ declared *Wi Parata* to be 'rightly decided' and he indicated that the Privy Council in *Nireaha Tamaki v Baker* 'does not seem to have been informed of the circumstances of the colony' when making remarks on the Native Rights Act 1865.⁷⁶ In mentioning the circumstances of the colony in 1902, Stout was referring to the statute laws on Native lands that the Privy Council had allegedly misunderstood. He emphatically rejected the notion of a common law in New Zealand that accorded weight to Māori customary rights of the sort that the Privy Council was prepared to countenance. It would have been preferable, in my view, if the Court of Appeal in 2003 had been a little more open about its realignment of New Zealand common law reasoning.

---

73. *Ngati Apa*, above n 3, para 134 Keith and Anderson JJ.
74. D V Williams 'Gold, The *Case of Mines* (1568) and the Waitangi Tribunal' (2003) 7 Aust J Leg Hist 157, 167–169.
75. *Skeet and Dillon v Nicholls* (1911) 30 NZLR 623 (SC).
76. *Hohepa Wi Neera v Bishop of Wellington*, above n 24, 667.

VI Do New Zealanders Wish to Return to Assimilation Policies?

The Court of Appeal's decision was novel but it was neither unexpected nor particularly startling. It may be that the vitriolic backlash against the court decision should be considered alongside similar outpourings of fear and concern in a number of recent controversies. The notion that New Zealand governments may have been responsible in the past for cultural oppression seems to cause a significant backlash in public opinion from within the majority culture. There was, for example, an acrimonious debate about the use of the word 'holocaust' in the Waitangi Tribunal's *Taranaki Report* in 1996 to describe nineteenth-century colonial government policies of war, land confiscations and the invasion of a pacifist Māori community engaged in non-violent resistance to the implementation of land confiscations.[77] There was a white-hot negative reaction to a speech by the Māori Party co-leader, Tariana Turia, when she was the Associate Minister of Health in 2000. In speaking of Māori mental health issues today, she commented on the adverse effects of cultural oppression in the past:[78]

> Do you consider for example the effects of the trauma of colonisation? I know that psychology has accepted the relevance of PTSD (Post Traumatic Stress Disorder).
>
> I understand that much of the research done in this area has focused on the trauma suffered by the Jewish survivors of the holocaust of World War Two. I also understand the same has been done with the Vietnam veterans.
>
> What seems to not have received similar attention is the holocaust suffered by indigenous people including Maori as a result of colonial contact and behaviour.

On the other hand, the speech on 'Nationhood' in January 2004 by the former Leader of the Opposition, Don Brash, received a very different reaction. These were his questions:[79]

> [W]hat sort of nation do we want to build?
> Is it to be a modern democratic society, embodying the essential notion of one rule for all in a single nation state?
> Or is it the racially divided nation, with two sets of laws, and two standards of

---

77. Waitangi Tribunal *The Taranaki Report Kaupapa Tuatahi: Wai 143* (GP Publications, Wellington, 1996) 312.
78. Hon T Turia (Speech to NZ Psychological Society Conference 2000, Waikato University, Hamilton, 29 August 2000) 3–4. See New Zealand Government Website <http://www.beehive.govt.nz> (last accessed 3 December 2004).
79. D Brash, 'Nationhood' (Orewa Rotary Club, 27 January 2004) 3. National Party Website <http://www.national.org.nz> (last accessed 3 December 2004)

citizenship, that the present Labour Government is moving us steadily towards?

And then he invoked the words that Lieutenant-Governor Hobson said in February 1840: '[h]e iwi tahi tātou.' The precise meaning and intention of Hobson in using those words has been mulled over at many Waitangi Day ceremonies in the past. Brash, following Colenso's contemporary account, translated them as '[w]e are one people'. A respected academic authority, Dame Joan Metge, has suggested that a better translation of the Māori words would be, '[w]e two peoples together make a nation', or, to give it a wider interpretation, '[w]e many peoples together make a nation'.[80] That interpretation points to acceptance of a vision that this is a nation with bicultural origins and a multicultural current reality.

It is apparent that there is no consensus in our understanding of Hobson's few words. Hobson's statement as he shook hands with each Māori signatory has come to be seen by many as crucial to our national origins. However, from different understandings of that symbolic event very different competing myths have been constructed. For Brash there is no doubt that '[w]e are one people' speaks of integration as crucial to our national origins and to our future:[81]

> Where there has been a clear breach of the Treaty – where land has been stolen, for example – then it is right that attempts to make amends should be made. But the Treaty is not some magical, mystical, document. Lurking behind its words is not a blueprint for building a modern, prosperous, New Zealand. The Treaty did not create a partnership: fundamentally, it was the launching pad for the creation of one sovereign nation. We should not use the Treaty as a basis for creating greater civil, political or democratic rights for Maori than for any other New Zealander. In the 21st century, it is unconscionable for us to be taking that separatist path.

This speech, it seems, has created a new, more volatile context for discussions about New Zealand's national identity.[82] The 'political correctness' of the notion that the Treaty of Waitangi is a foundation of our national origins and is of continuing importance to the nation's future has been challenged.

---

80. J Metge 'Ropeworks – He Taura Whiri' (Waitangi Rua Rau Tau (Waitangi Bicentenary lecture, February 2004) 10. See The FIRST Foundation <http://www.firstfound.org> (last accessed 3 December 2004).
81. Brash, above n 79, 13.
82. The tenor of the speech was not remarkably different to those of his predecessor as Leader of the Opposition, B English 'One Standard of Citizenship – One Rule for All' (New Zealand Institute of Directors, The Wellington Club, Wellington, 19 November 2002); B English 'Unity and Development are better than Division and Dependency' (Channel View Lounge, Takapuna, Auckland, 22 January 2003). The Brash speech at Orewa, however, made an immediate impact on talkback radio and in political polls (showing a dramatic rise in support for the National Party in the early months of 2004) quite unlike the muted responses to the English speeches.

According to Brash, the 'anachronism' of the Māori seats in Parliament should be removed and all statutory references to the Treaty of Waitangi or the principles of the Treaty should be eliminated.[83] Similarly, Parliament should take back from the judges the power to define Treaty principles that were only ever inserted because of 'an accident of litigation.'[84] Brash in succeeding speeches has capitalised on non-Māori resentment against biculturalism being rammed down people's throats. He talks of 'non-Māori' deliberately in order to avoid using the label 'Pākehā' (although that hardly moves discourse away from the 'racial' or cultural categories he claims to abhor). An apparent surge of popular support for his approach and for his National Party has the potential to transform the political landscape. Certainly, the Labour-led Government began scrambling to find defensible 'needs-based' (not 'race-based') positions that would not seriously alienate one group or another of its supporters.[85] Since the 'Nationhood' speech it is still unlikely, but no longer implausible, to suggest that government policy in the future may attempt to revert to the assimilation and integration policies of the past.

VII Māori Resistance to Assimilation and Integration

On the other hand, debates in Parliament and within the predominantly Pākehā media do not tell anything like the whole story. A Māori cultural and political renaissance may be traced back some decades to a number of significant events. Some of the more important include the opposition to the Maori Affairs Amendment Act 1967, the presentation of the Māori language petition to Parliament in 1972, the dramatic Māori Land March in 1975 (now often called the 'first Hīkoi'), the Hīkoi ki Waitangi and the national hui at Tūrangawaewae in 1984, the Hīrangi hui (and the various fiscal envelope hui) in 1995, and the Hīkoi of Hope in 1999.[86] Land-protest occupations over the years – such as those at Raglan/Whaingaroa, Bastion Point/Takaparawhau, Moutoa Gardens/Pākaitore and many others – were also hugely important. They helped in the development of Māori resistance strategies based on tino rangatiratanga principles in opposition to government policies of Pākehā hegemony. In 2004 the Māori renaissance was strikingly visible in the organisational skills that produced the very strong sense of Māori unity and massive support for the Hīkoi Takutaimoana. This mass hīkoi to Parliament

---

83. Brash, above n 79, 13–14.
84. Brash, above n 79, 7.
85. T Mallard 'First results of review of targeted programmes' (16 December 2004) Press Release, New Zealand Government Website <http://www.beehive.govt.nz> (last accessed 1 February 2005).
86. See M Durie *Te Mana, Te Kawanatanga: The Politics of Maori Self-Determination* (Oxford University Press, Auckland, 1998); A Harris *Hīkoi: Forty Years of Māori Protest* (Huia Publishers, Wellington, 2004).

was mounted in opposition to the Government's abandonment of due process in the courts, its rejection of a carefully crafted Waitangi Tribunal report and its discriminatory extinguishment of customary rights in the Foreshore and Seabed Bill 2004.[87] Calls for recognition of tino rangatiratanga rights affirmed by te Tiriti o Waitangi at the very least require some major reforms of the monistic constitutional structures based on the Westminster system of government currently in place. In the view of some Māori sovereignty advocates, constitutional reform would involve revolutionary challenges to the current legal order.[88]

VIII Parliamentary Sovereignty

Meanwhile, New Zealand retains perhaps the most 'pure' form of the Westminster version of parliamentary sovereignty anywhere in the world, albeit with a unicameral Parliament since 1950. Since that date the slim possibility of the upper house acting as a check on legislation being rammed through to meet the political needs and moods of the moment no longer exists here. On the other hand, the Parliaments in Australia and Canada have to operate within the restraints of federal constitutions, bicameral Parliaments and judicial review of the constitutionality of duly enacted legislation. In Canada's case there is an express protection for aboriginal and treaty rights in section 35 of the Constitution which is supreme law. The United Kingdom Parliament is subject to supranational law and human rights conventions from the European Community, on the one hand, and has devolved certain powers to the Scottish Parliament and the Welsh Assembly on the other hand.

In New Zealand, however, we have only the Constitution Act 1986, which is of course merely an ordinary statute (and a very brief one at that) without protection from amendment or repeal. It stipulates baldly that '[t]he Parliament of New Zealand continues to have full power to make laws.'[89] That is a proposition that Ministers of the Crown were most anxious to reaffirm in 2003 and 2004. The courts, the Waitangi Tribunal, indigenous rights claimants and human rights activists are perceived to be challenging the right of Parliament to overturn inconvenient court decisions and to reject

---

87. Te Ope Mana a Tai *Discussion Framework on Customary Rights to the Foreshore and Seabed, August 2003* <http://www.teope.co.nz> (last accessed 3 December 2004); Indigenous Research Institute *Te Takutai Moana: Economics, Politics & Colonisation*, vol 5, (2 ed, IRI, Auckland, 2003); *Report on the Crown's Foreshore and Seabed Policy*, above n 45; Harris, above n 86, 144–155; see also 'Media Releases and Photos', Converge <http://www.converge.org.nz> (last accessed 2 February 2005).
88. See C James (ed) *Building the Constitution* (Institute of Policy Studies, Wellington, 2000); A Mikaere 'The Treaty of Waitangi and Recognition of Tikanga Maori' in Belgrave, Kawharu and Williams (eds), above n 46, 334.
89. Constitution Act 1986, s 15(1).

tribunal recommendations. The Deputy Prime Minister, Michael Cullen, has assiduously proclaimed the importance of parliamentary sovereignty in a series of speeches in 2004.[90] Indeed his contribution to a special sitting of Parliament, on the 150th anniversary of its first session at Auckland in 1854, was devoted to insisting upon the 'settled doctrine that New Zealand is a sovereign State in which sovereignty is exercised by Parliament as the supreme maker of law, the highest expression of the will of the governed, and the body to which the Government of the day is accountable.'[91] This speech contained a very strong attack not only on Māori radicals who doubt that proposition, but also on the judicial activism of the current bench. His strongest barb was directed at the Chief Justice. He attributed to her three key statements:[92]

> Firstly, we have assumed the application of the doctrine of parliamentary sovereignty in New Zealand – why, is not clear. Secondly, whether there are limits to the lawmaking power of the New Zealand Parliament has not been authoritatively determined, which raises the interesting question of who has the authority to determine that. Thirdly, an untrammelled freedom of Parliament does not exist.

To those suggestions Cullen replied:[93]

> In my view, we are approaching the point where Parliament may need to be more assertive in defence of its own sovereignty, not just for its own sake but also for the sake of good order and government. In our tradition the courts are not free to make new law. It is fundamental to our constitution that lawmakers are chosen by the electorate and accountable to the electorate for their decisions.
>
> ...
>
> Governments, of whatever stripe, do not favour judicial activism. They almost inevitably favour a strict constructivist approach, because it involves far fewer political or fiscal risks. Activism does not always challenge parliamentary

---

90. M Cullen 'Waitangi Tribunal Report disappointing' (8 March 2004); 'Address to Labour Party Conference, Wanganui' (15 March 2004); 'Waipukurau Rotary Club' (15 March 2004); 'Address to Otago District Law Society' (8 April 2004); 'Human Rights and the Foreshore and Seabed' (1 June 2004), New Zealand Government Website <http://www.beehive.govt.nz/> (last accessed 3 December 2004).
91. M Cullen 'Address to Her Excellency the Governor-General' (150th Anniversary Sitting of Parliament, 24 May 2004) Office of the Clerk of the House of Representatives <http://www.clerk.parliament.govt.nz > (3 December 2004). For a gentle riposte from an MP in the Government coalition, see M Robson 'Sometimes it is best to be humble' (2 June 2004) Press Release, Progressive Party <http://www.progressive.org.nz> (last accessed 8 February 2005): 'Politicians are lawmakers. If some among us are unhappy at individual judges' interpretations of any particular law then all that really means is that clearly the law wasn't very well written.'
92. 'Address to Her Excellency the Governor-General', above n 91. For her own words, see S Elias 'Sovereignty in the 21st Century: Another Spin on the Merry-go-round' (2003) 14 Pub LR 148.
93. 'Address to Her Excellency the Governor-General', above n 91.

sovereignty, but it often does. And in New Zealand fundamental questions have been raised about that sovereignty. It is almost as if there is an emerging view that sovereignty is to be shared between Parliament and the judiciary, with Parliament being the junior and less-informed partner. That is so because where Parliament's sovereignty is questioned it is usually accompanied by the assertion or implication that it is the courts that have the final say as to the rules ... The point I make in response is not merely that this is a trend for which there is no democratic mandate, and which has never been part of the political discourse in New Zealand, but that it cannot exist as a one-sided development. It will inevitably lead to the politicisation of the process of judicial appointments and of the judiciary itself – something to be avoided.

IX Conclusion: Wi Parata Lives

The *Ngati Apa* decision finally and conclusively overruled the *Wi Parata* approach as a matter of judge-made law. It no longer has any authority as a precedent in court proceedings. But, at the end of the day, with the FSA now part of New Zealand law, it is apparent that the *Wi Parata* approach lives on. As I suggested at the outset, '[h]istory does not repeat itself, but it does rhyme a lot.' *Wi Parata* lives on not in the precedents that will be applied by the courts but in the thinking behind the Government's response to the *Ngati Apa* judgments. The Government's position in 2003 and 2004 was something of an historical rhyming with the views of Prendergast CJ and Richmond J in 1877, that 'the supreme executive Government must acquit itself as best it may, of its obligation to respect native proprietary rights, and of necessity must be the sole arbiter of its own justice.'[94] The Parliament today, like parliaments in the first decade of the twentieth century, does not like the authoritative reasoning of appellate court judges. The extremely restrictive nature of the territorial customary rights provided for in the 2004 Act is much closer to the views of Prendergast CJ, Richmond J, Stout CJ and other judges of the colonial era than to the Privy Council reasoning approved of in *Ngati Apa*. The Government, in its 2003 consultations with Māori and in its peremptory rejection of the Waitangi Tribunal's recommendations, has approached its task in line with Salmond's advice to Ngata in 1909. Salmond insisted, 'when a dispute arises between Natives and the Crown as to the right to customary land, the dispute shall be settled by Parliament and not otherwise.'[95] What the Deputy Prime Minister said in 2003 rhymes with Salmond's views; '[b]ut in the end, this matter will be resolved in the legislative arena so any solution

---

94. *Wi Parata*, above n 2.
95. See *Salmond: Southern Jurist*, above n 26.

must be able to attract a Parliamentary majority.'[96]

The application of the common law to the circumstances of Aotearoa/New Zealand, as now understood by the courts, permits much greater weight and credence to be given to Māori customary entitlements than was permitted for most of the New Zealand state's legal history. Yet in some respects the colonialist assumptions accompanying the reception of English law in British colonies in the nineteenth century remain powerful and persuasive for those acting on behalf of the Crown in Right of New Zealand today. The judiciary may have discarded 'the discredited authority' of *Wi Parata*. In this respect history has not repeated itself. The Court of Appeal judgments in 2003 endorsed Privy Council sentiments rather than publicly protesting about them as their predecessors had exactly 100 years before in 1903. Members of the executive and a very substantial majority in the legislature, however, still act on assumptions nearly identical to those that informed the reasoning in *Wi Parata*.[97] They still treat Māori customary property rights as an inferior and dispensable form of property right. They refuse to give credence to Māori petitions and protests. Faced with a fear that to recognise Māori custom would unsettle the claimed rights of the Pākehā population, Parliament moves in a rhyming fashion to 1902 when the Land Titles Protection Act was passed, as its preamble asserted, because of the considerable alarm caused among the European landholders of the colony at attacks upon their titles.

---

96. M Cullen 'Govt aiming for foreshore policy statement by Xmas' (23 October 2003) Press Release. New Zealand Government Website <http://www.beehive.govt.nz> (last accessed 17 February 2005).
97. The Government did find it difficult to attract a majority for its measure during the Bill's consideration by the House. Apart from the small number of Green and Māori Party MPs, however, those opposing the Bill would have been even more assertive of the need for a *Wi Parata*-type non-recognition of customary rights than the Government–New Zealand First majority.

An Australian Comparison on Native Title to the Foreshore and Seabed

Shaunnagh Dorsett[*]

I Introduction

In November 2004, the New Zealand Parliament passed the Foreshore and Seabed Act (FSA).[1] In so doing, it passed legislation which goes further towards denying Māori the opportunity to establish aboriginal title than comparative legislation which affects indigenous land rights in any other common law country. In essence the FSA removes the right of Māori to apply to Te Kooti Whenua Māori (the Māori Land Court) for territorial customary claims. It extinguishes aboriginal territorial claims to the foreshore and seabed and replaces such claims with a right to argue before the High Court that aboriginal title would have existed but for the legislation. However, there is no accompanying guarantee of compensation for this extinguishment. Finally, it allows for an application for recognition of a non-territorial customary right, known as a customary rights order, to be made to either the Māori Land Court or the High Court. Again, this statutory provision replaces common law jurisdiction. Not even Australia has gone so far as to extinguish common law native title rights and replace them with statutory entitlements. Although just such an attempt was made in 1993 by the Western Australian Government, the statutory rights were declared discriminatory, and hence void, by the High Court of Australia in *Western Australia v Commonwealth* (*The Native Title Act Case*).[2]

---

[*] Reader, Faculty of Law, Victoria University of Wellington.
[1] Foreshore and Seabed Act 2004 (NZ).
[2] See *Western Australia v Commonwealth* (1995) 183 CLR 373 (HCA). In 1993 Western Australia enacted the Land (Titles and Traditional Usages) Act 1993 (WA) which extinguished all surviving native title and substituted 'rights of traditional usages': section 7. The legislation was declared invalid as contrary to section 10 of the Racial Discrimination Act 1975 (Cth). In essence, this Act

This chapter is divided into three parts. The first will provide an overview of the basic distinction between Australian and Canadian law on native (or aboriginal) title so as to locate the New Zealand provisions within this wider context. Although the common law has been replaced in New Zealand by statutory provisions, as will be seen the particular wording of these provisions appears to contemplate aspects of Australian and Canadian jurisprudence. The second part will consider Australian case law on native title in the offshore. There have been few cases on aboriginal rights in the offshore. The majority of those thus far determined are from Australia. I will consider not only the major High Court of Australia decision in *Yarmirr v Northern Territory* (*Yarmirr*), but also *The Lardil People v State of Queensland* (*The Lardil People*), which is the most recent litigated determination of native title offshore, and consider what rights were recognised in *The Lardil People* by the Federal Court.[3] In some ways this case provides a better illustration of how native title claims fare in the offshore than the High Court of Australia decision in *Yarmirr*, a decision which was primarily concerned, as are all appeals, with the legal parameters of offshore native title, rather than the factual outcomes for claimants.[4] These cases illustrate well the paucity of rights that can result from claims to the offshore if a narrow view is taken of the doctrine of native or aboriginal title. The third part will look to six particular facets of the FSA, flag issues which may prove problematic, and try to provide some brief understanding of how these issues have played out in Australian native title law.

In looking to Australian jurisprudence I will in part be re-traversing the ground covered by Dr Paul McHugh in his evidence on behalf of the Crown to the Waitangi Tribunal, as well as his article on aboriginal title to the foreshore.[5] Dr McHugh provides a detailed account of jurisprudence in this area, particularly of Australian case law and the part it might play in

---

enacts into domestic law the International Convention on the Elimination of All Forms of Racial Discrimination (4 January 1969) 660 UNTS 195. For comments on the potentially discriminatory nature of the FSA see Waitangi Tribunal *Report on the Crown's Foreshore and Seabed Policy: Wai 1071* (Legislation Direct, Wellington, 2004).

3. *Yarmirr v Northern Territory* (1998) 156 ALR 370 (HCA); *The Lardil People v State of Queensland* [2004] FCA 298.
4. A word on terminology is perhaps important here. Throughout this paper I refer to native title in the offshore. Native title claims effectively cannot be made to the foreshore in Australia, as it has been confirmed in a number of cases that the Crown title to the foreshore and the beds of tidal rivers was not a radical title but an absolute one. See *Yarmirr*, above n 3, para 213 McHugh J; *The Lardil People*, above n 3, para 221 Cooper J. Effectively, therefore, native title has been extinguished. This is a significant point of difference between the High Court's approach in *Yarmirr* and that of the New Zealand Court of Appeal in *Attorney-General v Ngati Apa* [2003] 3 NZLR 643 (CA).
5. Dr Paul Gerard McHugh *Brief of Evidence to the Waitangi Tribunal, 13 January 2004, in the Matter of the Treaty of Waitangi Act 1975 and of Applications for an Urgent Inquiry into the Foreshore and Seabed Issues, Wai 1071*; Paul McHugh 'Aboriginal Title in New Zealand: A Retrospective and Prospect' (2004) 2 NZJPIL 139.

determining the parameters of any claims for territorial customary rights under the FSA. In general, I agree with his conclusions about what choices might need to be made by the courts in constructing a New Zealand aboriginal title jurisprudence, although we differ somewhat in our understanding of some of the intricacies of Australian native title doctrine. I would also sound a warning about use of Australian jurisprudence in any claims which may be made, particularly territorial claims under the inherent jurisdiction of the High Court. If Australian case law is followed too slavishly, a prospect which I hope is unlikely, this may well result in New Zealand, as it has in Australia, in a form of native title which is impoverished and which fails to recognise the realities of tikanga Māori.

II Approaches to Native Title in Canada and Australia: Territorial and Non-Territorial Rights

A CANADA

The FSA is predicated on a distinction between territorial and non-territorial customary rights. Strictly speaking, this dichotomy is not found in common law jurisprudence on native or aboriginal title either in Canada or Australia. However, it most resembles the bifurcation in Canada between 'aboriginal title' and 'aboriginal rights', and which derives from the jurisprudence of the Supreme Court of Canada relating to section 35(1) of the Constitution Act 1982. This is the provision which protects 'existing aboriginal rights', in other words those rights existing in 1982, the date at which the section was enacted. From a number of Supreme Court decisions, it is clear that aboriginal rights include, but are not limited to, aboriginal title. Nor has the Supreme Court of Canada made a rigid distinction between the two. Rather, it talks of a 'spectrum'. In *Delgamuukw v British Columbia* (*Delgamuukw*), Lamer CJ said that:[6]

> The picture which emerges ... is that the aboriginal rights which are recognized and affirmed by s 35(1) fall along a spectrum with respect to their degree of connection with the land. At one end, there are those aboriginal rights which are practices, customs and traditions that are integral to the distinctive culture of the group claiming the right. However, the 'occupation and use of the land' where the activity is taking place is 'not sufficient to support a claim of title to the land' (at para. 26 [of *R. v Adams* (1996) 138 DLR (4th) 657]) ... In the middle, there are activities which, out of necessity, take place on land and indeed, might

---

6. *Delgamuukw v British Columbia* (1997) 153 DLR (4th) 193, para 138 Lamer CJC (Cory and Major JJ concurring) (SCC).

be intimately connected with a particular piece of land. Although an aboriginal group may not be able to demonstrate title to land, it may nevertheless have a site-specific right to engage in a particular activity ... At the other end of the spectrum is aboriginal title itself ... What aboriginal title confers is the right to the land itself.

Thus, aboriginal rights in Canada are those which are 'integral to the distinctive culture of the group claiming the right.'[7] They may or may not be activities which are intimately connected with land, but they do not demonstrate the possession required to found aboriginal title. Aboriginal title, on the other hand, requires 'possession', generally demonstrated by occupation. While the Supreme Court of Canada has stated that 'mere occupancy' is not sufficient,[8] and that generally the use must be sufficiently regular and exclusive to comport with title at common law, that Court has acknowledged that possession is contextual, and has not ruled out the possibility that less-intensive, partly nomadic practices might amount to occupancy and thereby suffice to found aboriginal title. In the recent Supreme Court of Canada decision in *R v Marshall* (*Marshall*), McLachlin CJ stated that: 'whether nomadic people enjoyed a sufficient "physical possession" to give them title to land, is a question of fact, depending on all the circumstances, in particular the nature of the land and the manner in which it is commonly used.'[9]

Finally, where aboriginal title exists, it confers the right to use the land for a variety of activities, not all of which need be aspects of practices, customs and traditions which are integral to the distinctive cultures of aboriginal societies. Those activities are 'parasitic' on the underlying title.[10]

While the issue of aboriginal rights or title in the offshore has not been directly raised, there have been several cases in which the offshore rights have been involved. In *Marshall*, referred to above, the area claimed included coastal lands, including lands around bays. The Supreme Court of Canada did not appear to consider that the inclusion of coastal lands raised any particular questions.

In 2002, the Haida Nation began an action for aboriginal title to all lands and seas contained within the Haida Gwaii (Queen Charlotte Islands), which encompass not only the land and sea, but also the resources in and under the sea, including oil and gas reserves. It will undoubtedly be some time before this

---

7. *R v Van der Peet* (1996) 137 DLR (4th) 289 (SCC).
8. *R v Côté* (1996) 137 DLR (4th) 289, para 60 Lamer CJ, Sopinka, Gonthier, Cory, McLachlin, Iacobucci and Major JJ. (SCC).
9. *R v Marshall; R v Bernard* (2005) SCC 43, paras 58, 66. In *Delgamuukw*, above n 6, Lamer CJ held that any consideration of sufficient occupation to found possession should take into account both the aboriginal and common law perspectives: paras 147, 156.
10. *Delgamuukw*, above n 6, para 111 Lamer CJC (Cory and Major JJ concurring).

case is heard. However, in 2000 the Haida launched an action objecting to the re-issuance and transfer of several logging licences to companies which had operated since before the First World War in the forests of the Haida Gwaii. They based their objections on a number of grounds, including breach of fiduciary duty. All claims, however, were ultimately grounded in an assertion of aboriginal title. The Supreme Court of Canada held that the Government of British Columbia had a duty to consult with the Haida about logging, including the transfer or replacement of licences, even prior to aboriginal title being determined.[11] The scope of the duty is dependent on a preliminary assessment of the strength of the case for aboriginal title. On the facts at hand it was accepted by the Supreme Court of Canada that the chambers judge felt that the Haida had established a good prima facie case.[12] No suggestion was made that title to waters was to be treated differently to title to land.

B   AUSTRALIA

In Australia, by contrast, the High Court has taken a 'normative' approach.[13] No distinction is made between aboriginal title and aboriginal rights. Rather, the doctrine of native title potentially encompasses both. The content of native title is determined by examining the customs and traditions of the claimant group.[14] This could amount to an interest in land tantamount to beneficial ownership (as in *Mabo v State of Queensland (No 2)* (*Mabo (No 2)*) itself), or some lesser activity on land, such as hunting and fishing. However, since *Mabo (No 2)*, court decisions have continually narrowed the doctrine of native title so as to in reality only comprehend the middle part of the sliding scale identified by Lamer CJ in *Delgamuukw*.

On the one hand, aboriginal rights not intimately connected with land would not be recognised as native title because they would fail to meet the requirement of a connection to the land as required in the Native Title Act 1993 (NTA) and as interpreted by the High Court in *Yorta Yorta*. On the other hand, while the High Court has not ruled out the possibility of making determinations of exclusive possession, it appears increasingly unlikely to do

---

11. *Haida Nation v British Columbia (Minister of Forests)*, (2004) 245 DLR (4th) 33 (SCC), para 10 McLachlin CJC for the Court. See also *R v Sparrow* (1990) 70 DLR (4th) 385 (SCC); *Saanichtan Marina Ltd v Claxton* [1989] 3 CNLR 46. Further, the Canadian Federal Government's policy relating to the settlement of native claims recognises that negotiations may include offshore areas: Indian and Northern Affairs *Federal Policy for the Settlement of Native Claims* (Indian and Northern Affairs, Ottawa, 1993) 10.
12. *Haida Nation v British Columbia*, above n 11, para 69–71 McLachlin CJC for the Court.
13. *Members of the Yorta Yorta Community v Victoria* (2002) 194 ALR 538 (HCA) (*Yorta Yorta*).
14. See generally *Mabo v State of Queensland (No. 2)* (1992) 175 CLR 1 (HCA) particularly the judgment of Brennan J. The issue of proof has been significantly complicated by the provisions of the Native Title Act 1993 (Cth).

so.¹⁵ Of course the original doctrine as enunciated in *Mabo (No 2)* clearly can include territorial claims if it can be shown that the customs and traditions of the aboriginal peoples amounted to exclusive possession. That was the case in *Mabo (No 2)* itself. However, given the requirement that native title be determined by examination of traditional laws and customs, the High Court in *Western Australia v Ward* (*Ward*) in fact took the view that occupation is an insufficient basis on which to found native title as it 'says nothing of what traditional law or custom provided.'¹⁶ Thus, evidence of occupation itself will not found title. This is probably the most strident point of contrast with Canada and with the approach of the Supreme Court of Canada in both *Delgamuukw* and *Marshall*. The High Court of Australia is effectively holding indigenous Australians to a higher standard to show exclusive possession than was required in *Marshall*. Further, the failure, unlike in Canada, to take into account the aboriginal perspective almost guarantees that territorial rights and exclusive possession will be exceptionally difficult to prove.

Hence, native title rights recognised in Australia post-*Mabo (No 2)* have been almost exclusively confined to hunting and fishing rights. Thus, as it stands, native title includes only activities on land – what Lamer CJ labelled site-specific activities relating to a particular piece of land – but not amounting to aboriginal title.

There are a number of reasons which can be pointed to for the paucity of rights which can be recognised as native title in Australia, the most obvious of which is the increasing conservatism of the High Court of Australia itself. However, the particular approach of the current High Court of Australia to two matters has particularly led to the narrowing of native title rights: their interpretation of the relationship between the common law and section 223 of the NTA (the definition of native title); and the requirement to particularise each and every element of traditional law and custom relied upon as a foundation for native title rights and interests.

In 1993, when the NTA was enacted, there seemed to be a clear consensus on the relationship between the NTA and the common law doctrine of native title. In particular, there seemed to be a common understanding that the definition of native title in the Act was reflective of the common law. As Senator Minchin stated during debate on the 1998 amendments to the NTA, 'I repeat that our [A]ct preserves the fact of common law; who holds native title, what it consists of, is entirely a matter for the courts of Australia. It is a common law right.'¹⁷ 'Native title' was clearly dynamic, and as native title law

---

15. *Western Australia v Ward* (2002) 213 C.L.R. 1 (HCA).
16. *Ward*, above n 15, para 93, Gleeson CJ, Gaudron, Gummow and Hayne JJ.
17. Senate, *Parliamentary Debates* 2 December 1997 (Commonwealth Government Printer, Canberra, 1953) 10171; quoted in *Yorta Yorta*, above n 13, para 130 McHugh J.

matured and evolved, the definition in section 223 would remain reflective of the common law.

In *Ward* and *Yorta Yorta*, however, the main judgments took a different approach. Rather than commencing with the common law, it was determined that the correct approach was to begin with the NTA, and the definition of native title in section 223.[18] As a result, not only was the centrality of the common law displaced, Brennan J's judgment in *Mabo (No 2)* was relegated to an interpretational aid: [19]

> Much of the argument in the courts below, as in this Court, took as its starting point consideration of what was said in *Mabo* [*No 2*]. No doubt account may be taken of what was decided and what was said in that case when considering the meaning and effect of the NTA. This especially is so when it is recognised that paras (a) and (b) of s 223(1) plainly are based on what was said by Brennan J in *Mabo* [*No 2*]. It is, however, of the first importance to recognise two crucial points: that s 11(1) of the NTA provides that native title is not able to be extinguished contrary to the NTA and that the present appeals are claims made under the NTA for rights that are defined in that statute.

The Court further clarified in *Yorta Yorta* that paragraph (c) of the definition of native title — that the native title rights and interests are those which are recognised by the common law of Australia — meant no more than that recognition and protection of native title depends on that native title not having been extinguished and its not having incidents that are repugnant to the common law.[20] Thus, rather than embodying a dynamic jurisprudence, section 223 has been interpreted as definitional. As a result, recognition of native title is limited by section 223(1) to 'rights and interests … in land or waters.' The proper interpretation of section 223 meant that: '[t]hose rights and interests may be communal, group or individual rights and interests, but they must be "in relation to" land or waters.'[21] Examples of such 'rights and interests' are given in subsection (2). Section 223(2) provides that 'without limiting subsection (1), rights and interests in that subsection includes hunting,

---

18. Section 223(1) –
    The expression native title or native title rights and interests means the communal, group or individual rights and interests of Aboriginal peoples or Torres Strait Islanders in relation to land or waters, where:
    (a) the rights and interests are possessed under the traditional laws acknowledged, and the traditional customs observed, by the Aboriginal peoples or Torres Strait Islanders; and
    (b) the Aboriginal peoples or Torres Strait Islanders, by those laws and customs, have a connection with the land or waters; and
    (c) the rights and interests are recognised by the common law of Australia.
19. *Ward*, above n 15, para 16 Gleeson CJ, Gaudron, Gummow, Hayne JJ.
20. *Yorta Yorta*, above n 13, para 110 Gaudron and Kirby JJ.
21. *Yorta Yorta*, above n 13, para 33 Gleeson, Gummow and Hayne JJ.

gathering, or fishing rights and interests.' Similar kinds of activities are also specified in section 211. That section is designed to exempt native title holders in certain situations from licensing requirements. For example, if a licence is required under resource legislation, as long as the activity fits within the classes of activity specified by the section, the native title holder is exempted from requiring a licence. Section 211(3) specifies the classes of activity as hunting, fishing, gathering, and cultural or spiritual activities. In addition, these activities can only be undertaken for domestic or non-commercial purposes (section 211(2)). The High Court of Australia's approach to the definition and content of native title has received criticism not only from commentators, but from within the ranks of the High Court itself. McHugh J has reiterated in several decisions that the understanding of the majority of the relationship between common law and the statute is at odds with the legislature's intention.[22]

Further, as noted above, the majority in *Ward* required that each and every element of custom and tradition relied upon to found native title rights and interests be particularised. Again, this flowed from the language of section 223 of the Act. According to the majority, it required 'not only the identification of the laws and customs said to be traditional laws and customs, but, no less importantly, the identification of the rights and interests in relation to land or waters which are possessed under those laws or customs.'[23]

As a result of *Ward* and *Yorta Yorta* it seems that native title rights are confined to physical activities done on land in relation to land or water: hunting, fishing, gathering (those activities listed as examples in the NTA itself), as well as care for sites of special significance and access rights to areas for the above purposes, as well as for activities of ceremonial or spiritual significance.[24] The limitations of the High Court of Australia's approach can be starkly seen in the cases concerning native title in the offshore.

III Native Title in the Offshore: Yarmirr

In 2001, the High Court of Australia handed down its decision in *Yarmirr*. This is a significant decision because, along with decisions relating to Alaska,[25] it is one of the few in the common law world to consider native title to the offshore.

---

22. *Yorta Yorta*, above n 13, para 130 McHugh J.
23. *Ward*, above n 15, para 18 Gleeson CJ, Gaudron, Gummow and Hayne JJ.
24. For an attempt to argue wider rights see *Bulun Bulun*, in which von Doussa J held that matters normally covered by intellectual property law could not be comprehended within the doctrine of native title: *Bulun Bulun v R & T Textiles Pty Ltd* (1998) 157 ALR 193 (FCA).
25. *Inupiat Community of the Arctic Slope v United States* (1982) 548 F Supp 182 (Dist Alaska); *Native Village of Eyak v Trawler Diane Marie Inc* (1998) 154 F 3rd 1090 (9th Cir).

There was originally some supposition in Australia that native title did not extend to the offshore. This was certainly the position taken by the various state and federal governments. In the 1975 case of *New South Wales v Commonwealth* (*Seas and Submerged Lands Case*), the High Court of Australia, following *Reg v Keyn* (*Keyn's Case*), had suggested that the common law did not extend below the high water mark,[26] a rule which was derived originally from the fact that common law juries could not be empanelled outside the county, and the county ended at the low water mark. Hence there was no common law jurisdiction beyond that mark. Thus, went the argument in *Yarmirr*, as the common law does not operate in the offshore, it could not 'recognise' native title. Such an approach attributes to the common law a purely geographic rather than conceptual jurisdiction.

Second, the Crown also argued that even if recognition was possible, native title had been extinguished by the vesting of offshore waters and the seabed in the Northern Territory as part of the late 1970s offshore constitutional settlement. Third, it contended that there could be no exclusive native title rights in the offshore and even if there were they would be subject to the right of innocent passage, public right to navigate and rights of those with fishing licences.

On the other side, the argument was that even if the common law did not extend beyond the low water mark, aboriginal law did. This raised the question: could the common law give effect to the recognition of that aboriginal law in the form of native title?[27]

The High Court in *Yarmirr* held that native title could be recognised in the offshore. The problem, or disappointment, with the decision concerned what could be recognised as native title, and the other interests which could infringe on native title. It was certainly not a unanimous decision. Four justices, Gleeson CJ, Gaudron, Gummow and Hayne JJ gave a joint judgment in which they recognised native title in the offshore, but denied it could amount to exclusive possession. Kirby J would have given qualified exclusive possession and McHugh and Callinan JJ gave separate reasons in which rejected the extension of native title to the offshore.

As outlined earlier, the Commonwealth essentially argued that despite the fact that the NTA refers to native title over land and waters (including seas), the effect of subsection 223(1)(c) was that only native title which was recognised by the common law was claimable under, and protected by, the NTA. This brought into play a series of constitutional questions about the limits and

---

26. *New South Wales v Commonwealth* (1975) 135 CLR 337; *Reg v Keyn* (1876) 2 Ex D 63.
27. An excellent summary of the High Court decision in *Yarmirr* has been written by Lisa Strelein. I have relied upon this in part in the discussion of this case which follows: Lisa Strelein 'Native Title Offshore: *Commonwealth v Yarmirr; Yarmirr v NT*' Australian Institute of Aboriginal and Torres Strait Islander Studies http://www.aiatsis.gov.au/ (last accessed 2 December 2004).

nature of sovereignty in the offshore, and the ability of the common law, if you will, to step off the land and into the offshore.

The main issue in determining whether or not the common law would recognise native title rights and interests was one of inconsistency between the claimed rights and the common law.[28] The majority held that this was an issue of 'inconsistency'. In determining this, they amalgamated doctrine from *Mabo (No 2)*, *The Native Title Act Case*; and *The Wik Peoples v Queensland (Wik)*.[29] From *Mabo (No 2)* the majority took the principle that 'at common law the native title rights and interests survived the acquisition of sovereignty because only so much of the common law was brought in as was applicable to the circumstances of the colony.'[30] Obviously this is a well-known and important principle, but it did not receive much emphasis in *Mabo (No 2)* itself. In contrast, in *Ngati Apa* the reception doctrine received considerably more attention and was important to the outcome of the decision. From *The Native Title Act Case*, the High Court took the principle that on acquisition of sovereignty the new sovereign may extinguish rights and interests 'in the course of the act of state acquiring the territory.'[31] This was restatement of *Mabo (No 2)*. From *Wik* came the principle of inconsistency – extinguishment of native title is determined by the inconsistency between native title interests and common law interests. However, in *Yarmirr* this was transmuted into a new context. The majority reinterpreted the decision in *Mabo (No 2)* to be whether there was an inconsistency between the common law itself and the continued recognition of native title rights and interests. In the case of an inconsistency, the common law prevails.[32]

So what are the sovereign rights and interests which are asserted over the territorial sea? Only by knowing these can the issue of inconsistency be examined. Despite this, the majority felt that it was too difficult and unnecessary to actually define or describe state sovereignty. They held that assertion of, and recognition of, Australia's sovereignty over the offshore did not amount to a claim of ownership, or even radical title. Authority for this was *Keyn's Case*. However, they accepted from *Keyn's Case* that the territorial sea is not part of the territory of England, and hence not part of the territory of Australia. They did not accept, however, that *Keyn's Case* necessarily meant that the common law did not extend below the low water mark.

Despite this, the majority did not actually hold that the common law extends beyond the low water mark. Rather, they simply said that any 'proposition

---

28. *Yarmirr*, above n 3, para 40, Gleeson CJ, Gaudron, Gummow and Hayne JJ.
29. *The Wik Peoples v Queensland* (1996) 187 CLR 1 (HCA). See Strelein, above n 27.
30. *Yarmirr*, above n 3, para 41 Gleeson CJ, Gaudron, Gummow and Hayne JJ.
31. *Yarmirr*, above n 3, para 41 Gleeson CJ, Gaudron, Gummow and Hayne JJ.
32. *Yarmirr*, above n 3, para 42 Gleeson CJ, Gaudron, Gummow and Hayne JJ.

in those general and unqualified terms could not be accepted.'[33] In fact, they avoided the question. What was important according to the majority was that the common law is not inconsistent with the continued existence of native title rights and interests offshore. They further held that legislation passed in furtherance of sovereign rights in the offshore was only an assertion of sovereignty, not ownership, and therefore not inconsistent with native title.[34]

However, the assertion of sovereignty did have important consequences for what was recognised. In effect it amounted to a qualification on the continued recognition of native title rights and interests, in particular in relation to claimed exclusivity of rights. Specifically, they noted a number of 'terms' of the assertion of sovereignty, derived from international law, which qualified this claim: the right of innocent passage under international law, and public rights of navigation and fishing. In essence, these were inconsistent with native title. This is, as Strelein has pointed out, a significant shift in thinking about inconsistency.[35] In earlier cases inconsistency referred to inconsistency between common law rights and native title rights, for example, between a fee simple and a native title interest. This is turn is just a twist on the extinguishment test in *Wik*: that native title is extinguished by that with which it is inconsistent, most obviously a fee simple estate.[36] In *Yarmirr*, however, they blur the two to say that the inconsistency between native title rights and the assertion of sovereignty is 'of no different quality' to that which arises where as a result of the exercise of sovereign power a fee simple estate is granted which extinguishes native title as a result of the inconsistency between them.[37] As a result, there is a 'fundamental inconsistency between the asserted native title rights and interests and the common law public rights of navigation and fishing as well as the right of innocent passage.'[38]

Kirby J, on the other hand, took a different view. He was prepared to find that there was a qualified right of exclusivity. He looked at the reasons for, or principles behind, the public rights to see if they were inconsistent with native title. He held that the principle behind innocent passage and navigation is the fundamental principle of freedom of movement and the common heritage of humanity. Even so, they only qualify, not destroy, exclusivity. The public right to fish, Kirby J felt, was also capable of being subject to native title.[39] He stated:[40]

> It follows that the above three qualifications do not extinguish otherwise

---

33. *Yarmirr*, above n 3, para 39 Gleeson CJ, Gaudron, Gummow and Hayne JJ.
34. *Yarmirr*, above n 3, para 61 Gleeson CJ, Gaudron, Gummow and Hayne JJ.
35. See Strelein, above n 27.
36. See for example, *Fejo v Northern Territory* (1998) 195 CLR 96 (HCA).
37. *Yarmirr*, above n 3, para 100 Gleeson CJ, Gaudron, Gummow and Hayne JJ.
38. *Yarmirr*, above n 3, para 98 Gleeson CJ, Gaudron, Gummow and Hayne JJ.
39. *Yarmirr*, above n 3, para 285–286.
40. *Yarmirr*, above n 3, para 285 footnotes omitted.

exclusive native title rights and interests. As the claimants submitted, rights of passage and navigation and rights of fishing under statutory licences are all rights 'defined and limited by purpose'. Although extensive, such purposes do not by any means cover *all* the potential activities and uses of the claimed waters. A power to exclude, for example, persons who move through the waters of the determination area to fish without licence, to conduct tourist activities or to extract natural resources without the consent of the native title holders remains a very significant power. Such a power is currently exercisable by the Northern Territory (up to three nautical miles) and the Commonwealth, subject to the recognition of pre-existing exclusive native title rights in the determination area. The rights which the claimants assert in these proceedings are similar. Viewed apart, they appear completely reasonable. But does the law recognise and uphold them? The other members of this Court think not. I disagree.

Importantly, he went on to say that:[41]

The claimants assert 'qualified exclusive' native title rights and interests to waters, as that term includes the sea, sea-bed or subsoil beneath the sea and airspace over the sea. Following *Yanner*, such a right is proprietary in nature, in the sense that the right to exclude others from, and to control access to, a resource produces a proprietary relationship. The common law has recognised a proprietary community title. It has done so in the face of significant difficulties of proof of boundaries, of membership of the community and of representatives of the community. So much is as clear for the sea as for the land. Modern approaches to the concept of property, embraced by the common law and this Court, acknowledge this possibility. I agree with Merkel J that the former uncertainty as to the ability of the Crown to assert proprietary rights in the sea-bed of the territorial sea, expressed outside of the context of the special status of native title under the common law and the Act, does not defeat this proposition.

If the Aboriginal laws and customs observed by the claimants establish otherwise a traditional entitlement to the exclusion of others to control the access of other persons to their sea country, and to fish in their sea country, such an entitlement is proprietary in nature.

The majority actually also acknowledged that there was not necessarily any reason why the qualified exclusivity proposed by the claimants could not accommodate the common law public rights and international rights. They just felt that the doctrine of inconsistency was too strong to resist.[42]

Most recently, native title has been recognised in the offshore in *The Lardil People*. The original application was lodged in 1996 (which demonstrates the

---

41. *Yarmirr*, above n 3, para 286–287 footnotes omitted.
42. See Strelein, above n 27.

average timeline for an outcome of a native title claim). A number of sea claims were lodged around this time. The original application sought a determination of exclusive ownership of land and waters, with each of four claimant groups claiming exclusive ownership of their respective traditional territory. These territories were adjoining, and in certain places, shared.

Evidence was prepared and tendered to support the 'claim to ownership with the right to hold and enjoy all of the incidents which flowed from ownership of the land and waters in the claim area.'[43] However, between the conclusion of evidence and the determination, the High Court of Australia's decisions in *Yarmirr*, *Ward* and *Yorta Yorta* were handed down. The effect was that the claim was amended to remove the claim to exclusive possession and occupation.[44] These three High Court decisions had a profound effect on many claims. *Yarmirr* forced the amendment of many sea claims to remove the claims of exclusive possession, while on land *Yorta Yorta* caused many indigenous groups to consider whether they would continue with their claims, given the difficulties that many will face in proving a continuing connection to the land post-*Yorta Yorta*.

The applicants claimed native title rights and interests in the sea 'as far as the eye could see.'[45] This area extended to the horizon and included the observable deep waters and any island or reef which could be seen between the land and the horizon. Cooper J accepted that this was the traditional method of determining respective sea countries. However, native title claims are required to be lodged with precise geographic co-ordinates and so the claimants plotted the location of the horizon from various high points on the land and the extreme ranges at sea from which those high points were visible from a boat. In the upshot, however, this method of defining their claim was rejected by Cooper J, who found that the claimants observed the seas in front of their countries from the dunes and beach, not high points, and that there was no evidence that at sovereignty people stood on the outlying islands looking seaward and claiming seas to the distant horizons.[46]

The applicants also asserted that the claimant groups owned the seas, the seabed, the subsoil below the seabed and the resources of the seas in their respective territories. Cooper J found, however, that the concept of ownership held by the applicants was not one based on common law concepts of property. Rather, it was 'a concept born out of the connection of the peoples to each of the elements through their spirituality.'[47] For the Lardil, the concept of ownership was essentially the 'right to be asked' and to control

---

43. *The Lardil People*, above n 3, para 12 Cooper J.
44. *The Lardil People*, above n 3, para 13 Cooper J.
45. *The Lardil People*, above n 3, para 15 Cooper J.
46. *The Lardil People*, above n 3, paras 91, 228 Cooper J.
47. *The Lardil People*, above n 3, paras 115, 147 Cooper J.

access and conduct.[48] The NTA as interpreted by the High Court of Australia in *Ward* requires each individual native title right or interest to be identified. This means that indigenous relationships to country, including of course sea country, must be 'translated' into individual rights and interests: [49]

> The Act requires that the relationship between a community or group of Aboriginal people and the land is to be expressed in terms of rights or interests in relation to that land. This means that a relationship which is essentially religious or spiritual, must be translated into law. This requires the fragmentation of an integrated view of the ordering of affairs into rights and interests which are considered apart from the duties and obligations which go with them.

In particular, Cooper J found that it was not helpful or useful to attempt to state native title rights in a broad and expansive way, subject to the common law rights of navigation and fishing and the international right of free passage.[50] Nor was a non-exclusive composite claim (that is, the non-exclusive right to occupy, use and enjoy the waters and land) appropriate because at common law the notions of possession and occupation involve notions of control of access. Applying *Yarmirr* and *Ward*, Cooper J found that control of access to the land and waters of the inter-tidal zone and the territorial seas, as a right of exclusion, even though part of traditional law, could not be recognised at common law.[51] According to Cooper J: [52]

> When the unity of the relationship between indigenous people and the land and waters is fragmented, and the rights to control access to, and use of and activities in the land and waters are excluded, little may remain which is capable of being translated into rights and interests in relation to that land and waters capable of recognition and protection under the NTA. What is left may amount to little more than non-exclusive rights to engage in specified activities in relation to the land and waters. Because the content of those rights or interests was fixed at sovereignty, no subsequent enlargement of these rights will be recognised under the Act.

So as a result, Cooper J held that:

- the claim of a 'right to speak for country' was too imprecise for the NTA;[53]
- the right to enjoy the amenity of the determination area was not recognisable

---

48. *The Lardil People*, above n 3, para 152 Cooper J.
49. *The Lardil People*, above n 3, para 173 Cooper J.
50. *The Lardil People*, above n 3, para 171 Cooper J.
51. *The Lardil People*, above n 3, para 164 Cooper J.
52. *The Lardil People*, above n 3, para 175, referring to *Yorta Yorta*, above n 13, para 43–44 Gleeson, Gummow and Hayne JJ.
53. *The Lardil People*, above n 3, para 71.

by the NTA as it was not a right in relation to land or waters at sovereignty, and any right that did exist at sovereignty to control the amenity of the area in relation to access and use by members and non-members of the claimant group did not survive the acquisition of sovereignty;[54]
- rights with respect to spiritual sites within the inter-tidal zone and adjacent seas had also been diminished by sovereignty;[55]
- claims of rights to control access to, and right to use, waters and land were inconsistent with the common law rights which enured at the assertion of sovereignty;[56] and
- a claimed right to protect the resources of the land and waters by taking steps to prevent acts which are inconsistent with reasonable and lawful use of the area and which may cause damage or destruction of habitat or wildlife were also rights of control and therefore did not survive sovereignty and because they were inconsistent with public rights to fish and navigate and innocent passage.[57]

What then, was recognised?[58]

- hunting, fishing and gathering for domestic or non-commercial communal consumption;
- the right to take and consume fresh drinking water from springs in the inter-tidal zone; and
- access to land and waters seaward of the high water line for hunting, gathering and religious, spiritual or ceremonial purposes.

The Lardil People demonstrates the paucity of rights that can result from aboriginal claims in the offshore when a narrow view is taken of the native title doctrine. In essence, while the Lardil did succeed in a claim for native title, the actual content of native title was significantly less than they originally claimed. It is also, like all native title determinations in Australia have become, incommensurate with their relationship to their sea country. This was, of course, also the critique made by many of the outcome of the original offshore case, *Yarmirr*. These rights are, in fact, little more than those held by non-indigenous peoples in the relevant area. In some states, for example, no licence is required by non-indigenous fishers to take fish or aquatic life for subsistence or personal use, subject to relevant catch and gear limits.[59] Further, some state-fisheries legislation specifically exempts from

---

54. *The Lardil People*, above n 3, para 179.
55. *The Lardil People*, above n 3, para 185.
56. *The Lardil People*, above n 3, para 185.
57. *The Lardil People*, above n 3, para 193.
58. The *Lardil People*, above n 3, paras 7, 194 Cooper J.
59. See for example, Fisheries Act 1988 (NT), s 10.

their provisions the right of indigenous peoples to continue to use resources in accordance with traditional practices.[60]

IV The Foreshore and Seabed Act: Lessons From Australia

As can be seen from the brief discussion of Australian and Canadian case law above, the language of the FSA is, in places, a curious amalgam of Canadian and Australian jurisprudence. References, for example, to 'integral' call to mind the tests relating to the doctrine of aboriginal rights in Canada, while the provisions on extinguishment appear to contemplate the inconsistency test of Australian jurisprudence. Inevitably, the Government's understanding of aboriginal, or native title, doctrine informs the legislation. As McHugh explains:[61]

> With the decision to replace the common law jurisdiction with a statutory version, it became necessary to form some idea, however speculative, of what was being replaced. By that measure the Government's proposals could be gauged. Political circumstance made inevitable the speculative exercise that the Court of Appeal had properly seen as unnecessary.

Section 50, for example, relates to determinations of applications for customary rights orders.[62] Before issuing an order, the Māori Land Court must be satisfied, *inter alia*, that:

> [T]he activity, use, or practice for which the applicant seeks a customary rights order –
> (i)   is, and has been since 1840, integral to tikanga Maori;
> (ii) has been carried on, exercised, or followed in accordance with tikanga Maori in a substantially uninterrupted manner since 1840, in the area of the public foreshore and seabed specified in the application; and
> (iii) continues to be carried on, exercised, or followed in the same area of the public foreshore and seabed in accordance with tikanga Maori ...

Thus, the non-territorial customary rights provisions substantially reproduce the Australian normative approach, although the use of the word 'integral' indicates a reference to the Canadian jurisprudence on aboriginal rights.

The territorial customary rights provisions, on the other hand, incorporate a factual approach which is similar to that of the Canadian case law, in particular *Delgamuukw*. Section 32 defines territorial customary rights, and provides that:

---

60. See for example, Fisheries Act 1988 (NT), s 53; Fisheries Act 1994 (Qld), s 14(1).
61. 'Aboriginal Title in New Zealand: A Retrospective and Prospect', above n 5, 3.
62. See also section 74, which is the parallel provision under which the High Court may make customary rights orders.

(1) In this Act, territorial customary rights, in relation to a group, means a customary title or an aboriginal title that could be recognised at common law and that –
(a) is founded on the exclusive use and occupation of a particular area of the public foreshore and seabed by the group; and
(b) entitled the group, until the commencement of this Part, to exclusive use and occupation of that area.

While it may be possible in Australia, as will be discussed below, to claim exclusive rights to an area, it is not exclusive use and occupation on which the test is based, but traditional laws and customs. Again this is a normative rather than strictly factual occupation-based approach, although these laws and customs may virtually amount to exclusive possession in particular factual circumstances.[63]

Are there lessons that can be learned from Australia? Given the way in which the legislation blends Canadian and Australian approaches it is perhaps possible at this stage to at least 'flag' some provisions with respect to which Australian (and undoubtedly Canadian) experience may turn out to be important.

A   'SUBSTANTIALLY UNINTERRUPTED'

The requirement that the uses, practices and traditions which are relied upon to found aboriginal title be substantially uninterrupted is a facet of both Australian and Canadian aboriginal title doctrine. However, just what is meant by this requirement has proven complex in the Australian context. In Australia, 'substantially uninterrupted' is really part of the requirement that there be an ongoing connection with the land. This is a requirement that has proven controversial in practice because of the widespread dislocation of indigenous Australians which occurred in colonial Australia. Peoples were frequently relocated, removed from and locked out of their country. This has made it difficult for some to meet the requirement of a continuing connection. Such problems have been exacerbated by the restrictive approach taken by the High Court of Australia to this issue, particularly with respect to the effect of forcible removals. The onus is on the claimants to demonstrate that they have not ceased to maintain a connection to the land. Further, the requirement of connection to the land does not take into account forcible removal of indigenous Australians from their land nor the dislocating effects of European culture. In fact, in most cases forcible removal will result in a loss of connection, and hence inability to prove native title. The High Court of Australia has not definitely ruled out the possibility that a spiritual connection would in

---

63.   An obvious example of this is the decision in *Mabo* (*No 2*) itself.

appropriate circumstances be sufficient to found a native title claim.[64]

However, it is difficult to point to a case in which it has not been held that connection was lost because of physical dislocation. The Federal Court of Australia decision in *De Rose v South Australia* is a good example.[65] In that case, O'Loughlin J held that the claimant group had failed to show a continuing connection after 1978 as they had not proven continuing acknowledgement of traditional laws, particularly in the form of rituals and ceremonies. In 1978 the claim group had been forced to leave the pastoral station which was located on their traditional country as there was no work and because of the conduct of the pastoral operator. They were held to have lost their connection, despite the recent nature of the physical loss of connection and the reasons for it. Whether this will be an issue in a practical sense in New Zealand is unclear. In many cases Māori have retained significant connections with coastal areas. Nevertheless, any requirement such as this will need elaboration.

The issue of substantial connection is bound up with another complex issue which may well have to be addressed by New Zealand courts, that of evolution of rights and the notion of 'traditional'. What does it mean to carry on a practice since 1840? How similar does it have to be in 2007 to practices undertaken in 1840? Can it have evolved and changed? How does one prove what activities, uses or practices were undertaken in 1840?

These questions have engaged both the High Court of Australia and the Supreme Court of Canada. While the High Court of Australia has been significantly criticised for its restrictive approach to this issue in *Yorta Yorta*, the Supreme Court of Canada has similarly been less than generous in its approach.[66] The High Court of Australia has constantly reiterated that aboriginal laws and customs can change. They are dynamic, rather than static. However, in practice virtually no real evolution or change has been accepted. To the contrary, the courts are quick to find that claimants no longer observe traditional laws and customs. In *Yorta Yorta*, the trial judge, Olney J, held that the Yorta Yorta people had failed to prove the required continuing observance of traditional laws and customs. He characterised their fishing practices as for 'recreation', rather than 'subsistence', and therefore 'not the continuation of a traditional custom.'[67] Similarly, in *Daniel v Western Australia*, Nicholson J stated that the 'applicants ... from time to time ... build shelters (including boughsheds, mias (may as) and humpies) and live there. I do not consider the evidence establishes the activity extends to building

---

64. *Ward*, above n 15, para 64 Gleeson CJ, Gaudron, Gummow, Hayne JJ.
65. *De Rose v South Australia* [2002] FCA 1342.
66. See *R v Van der Peet*, above n 7; *R v Gladstone* (1996) 137 DLR (4th) 648 (SCC); *R v NTC Smokehouse* (1996) 137 DLR (4th) 528 (SCC).
67. *Yorta Yorta*, above n 13, para 123 Gaudron and Kirby JJ.

shelters other than houses.'[68] Probably the best known comment in relation to this matter is that of Callinan J in *Yorta Yorta*. While his Honour does not deny that change can occur, he stated that: 'The matter [of how far custom may evolve] went uncontested in *Yanner v Eaton*, although I myself may have questioned whether the use of a motorboat powered by mined and processed fuel, and a steel tomahawk, remained in accordance with a traditional law and custom, particularly one of alleged totemic significance.'[69]

B 'ACTIVITY, USE OR PRACTICE'

While the NTA was not intended to replace the common law with a statutory jurisdiction, the decision by the High Court of Australia that any examination of the existence of native title must start at the definition of native title in section 223 has had the practical effect of limiting the potential of native title at common law. The limiting of native title rights to 'rights and interests' in 'land or waters' has resulted in the content of native title being restricted to a range of physical activities done on land or in waters. The provisions relating to customary rights orders under section 50 of the FSA refer to 'activity, use or practice ... in the area of the public foreshore and seabed specified in the application.' These words potentially show a wider scope than those in section 223. However, care should be taken to ensure that the customary rights order provisions of the FSA are not interpreted too strictly so as to limit orders only to particularised, physical activities on land. A generous interpretation needs to be given to any statutory provisions which purport to define the parameters of indigenous rights as the static nature of such provisions can stifle the development of a dynamic body of law.

C INCONSISTENCY/REGULATION

What I would call the extinguishment provisions of the legislation echo Australian approaches to this issue. Section 51, for example, sets out the basis on which customary orders can be determined by the Māori Land Court. In essence, this is a provision which, rather than setting up a positive basis for orders, confirms that certain events extinguish customary rights, and that if any of these apply no order can be made.[70] Like Australian law, these provisions emphasise that it is *legal* interests, rather than *factual* circumstances that extinguish customary rights.[71] The latter would be more consistent with

---

68. *Daniel v Western Australia* [2003] FCA 666, para 260 R D Nicholson J.
69. *Daniel v Western Australia*, above n 68, para 592 R D Nicholson J.
70. The parallel provision for orders made by the High Court with respect to non-territorial customary rights is section 75.
71. See *Wik*, above n 29; *Ward*, above n 15.

the approach in Canada. In particular, section 51(2)(c) provides that the right to carry on activities, uses or practices, which are in turn to be relied upon to establish customary rights, have been extinguished where 'an interest has been established that is legally inconsistent with the activity, use, or practice for which the customary rights order is sought.'

The FSA contains no definition of 'legally inconsistent'. While this may seem to be a straightforward concept, it has not proved always to be in Australia. While interests which establish rights of exclusive possession are considered to be legally inconsistent, the High Court of Australia has developed a significant jurisprudence with respect to lesser interests, in other words those which do not necessarily carry exclusive possession. The extent to which these are legally inconsistent, and hence the extent to which they extinguish customary rights, may well be problematic.[72] The more rights are individualised and conceptualised as constituting a 'bundle', the more difficult the issue of extinguishment becomes, and the more complex the interrelationship between legal interests and customary rights can be.[73]

Further, and particularly in the context of the offshore, the distinction between extinguishment and regulation may be important. The High Court of Australia has held, as has the Supreme Court of Canada, that a distinction must be drawn between acts which regulate, and those which extinguish, customary rights.[74] Fisheries legislation and conservation legislation can affect customary rights by requiring licensing, setting catch or gear restrictions, or banning hunting and fishing of certain species. New Zealand courts will need to determine whether they will recognise a distinction between regulation and extinguishment, and where the dividing line between the two falls. The problems of making this determination can be seen in the Australian case of *Ward*. At both first instance, and in the Federal Court of Appeal, it was held that certain by-laws which prohibited interference with flora and fauna were a regulation, rather than an extinguishment of native title, while the majority of the High Court held that the by-laws amounted to extinguishment.[75]

D Territorial Customary Rights

The problems in Australia of showing exclusivity of title to the offshore have been outlined above, particularly in the context of *The Lardil People*. However,

---

72. See *Wik*, above n 29; *Ward*, above n 15.
73. See Sean Brennan 'Native Title in the High Court of Australia a Decade after *Mabo*' (2003) 14 Public LR 209; Shaunnagh Dorsett '"Clear and Plain Intention": Extinguishment of Native Title in Australia and Canada Post-*Wik*' (1997) 6 GLR 96.
74. See *Yanner v Eaton* (1999) 166 ALR 258 (HCC); *R v Gladstone*, above n 66.
75. *Ward v Western Australia* (1998) 159 ALR 483, 583 Olney J (FCA); *Western Australia v Ward* (2000) 170 ALR 159, 262 (FFC); *Ward*, above n 15.

in emphasising the importance of section 223 of the NTA to the way in which native title is recognised I hope both to signal that a broader notion of aboriginal title to the offshore should be possible, and to show the way in which statutes can come to dominate the way in which rights develop at common law.

The particularised nature of the interests recognised resulted not only from the limitations or qualifications posed by the common law rights of navigation and public fishing, as well as the international law right of innocent passage, but also from the requirements of the NTA, as interpreted in *Ward*, that every native title right be particularised. If this requirement is followed, it becomes virtually impossible to construct a claim of qualified exclusive possession.

In saying this I therefore have to disagree with McHugh that aboriginal title to the foreshore cannot amount to exclusive possession, or even qualified exclusive possession.[76] With respect, I think his analysis of Australian case law misses the impact of the NTA on the way in which rights are constructed. In so saying, I am, however, not indicating that even absent this provision the High Court of Australia would grant exclusive rights. However, the importance of section 223 as a starting point makes such an analysis even less likely. Recent Canadian case law can also be pointed to in this context. The 2004 decision in *Haida Nation v British Columbia*, for example, indicates that there is still the substantial possibility that territorial rights in the offshore will be recognised.[77]

Nor would I predicate legislation on the basis that such a claim is not possible. It is simply an unanswered question. It is true that the possibility of exclusive claims to the foreshore and seabed was not entirely ignored by the legislation. However, the form in which it was acknowledged, the claim that could be made 'but for' extinguishment by the legislation,[78] is even more problematic if a real possibility does exist that territorial customary rights could be claimed in the form of aboriginal title at common law. It is one thing to effectively confiscate rights through extinguishment in a context in which it seems unlikely they will ever be found, and another to do so if there remains a possibility that they could be. In removing any genuine opportunity for Māori to test these claims (other than for the purposes of redress), New Zealand has gone further in denying aboriginal rights than arguably even Australia. And in so doing the understanding of aboriginal title which underpins the legislation appears too restrictive and too reliant on a body of jurisprudence which has arisen within a quite different legal framework. In particular, it has arisen not only in the context of the NTA, but it has arisen in the context of

---

76. 'Aboriginal Title in New Zealand: A Retrospective and Prospect', above n 5, 21.
77. It should be noted that this decision was handed down after McHugh's article in the NZJPIL and his presentation of evidence to the Waitangi Tribunal.
78. See FSA, s 33.

a country in which there is no instrument like the Treaty of Waitangi, and no tradition of reconciling indigenous and non-indigenous interests such as that characterises recent history in New Zealand.

McHugh suggests that the fact that section 33 of the Act allows for an order by the High Court of New Zealand that territorial customary rights would have existed but for the vesting of ownership should 'answer the recognition question in the affirmative' for New Zealand courts.[79] In other words, as a result of this provision, '[a] New Zealand court would reason that in enacting [section 33] Parliament was recognising the legal possibility of exclusive Māori ownership, and in that regard has provided for more than the common law by itself would have allowed.'[80]

With respect, however, such a view is only sustainable if one is convinced in advance about the form that aboriginal title claims would take in New Zealand, and that only a restrictive set of rights would be granted. One must remember that the doctrine would be developed by a court substantially composed of the same justices who determined *Ngati Apa*. It seems unlikely that they were not fully aware of the potential and consequences of their determination that the Māori Land Court had jurisdiction, and that the common law was the underlying source of Māori rights. In any case, even allowing such a 'legal possibility' can only lead to negotiations for redress, not recognition of title itself.

It is probably trite to point out that the development of doctrine is always significantly influenced by the legal framework and culture in which it is developed. The legal culture within which such a doctrine as aboriginal title will develop in New Zealand is significantly different to that of Australia and Canada. The impact of the Treaty of Waitangi on legal culture appears to be an extraordinarily powerful facet of the New Zealand legal system, regardless of the fact that the Treaty is not directly enforceable, as McHugh points out:[81]

> [I]n constructing a common law jurisprudence ... it is likely that New Zealand court[s] will consciously strive to build one consistent with the Treaty ... There are a number of choices New Zealand judges would face in exercising the inherent jurisdiction. It seems inescapable that the Treaty would influence their route.

It seems a pity that the Government chose to intervene, and did not, as governments largely have in other jurisdictions, leave the courts to develop doctrine and to balance the claims of indigenous and non-indigenous peoples.

---

79. 'Aboriginal Title in New Zealand: A Retrospective and Prospect', above n 5, 21.
80. 'Aboriginal Title in New Zealand: A Retrospective and Prospect', above n 5, 21.
81. 'Aboriginal Title in New Zealand: A Retrospective and Prospect', above n 5, 5.

While we may not always approve of the way balance is achieved, courts do develop doctrine which takes into account the rights of all.

E 'INTEGRAL'

As intimated above, the use of the word 'integral' in the FSA provisions relating to non-territorial customary rights brings to mind the Canadian test for aboriginal rights. In essence, section 51 of the FSA layers two strands of aboriginal rights doctrine. In addition to showing that the customary rights claimed are *tikanga*, it must also be shown that they are *integral*. This potentially 'ups the ante' because it implies that not all rights will be recognised, but that some higher threshold must be reached. Only those rights which are also *integral* can be the subject of a customary rights order. How does one determine which rights are integral, and which are only peripheral? While not venturing too far into Canadian jurisprudence, a task I leave to Kent McNeil, this requirement in Canadian case law has spawned a significantly different body of jurisprudence from that in Australia.[82] How these two will be amalgamated, if at all, remains of course to be seen. Whether the legislature intended to incorporate two different strands of aboriginal rights doctrine into this provision is unclear. However, once sections are enacted they can take on a life of their own. Courts have a tendency to take words in legislation seriously, and to accord meaning to them. The Australian experience with the NTA is testament to that tendency.

F REDRESS

Perhaps one of the most unfortunate parts of the FSA is that there is no guarantee of compensation once an order recognising that territorial customary rights would have existed had it not been for the FSA. Rather, the FSA only provides that the High Court may make an order referring a finding of territorial customary rights to the Attorney-General and Minister of Māori Affairs (section 36). Section 37 further provides that 'the Ministers must enter into discussions with the applicant group for the purpose of negotiating an agreement as to the nature and extent of the redress to be given by the Crown in recognition of the finding of the High Court.'

The FSA neither mandates the way or manner in which redress is to be given, or the form of that redress. Nor does it mandate that compensation be given. As intimated above, even in Australia, notably a conservative native title jurisdiction, claims for compensation can be made in all cases of extinguishment.

---

82. See *R v Van der Peet*, above n 7; *R v Gladstone*, above n 66; *R v NTC Smokehouse*, above n 66.

Undoubtedly as a result of settlements made as a result of reports of the Waitangi Tribunal there is much expertise to be drawn upon in determining claims for redress. However, if compensation is to be given for extinguishment of aboriginal title this brings into play a potentially different array of principles and need for a mechanism to determine how to value that aboriginal title.

G COHERENCE?

My last point on this is a general one and returns to the beginning of my critique of the FSA. Although it is difficult to tell from the terms of the FSA itself exactly what the understanding of aboriginal title/rights was which underpinned the legislation, it is a curious amalgam of Canadian and Australian approaches. To that extent, the legislation lacks a consistent approach to the recognition of rights. The territorial and non-territorial bifurcation seems to suggest that a (more generous) Canadian approach should be taken. However, layered on top of this, as intimated above, are echoes of Australian law. Whether this will prove problematic only time can tell. I have to suggest, however, that it may have been better to have either taken one approach, or left the resolution of, particularly non-territorial rights, to the courts themselves. This is, of course, the problem which arises when a government legislates to deal with a body of doctrine which does not actually yet exist.

V Conclusion

It is difficult to make any predictions at this stage about what will result from the FSA. As I have suggested above, there are a number of particular issues which will require resolution, and will undoubtedly along the way to so doing spawn a significant body of new jurisprudence. If Australian experience is any guide, in the foreseeable future at least most, if not all, of the applications will end up in the Supreme Court. It is only this peak body which can really construct the new law required.

Legal Rights and Legislative Wrongs: Māori Claims to the Foreshore and Seabed

*Kent McNeil**

I Introduction

As other chapters in this book demonstrate, the legal and political debate over Māori rights to the foreshore and seabed probably goes back to the time of the British colonisation of New Zealand. I am nonetheless going to take the Court of Appeal's recent decision in *Ngati Apa v Attorney-General* (*Ngati Apa*) as my starting point.[1] I will attempt to show that the main elements of that decision are generally consistent with the common law in other jurisdictions, especially the law on aboriginal title developed by the Supreme Court of Canada over the past twenty-five years. I will then focus on certain aspects of the legislative response to that decision in the Foreshore and Seabed Act 2004 (FSA). In particular, I will criticise the legislation for selectively adopting two of the more problematic aspects of the jurisprudence on indigenous rights in Canada and Australia, namely the Supreme Court of Canada's 'integral to the distinctive culture' test for aboriginal rights apart from title,[2] and the High Court of Australia's requirement of substantial maintenance of a continuing connection with the land in accordance with traditional laws and customs for native title.[3] I will also argue that the legislative treatment of foreshore and

---

* I would like to express my gratitude to Leah Mack for her indispensable assistance with the research for this chapter. The financial assistance of the Social Sciences and Humanities Research Council of Canada is also gratefully acknowledged. The title of this chapter borrows from the heading, 'Aboriginal Rights and Judicial Wrongs', in David Bloch's illuminating article on off-shore aboriginal rights in Alaska, cited below n 19.

1. *Attorney-General v Ngati Apa* [2003] 3 NZLR 643.
2. *R. v Van der Peet* [1996] 2 SCR 507, para 46 Lamer CJ.
3. *Mabo v Queensland (No 2)* (1992) 175 CLR 1, 59 Brennan J; *Members of the Yorta Yorta Aboriginal Community v Victoria* (2002) 194 ALR 538.

seabed rights in the FSA is discriminatory because it privileges ownership by private individuals and corporations over Māori customary rights.

II The Common Law Basis for Māori Rights to the Foreshore and Seabed: Ngati Apa

The *Ngati Apa* case involved a dispute over the jurisdiction of the Māori Land Court to hear a Māori customary land claim to the foreshore and seabed in the Marlborough Sounds of the South Island. The Crown argued that the Māori Land Court lacked jurisdiction because the foreshore and seabed could not be Māori customary land, either as a matter of law or because customary rights to those coastal areas had all been extinguished by legislation. In four judgments, the Court of Appeal unanimously rejected these arguments and decided that the Māori Land Court did have jurisdiction because Māori customary rights to the foreshore and seabed could exist as a matter of law and had not been generally extinguished by legislation. The Court of Appeal did not, however, decide whether any such rights exist in New Zealand, as that was mainly a matter of fact to be determined by the Māori Land Court.

In reaching this decision, the Court of Appeal judges relied upon the jurisprudence on indigenous land rights in other common law jurisdictions, especially Australia, Canada and Nigeria. They decided that some New Zealand authorities denying the existence of Māori land rights as enforceable legal entitlements (such as *Wi Parata v Bishop of Wellington* (*Wi Parata*)[4]) had not only been rejected in Privy Council appeals from New Zealand (especially in *Nireaha Tamaki v Baker*),[5] but were also inconsistent with the case law in other parts of the British Commonwealth. The Court held that, from the time of Crown acquisition of sovereignty over New Zealand, any rights to land held by virtue of tikanga Māori (Māori custom and practice/usage)[6] continued as a burden on the Crown's radical title. The Court held further that the foreshore and seabed could also be Māori customary land, if rights to those coastal areas could be proven as a matter of fact in accordance with tikanga Māori. This would displace any presumption of Crown ownership that might arise at common law. Moreover, any Māori rights to the foreshore and seabed had not been generally extinguished by legislation such as the Harbours Acts of 1878

---

4. *Wi Parata v Bishop of Wellington* (1877) 3 NZ Jur (NS) 561.
5. *Nireaha Tamaki v Baker* [1901] AC 561. See also *Wallis v Solicitor-General for New Zealand* [1903] AC 173.
6. For a more detailed explanation of tikanga Māori, see Waitangi Tribunal *Report on the Crown's Foreshore and Seabed Policy: Wai 1071* (Legislation Direct, Wellington, 2004) 1–2 (Waitangi Tribunal Report).

and 1955, the Territorial Sea and Fishing Zone Act 1965, the Territorial Sea, Contiguous Zone and Exclusive Economic Zone Act 1977, and the Foreshore and Seabed Endowment Revesting Act 1991.[7] Finally, a majority of the Court overruled *In re the Ninety-Mile Beach*,[8] where the Court of Appeal had held that, when land bordering the sea ceased to be Māori customary land, no Māori rights to the foreshore adjoining that land could be claimed. In *Ngati Apa* the Court decided that such rights can still exist as a matter of law, though whether they exist as a matter of fact depends on tikanga Māori and the findings of the Māori Land Court.

The *Ngati Apa* decision relied on what is commonly known as the doctrine of continuity, whereby the property rights of the inhabitants of a territory over which the Crown has acquired sovereignty continue, in the absence of Crown taking by act of state in the course of the acquisition.[9] In New Zealand, Māori lands were not seized by act of state; on the contrary, Māori property rights were expressly acknowledged and guaranteed by the Crown in the Treaty of Waitangi of 1840.[10] As recognised by the Court in *Ngati Apa*, a statutory process was initiated in the 1860s for conversion of Māori customary land into common law fee simple title through the deliberations of the Native Land Court.[11] That process constituted further recognition, this time by legislation, of the legal existence of Māori land rights.[12] However, as pointed out by the Court, the continuation of those rights did not depend on recognition by treaty or statute. As confirmed by leading authorities relied on by the Court, continuation of property rights in colonised territories is an established principle of both the common law[13]

---

7. Legislative extinguishment may have occurred with respect to specific portions of the foreshore and seabed, but the Court did not decide whether that had actually happened: *Ngati Apa*, above n 1, para 58 Elias CJ.
8. *In re the Ninety-Mile Beach* [1963] NZLR 461 (apparently Gault P would have allowed this decision to stand: see *Ngati Apa*, above n 1, paras 118–122). For further discussion of this decision, see Richard Boast's chapter in this book, 9–30.
9. See Kent McNeil *Common Law Aboriginal Title* (Clarendon Press, Oxford, 1989) 161–92; Mark Walters 'The "Golden Thread" of Continuity: Aboriginal Customs at Common Law and under the Constitution Act, 1982' (1999) 44 McGill LJ 711; Russel Lawrence Barsh, 'Indigenous Rights and the *Lex Loci* in British Imperial Law' in Kerry Wilkins (ed) *Advancing Aboriginal Claims: Visions/Strategies/Directions* (Purich Publishing, Saskatoon, 2004) 91–126.
10. *Common Law Aboriginal Title*, above n 9, 188–189. More generally, see Claudia Orange *The Treaty of Waitangi* (Allen & Unwin/Port Nicholson Press, Wellington, 1987); Paul McHugh *The Māori Magna Carta: New Zealand Law and the Treaty of Waitangi* (Oxford University Press, Auckland, 1991); Michael Belgrave, Merata Kawharu, and David Williams (eds) *Waitangi Revisited: Perspectives on the Treaty of Waitangi* (Oxford University Press, Melbourne, 2005).
11. See generally David V Williams *'Te Kooti tango whenua': The Native Land Court 1864–1909* (Huia Publishers, Wellington, 1999).
12. *Ngati Apa*, above n 1, paras 39–40 Elias CJ.
13. For example see *Amodu Tijani v Secretary, Southern Nigeria* [1921] 2 AC 399 (PC); *Mabo (No 2)*, above n 3; Sir Kenneth Roberts-Wray *Commonwealth and Colonial Law* (Stevens & Sons, London, 1966) 625–36.

and international law.[14]

In deciding that Māori customary lands rights continued as a matter of law in the absence of valid extinguishment or conversion into English law titles, the Court relied upon the long-standing distinction between sovereignty and property.[15] Crown acquisition of sovereignty over New Zealand was accompanied by acquisition of the radical or underlying title to lands, but this proprietary title was subject to Māori customary rights.[16] In this regard, the Court did not think a distinction could be drawn between dry land and land below the coastal high water mark.[17] Both would be subject to Māori customary rights existing at the time of Crown acquisition of sovereignty, apparently dating from the Treaty of Waitangi in 1840.[18] Although the Court of Appeal did not address the issue directly, it is thus clear that the judges did not regard Māori customary rights to the foreshore and seabed as being incompatible with Crown sovereignty.[19] This conclusion is supported by the

---

See also *Guerin v The Queen* [1984] 2 SCR 335, 376–79 Dickson J; *Delgamuukw v British Columbia* [1997] 3 SCR 1010, para 114, 147–148 Lamer CJ.

14. *Ngati Apa*, above n 1, paras 136–38 Keith and Anderson JJ, relying on M de Vattel *Le Droit des Gens ou Principles de la Loi Naturelle Appliqués à la Conduite & aux Affaires des Nations & des Souverains* (A Leide, aux Dépens de la Compagnie, 1758), English translation by Charles G Fenwick (Carnegie Institution of Washington, Wellington, 1916), Bk III, ch 13, §§ 200–1; *United States v Perchman* 7 Pet 51 (1833) 86–87; PD O'Connell *State Succession in Municipal and International Law* (University Press, Cambridge, 1967) vol I, 237–250. See also *Cook v Sprigg* [1899] AC 572, 578; A Berriedale Keith *The Theory of State Succession, with Special Reference to English and Colonial Law* (Waterlow & Sons, London, 1907) 78–81.
15. *Ngati Apa*, above n 1, paras 26–28 Elias CJ, 132, 136–140 Keith and Anderson JJ, 183, 204 Tipping J.
16. *Ngati Apa*, above n 1, paras 29–31 Elias CJ, 101–102 Gault P, 160 Keith and Anderson JJ, 183, 197, 204, 211 Tipping J.
17. *Ngati Apa*, above n 1, paras 48–55 Elias CJ, 133–135, 171–180 Keith and Anderson JJ, 187–188, 205 Tipping J.
18. *Ngati Apa*, above n 1, para 14 Elias CJ. See also Simon John Young 'The Trouble with Tradition: Menagerie Theory in Judicial Understanding of Native Title' (PhD thesis, University of Western Australia Faculty of Law, 2004) 152–153. For criticism of using 1840 as the date, see Bryan D Gilling 'Engine of Destruction? An Introduction to the History of the Maori Land Court' (1994) 24 VUWLR 115, and '"The Queen's Sovereignty Must be Vindicated": The 1840 Rule in the Maori Land Court' (1994) 16 NZULR 136. Note, however, that the time of Crown acquisition of sovereignty over areas of the territorial sea beyond the limits claimed in 1840 would probably be more recent.
19. This is consistent with the High Court of Australia's decision in *Commonwealth v Yarmirr* (2001) 184 ALR 184 (*Yarmirr*), and with *Lardil People v Queensland* [2004] FCA 298, discussed in Shaunnagh Dorsett's chapter in this book, 59–82. Compare *Native Village of Eyak v Trawler Diane Marie Inc* 154 F 3d 1090 (9th Cir 1998) cert denied 527 US 1003 (1999), where the Court held that exclusive aboriginal title rights to the seabed in Alaska are incompatible with American offshore sovereignty. However, the 9th Circuit en banc has since opened the door to a reassessment of that issue in the context of non-exclusive aboriginal rights, see *Native Village of Eyak v Evans* 375 F 3d 1218 (2004), vacating the District Court's summary judgment (D Alaska, 25 Sept 2002) that had been based on the paramountcy of federal sovereignty, and remanding 'with instructions that the district court decide what aboriginal rights to fish beyond the three-mile limit, if any, the plaintiffs have', assuming '[f]or the purposes of this limited remand ... that the villages' aboriginal rights, if any, have not been abrogated by the federal paramountcy doctrine or other federal law.' For critical commentary, see David J Bloch 'Colonizing the Last Frontier' (2004) 29 Am Indian L Rev 1.

fact that private rights to the foreshore and seabed can also exist in England, as a result of custom and usage or Crown grant.[20] Māori customary rights might, however, be subject to common law public rights of navigation and fishing, and the international-law right of innocent passage, though the Court appears to have left this open.[21]

I have no doubt that the *Ngati Apa* case was correctly decided. In it the Court simply adopted well-established common law principles and precedents and applied them to the foreshore and seabed. In doing so, they resolved some fundamental contradictions regarding the legal existence of Māori land rights that have plagued New Zealand's jurisprudence for well over a century. Given the dual doctrines that land rights continue after Crown acquisition of sovereignty and that the common law is received into a colony only to the extent that local circumstances allow,[22] the presumption – and it needs to be emphasised that it is *only a presumption* – of Crown ownership of the foreshore and seabed can be displaced, as the Court held, by proof that specific portions of them are Māori customary lands.[23] Without doing so explicitly, the Court also appears to have accepted an approach to proof of Māori customary land rights that is less rigid than that of the High Court of Australia. In Australia, native title rights depend on proof of the existence at the time of Crown acquisition of sovereignty of traditional laws and customs, which are then used to define the nature and content of the rights.[24] As applied by

20. *Ngati Apa*, above n 1, paras 50–51 Elias CJ, 133–134 Keith and Anderson JJ.
21. *Ngati Apa*, paras 50–51 Elias CJ, 132–135, 146 Keith and Anderson JJ. See also *Yarmirr*, above n 19, holding that native title rights to the seabed in Australia cannot be exclusive because they are subject to these public and international law rights. It can be argued, however, that the rule that the common law is received in a colony only to the extent it is applicable to local circumstances would exclude the public rights of navigation and fishing where exclusive Māori rights could be established on the basis of tikanga Māori (in *Ngati Apa*, this rule was used by Elias CJ, paras 28, 49, to exclude Crown ownership of the seabed by prerogative right; see also Keith and Anderson JJ, paras 133–134, 146). Note also that fishing rights in New Zealand are now largely governed by statute. See for example the Treaty of Waitangi (Fisheries Claims) Settlement Act 1992 and the Maori Fisheries Act 2004.
22. On application of these doctrines in the context of tidal and non-tidal waters, and their impact on aboriginal fishing rights in New Zealand and Canada, see Mark D Walters 'Aboriginal Rights, *Magna Carta* and Exclusive Rights to Fisheries in the Waters of Upper Canada' (1998) 23 Queen's LJ 301, 318–352.
23. See *Common Law Aboriginal Title*, above n 9, 103–105, 217 n 88; *Hanasiki v Symes* (1951, Solomon Islands JC) in Barbara Hocking 'Native Land Rights' (LLM thesis, Monash University, 1970) 254. Compare Dr Paul McHugh *Brief of Evidence to the Waitangi Tribunal* (Wai 1071) 13 January 2004, paras 52–56.
24. See *Mabo (No 2)*, above n 3, 58 Brennan J. His definition was incorporated into the Native Title Act 1993 (NTA), as interpreted and applied in *Western Australia v Ward* (2002) 191 ALR 1 and *Yorta Yorta*, above n 3. For an interpretation of *Mabo (No 2)* more in keeping, in my respectful opinion, with the order of the Court in the case, see 'The Relevance of Traditional Laws and Customs to the Existence and Content of Native Title at Common Law' ('Relevance of Traditional Laws') in Kent McNeil *Emerging Justice? Essays on Indigenous Rights in Canada and Australia* (Saskatoon: University of Saskatchewan Native Law Centre, 2001) 416, 418–423 (*Emerging Justice?*).

the High Court of Australia, this approach involves a strict application of the doctrine of continuity, whereby only 'rights' that can be identified and defined as such in the pre-existing legal systems are continued.[25] By contrast, in *Ngati Apa* the Court said that the tikanga Māori on which Māori land rights are based includes custom *and* practice or usage.[26] While this reflects a statutory definition different from the statutory definition for native title in Australia,[27] it is nonetheless clear that the Court did not regard the Māori lands legislation as creating any *new* rights; instead, it provided a mechanism for converting *existing* Māori customary rights into common law titles.[28] The New Zealand approach to Māori land rights therefore appears to be closer to the Canadian approach, which bases aboriginal land rights either on practices, customs and traditions (where rights less than title are concerned),[29] or on exclusive occupation which may be supported by aboriginal law (where title is concerned).[30] So in New Zealand, while Māori custom, practice or usage commonly involves exclusive occupation giving rise to ownership

---

25. See 'Relevance of Traditional Laws', above n 24, 454–463; Young, above n 18, 183–301.
26. *Ngati Apa*, above n 1, paras 14, 32, 49, 89 Elias CJ, 101 Gault P, 184 Tipping J.
27. The Te Ture Whenua Maori Act 1993, upon which the jurisdiction of the Māori Land Court is currently based, defines 'Maori customary land' in s129(2)(a) as '[l]and that is held by Maori in accordance with tikanga Maori', which is defined in section 3 as 'Maori customary values and practices'. See also the Native Rights Act 1865, s 4: 'Every title to or interest in land over which the Native Title shall not have been extinguished shall be determined according to the Ancient Custom and Usage of the Maori people so far as the same can be ascertained.' For a list of equivalent definitions of native land up to 1909, see *'Te Kooti tango whenua': The Native Land Court 1864–1909*, above n 11, App 3, 255–259. By contrast, the Australian NTA, above n 24, section 223(1), adopted a description of native title provided by Brennan J in *Mabo (No 2)*, above n 3, 58, and defined native title as rights and interests 'possessed under the traditional laws acknowledged, and the traditional customs observed, by the Aboriginal peoples or Torres Strait Islanders' (see below n 100). For criticism of the way the High Court has used this definition, see Noel Pearson 'Land Is Susceptible of Ownership' (10 October 2003) Cape York Partnerships website <http://www.capeyorkpartnerships.com> (last accessed 14 June 2005).
28. *Ngati Apa*, above n 1, paras 31–47 Elias CJ, para 47: 'The Maori lands legislation was not constitutive of Maori customary land. It assumed its continued existence.' See also *Ngati Apa*, paras 183–186, 197, 204–208, 213–214 Tipping J.
29. *Van der Peet*, above n 2.
30. *Delgamuukw*, above n 13. See Kent McNeil 'Aboriginal Rights in Canada: From Title to Land to Territorial Sovereignty' (1998) 5 Tulsa J of Comp & Int'l L 253 (also in *Emerging Justice?*, above n 24, 58). Note, however, that in Canada there are now three different dates for proof of these rights: (1) contact with Europeans where *Indian* (and no doubt Inuit) rights based on practices, customs or traditions are involved (*Van der Peet*, above n 2); (2) effective European control where *Métis* rights based on practices, customs or traditions are involved (*R. v Powley* [2003] 2 SCR 207); and (3) Crown assertion of sovereignty where aboriginal title based on exclusive occupation is concerned (*Delgamuukw*). Where the time-frames used are not acquisition of Crown sovereignty, however, it is questionable whether Canadian approaches really involve an application of the doctrine of continuity. See Walters, above n 9, 735–749; compare McLachlin J's dissenting judgment in *Van der Peet*.

equivalent to a fee simple estate,[31] Māori customary rights can also entail lesser interests.[32]

As is well known, the *Ngati Apa* decision provoked a political debate over rights to the foreshore and seabed that resulted in the FSA.[33] I will now turn to examine some of what I think are the more problematic aspects of that statute, in particular the extinguishment of territorial customary rights, and the adoption of versions of the Canadian integral to the distinctive culture test and the Australian requirement of substantial maintenance of a connection with the land in accordance with traditional laws and customs where non-exclusive rights of use are concerned.

III The Political Reaction: The Foreshore and Seabed Act 2004

The problems with the FSA begin with section 3, stating the legislation's objective:

> The object of this Act is to preserve the public foreshore and seabed in perpetuity as the common heritage of all New Zealanders in a way that enables the protection by the Crown of the public foreshore and seabed on behalf of all the people of New Zealand, including the protection of the association of whānau, hapū, and iwi with areas of the public foreshore and seabed.

The definitions in section 5 provide that 'public foreshore and seabed – (a) means the foreshore and seabed; but (b) does not include any land that is, for the time being, subject to a specified freehold interest.' Section 4 states one of the Act's purposes to be 'vesting the full legal and beneficial ownership of the public foreshore and seabed in the Crown.' This vesting is then accomplished by section 13. It is therefore apparent that, despite the Act's stated object, it is not intended to *'preserve the public* foreshore and seabed in perpetuity as the

---

31. This is illustrated by the conversion work of the Native Land Court and more recently the Māori Land Court: *Ngati Apa*, above n 1, paras 40–42 Elias CJ. See also Young, above n 18, 28, 41, 148–176. On the work of the Native Land Court, see *'Te Kooti tango whenua': The Native Land Court 1864–1909*, above n 11. One reason why a statutory conversion process was deemed necessary was that at common law Māori customary land is inalienable other than by surrender to the Crown: see *The Queen v Symonds* (1847) NZPCC 387 (NZSC) (*Symonds*), and discussion in *Common Law Aboriginal Title*, above n 9, 229–234. For analysis of the inalienability rule in North America, see Kent McNeil 'Self-Government and the Inalienability of Aboriginal Title' (2002) 47 McGill LJ 473.
32. *Kauwaeranga* Judgment (1870, NLC), reproduced by A Frame in (1984) 14 VUWLR 227. In *Ngati Apa*, above n 1, para 46 Elias CJ acknowledged that Māori land rights could either be equivalent to fee simple ownership or be lesser interests, though she said 'the common law recognition of property interests in land under native custom is little developed' in New Zealand. See also *Ngati Apa*, para 106 Gault P.
33. See David Williams's chapter in this book, 31–58.

common heritage of all New Zealanders', but to *convert* foreshore and seabed that is not already owned by the Crown or held in freehold into Crown land. The Act is therefore specifically aimed at extinguishing, without obligation to pay compensation, any exclusive Māori customary rights to the foreshore and seabed that, as a result of the *Ngati Apa* decision, might have been found by the Māori Land Court to exist in accordance with tikanga Māori. The stated object of the Act is therefore misleading, as it conveys the impression that foreshore and seabed lands subject to Māori customary rights are *already* public lands that are the heritage of all New Zealanders and therefore should be preserved as such. This is in direct contradiction to the Court of Appeal's decision in *Ngati Apa*. Moreover, the Act's real objective of extinguishing exclusive Māori customary rights makes a mockery of the concluding words of section 3, stating that protection by the Crown includes 'the protection of the association of whānau, hapū, and iwi with areas of the public foreshore and seabed.' Under the statute this so-called protection is a matter of political grace insofar as exclusive rights are concerned, replacing the much more robust legal protection accorded by the *Ngati Apa* decision.

This negative assessment of the FSA is confirmed by a more detailed examination of some of its provisions. Section 10(1) completely replaces the inherent and previous statutory jurisdiction of the High Court to hear and determine any 'customary rights claim'[34] with 'the jurisdiction of the High Court under section 33 and Part 4, and the jurisdiction of the Māori Land Court under Part 3.' This applies retroactively to customary rights claims already commenced in the High Court.[35] Similarly, section 12 removes the jurisdiction of the Māori Land Court to hear applications in relation to the 'public foreshore and seabed' brought before that section came into force.

Turning to the jurisdiction of the High Court under the FSA, section 33 provides:

> The High Court may, on the application of a group, or on the application of a person authorized by the Court to represent the group, make a finding that the group (or any members of that group) would, but for the vesting of the full legal and beneficial ownership of the public foreshore and seabed in the Crown by section 13(1), have held territorial customary rights to a particular area of the public foreshore and seabed at common law.

The term 'territorial customary rights' is defined in section 32(1) as 'a customary title or an aboriginal title that could be recognized at common law and that – (a) is founded on the exclusive use and occupation of a particular area of the

---

34. These words are broadly defined in section 10(2).
35. FSA, s 11.

public foreshore and seabed by the group; and (b) entitled the group, until the commencement of this Part, to exclusive use and occupation of that area.'[36] Subsections (2) to (6) then limit this definition by specifying that the use and occupation must have been 'without substantial interruption' from 1840 to the commencement of this Part of the Act (I will come back to this requirement later in the context of the jurisdiction of the Māori Land Court), and must be supported by 'continuous title to contiguous land' (basically meaning land above the high water mark contiguous to the foreshore or seabed being claimed).

In addition to the restrictions on the definition of territorial customary rights, what is particularly remarkable about sections 32 and 33 is that they effectively reduce the jurisdiction of the High Court to a fact-finding mission, removing any significant legal consequences from a finding by the Court that territorial customary rights would have existed but for the statutory vesting of ownership of the foreshore and seabed in the Crown. Section 36(1) provides that, if the Court makes a finding in favour of an applicant group under section 33, the group can ask the Court either for '(a) an order referring the finding to the Attorney-General and the Minister of Māori Affairs; or (b) an order under section 43.' If an order is made under section 36(1)(a) referring the finding, 'the Ministers must enter into discussions with the applicant group for the purpose of negotiating an agreement as to the nature and extent of the redress to be given by the Crown in recognition of the finding of the High Court under section 33.'[37] But section 38(1) provides that the only forms of redress available are either those 'the Crown may give ... following discussions under section 37(1),' or as 'provided in accordance with sections 40 to 43.' Section 38(3) then makes clear the discretionary political rather than legal nature of the redress that may result from a section 37 agreement: 'No court has jurisdiction to consider the nature or the extent of any matter that the Crown proposes, offers, or gives for the purposes of any redress of the kind described in subsection (1).'

An order under section 43, the other option to an order to negotiate, would create a foreshore and seabed reserve to be administered by a board governed by a charter negotiated by the applicant group, the regional council for the area to which the finding relates, and the Attorney-General and Minister of Māori Affairs. Section 40 nonetheless makes clear that use of the reserve by the applicant group would co-exist with free public access and use, and would not affect 'the status of the area as public foreshore and seabed vested in the

---

36. This definition, were it not for the restrictions on it in section 32(2)-(6), essentially adopts the approach to aboriginal title of the Supreme Court of Canada in *Delgamuukw*, above n 13: see above n 30 and accompanying text.
37. FSA, s 37(1).

Crown under section 13(1).' Extinguishment of territorial customary rights, as defined in section 32(1), is therefore confirmed.

In addition to its section 33 jurisdiction regarding territorial customary rights, the High Court has jurisdiction under Part 4 of the FSA to issue 'customary rights orders' for activities, uses or practices in relation to specified areas of the public foreshore and seabed on application by the 'authorized representative of a group of natural persons with a distinctive community of interest.'[38] Specifically excluded, however, is jurisdiction to determine applications in relation to customary rights that could be made to the Māori Land Court under Part 3 of the Act.[39] The effect of this exclusion would appear to be to limit the High Court's jurisdiction under Part 4 in most if not all cases to applications brought on behalf of groups of persons who are not Māori.[40] So instead of examining Part 4, it is more relevant for us to consider the equivalent jurisdiction of the Māori Land Court in relation to Māori groups in Part 3 (sections 46 to 65 of the Act).

Section 46 confers jurisdiction on the Māori Land Court to inquire into and determine applications for customary rights orders made under section 48(1), which provides: 'A whānau, hapū, or iwi, through its authorised representative, may apply to the Māori Land Court for a customary rights order that relates to a specified area of the public foreshore and seabed.'[41]

Excluded from claim, however, are Māori fishing rights dealt with by the Treaty of Waitangi (Fisheries Claims) Settlement Act 1992 and wildlife and marine mammals coming under other statutes, as well as claims 'in respect of an activity, use, or practice on the basis of a spiritual or cultural association, unless that association is manifested by the relevant whānau, hapū, or iwi in a physical activity or use related to a natural or physical resource.'[42]

Section 50(1) places further restrictions on claims that can be made under Part 3 by providing that the Māori Land Court has to be satisfied that the claimed right has not been extinguished and:

(b) the activity, use, or practice for which the applicant seeks a customary rights order –
    (i) is, and has been since 1840, integral to tikanga Māori; and
    (ii) has been carried on, exercised, or followed in accordance with tikanga Māori in a substantially uninterrupted manner since 1840, in the area of the public foreshore and seabed specified in the application; and

---

38. FSA, ss 67–75.
39. FSA, s 73(1)(a).
40. There may not be any such groups, given that section 74(1)(b)(i) provides that the activity, use, or practice for which the order is sought 'is, and has been *since 1840*, integral to the distinctive cultural practices of the group' (emphasis added).
41. There is, however, a time limit of 31 December 2015 for bringing an application: FSA, s 48(2).
42. FSA, s 49.

(iii) continues to be carried on, exercised, or followed in the same area of the public foreshore and seabed in accordance with tikanga Māori; and
(iv) is not prohibited by any enactment or rule of law.

Section 51(1) then specifies that 'an activity, use, or practice has not been carried on, exercised, or followed in a substantially uninterrupted manner if it has been or is prevented from being carried on, exercised, or followed by another activity authorised by or under an enactment or rule of law.' Section 51(2) provides that the vesting of a legal title, whether by Crown grant, common law, statutory vesting, or administrative action, or creation of an interest 'legally inconsistent with the activity, use, or practice for which the customary rights order is sought', extinguishes the customary right. Section 51(4) specifies that this extinguishment occurs 'whether or not legal title has subsequently been resumed by the Crown.'

Issuance of an order by the Māori Land Court under Part 3 of the FSA has the effect of conferring 'a right on the whānau, hapū, or iwi on whose behalf the order is made to carry out a recognised customary activity in accordance with [provisions of] the Resource Management Act 1991.'[43] This right, however, is subject to public rights of access and navigation set out in sections 7 and 8 of the FSA.[44] Moreover, the Māori Land Court cannot make an order that confers an *exclusive* right to engage in an activity, use, or practice 'if, at any time after 1840 ... persons who did not belong to the applicant whānau, hapū, or iwi carried on, exercised, or followed that activity, use, or practice in the specified area' without the express or implied permission of the whānau, hapū, or iwi and without recognising their authority to prohibit others from engaging in the activity, use, or practice.[45] In other words, past violation of an exclusive customary right, even though that right would have been entitled to common law protection according to the decision in *Ngati Apa*, destroys the exclusivity of the right.

To sum up, the provisions of the FSA we have examined distinguish between territorial customary rights entailing exclusive occupation and use of specified areas of the foreshore and seabed, and more limited rights to engage in an activity, use, or practice in relation thereto. Territorial customary rights are extinguished by the statutory vesting of ownership of the public foreshore and seabed in the Crown, and by removal of the jurisdiction of the High Court to give legal effect to those rights. In place of this jurisdiction, the Court's role is to find whether those rights would have existed if it had not been for the vesting of ownership in the Crown, and if so to order either that the matter be

---

43. FSA, s 52(1)(a).
44. FSA, s 55(1).
45. FSA, s 57.

referred to the Government for discussion of redress with the applicant group, or that a foreshore and seabed reserve be created. There is, however, no legal obligation on the Crown to make any redress, as that is a political matter in the discretion of the Government.

Where customary rights to engage in an activity, use, or practice not involving exclusive occupation and use are concerned, the Māori Land Court has primary jurisdiction. However, the customary rights that can be claimed have been severely reduced by the statute from those that could have been claimed in accordance with the *Ngati Apa* decision. For example, any claims based on a spiritual or cultural association not manifested in a physical activity or use in relation to a natural or physical resource have been eliminated. So have claims in relation to foreshore or seabed to which legal title has been created or that would be legally inconsistent with other interests. Priority over Māori customary rights has therefore been given to third-party rights whenever the two conflict. Moreover, the FSA introduces two requirements for Māori customary rights that do not appear to have been elements of New Zealand law before, namely that they be integral to tikanga Māori and exercised in a substantially uninterrupted manner since 1840. As discussed below, these requirements borrow from two of the most severely criticised aspects of Canadian and Australian jurisprudence on aboriginal rights. The practical effect of this statutory adoption of these requirements is to extinguish any Māori customary rights that do not comply with them because neither the Māori Land Court nor the High Court has jurisdiction to issue orders for customary rights unless these requirements have been met.[46] Furthermore, the FSA places the burden of proof of these requirements on the applicants because the courts have to be satisfied that they have been met.[47]

The discriminatory nature of the FSA is revealed by the contrast between the way Māori customary rights and freehold interests in the foreshore and seabed are treated. Where Māori territorial rights are concerned, we have seen that they have been extinguished by the FSA and replaced with political discretion in the Government to provide redress. Freehold interests, on the other hand, are preserved because they are excluded from the definition in section 5 of 'the public foreshore and seabed' and therefore from the vesting of legal title thereto in the Crown by section 13.[48] Moreover, we have seen that Māori customary rights to engage in activities, uses or practices have been extinguished by section 51 if they are legally inconsistent with any other legal

---

46. The relevant parts of sections 50 and 74 (relating to the jurisdiction of the Māori Land Court and the High Court respectively) contain the same restrictions.
47. FSA, ss 50 and 74.
48. On the extent of these freehold interests, a small minority of which are held by Māori, see Tom Bennion, Malcolm Birdling and Rebecca Paton *Making Sense of the Foreshore and Seabed, A Special Edition of the Maori Law Review* (Maori Law Review, Wellington, 2004) 67.

title. While it might be argued that this treatment of non-territorial Māori rights is not discriminatory because Pākehā customary rights are treated in the same way in Part 4 of the Act, the reality is that few if any such Pākehā rights will ever be found to exist because they must predate 1840 and be integral to the distinctive cultural practices of the group of natural persons claiming them.[49] In my opinion, Part 4 is little more than a statutory smokescreen designed to mask some of the Act's discriminatory effect, which is clearly aimed at Māori customary rights.

The discrimination in the FSA has been pointed out by the United Nations Committee on the Elimination of Racial Discrimination (CERD) in its recent decision on the FSA.[50] This confirms the opinion of the Waitangi Tribunal that the Government's policy in relation to the foreshore and seabed is unfair and prejudicial to Māori.[51] Further confirmation of the discriminatory nature of legislation aimed at extinguishing indigenous land rights while leaving other rights intact can be found in two significant decisions of the High Court of Australia.

In *Mabo v Queensland (No 1)* (*Mabo (No 1)*),[52] the High Court struck down a Queensland statute that purported to take away the land rights of the Meriam people by declaring that, at the time the Torres Strait Islands were annexed to Queensland, all lands on them 'vested in the Crown in right of Queensland freed from all other rights.'[53] Brennan, Toohey and Gaudron JJ described the effect of the statute in these terms:[54]

> By extinguishing the traditional legal rights characteristically vested in the Meriam people, the 1985 Act abrogated the immunity of the Meriam people from arbitrary deprivation of their legal rights in and over the Murray Islands. The Act thus impaired their human rights while leaving unimpaired the corresponding human rights of those whose rights in and over the Murray Islands did not take their origins from the laws and customs of the Meriam people.

The Court found the statute to be invalid because it conflicted with the Racial Discrimination Act 1975 (Cth), a federal statute that is paramount over state legislation due to section 109 of the Australian Constitution. Significantly,

---

49. FSA, s 74(1); See Bennion, Birdling and Paton, above n 48, 78.
50. Decision 1(66): New Zealand *Foreshore and Seabed Act 2004* (11 March 2005) CERD/C/66/NZL/Dec.1. For illuminating commentary, see C Charters and A Erueti, 'Report: the CERD Committee's Review of the Foreshore and Seabed Act' (2005) 36(2) VUWLR 257.
51. Waitangi Tribunal Report, above n 6, 123–125, 136–138.
52. *Mabo v Queensland (No 1)* (1988) 166 CLR 186. For commentary, see Kent McNeil 'Racial Discrimination and Unilateral Extinguishment of Native Title' (1996) 1 AILR 181, 216–218 (also in *Emerging Justice?*, above n 24, 357, 402–404).
53. *Queensland Coast Islands Declaratory Act 1985* (Qld), s 3.
54. *Mabo (No 1)*, above n 52, 218.

the Court relied on section 10 of that Act, which was designed to implement and which expressly includes protection of rights referred to in article 5 of the International Convention on the Elimination of All Forms of Racial Discrimination, the same Convention applied by CERD in its decision on Māori rights to the foreshore and seabed. Specifically, the Court held that the rights in article 5(d)(v) and (vi) 'to own property alone as well as in association with others' and 'to inherit' had been violated by the Queensland statute because it purported to extinguish property rights of the Meriam people while leaving the property rights of others untouched. As we have seen, the same conclusion can be reached regarding the extinguishment of Māori customary rights by the FSA.

Consistently with *Mabo (No 1)*, the High Court of Australia in *Western Australia v The Commonwealth*[55] held the Land (Titles and Traditional Usage) Act 1993 (WA) to be inconsistent with section 10 of the Racial Discrimination Act 1975 (Cth) and therefore invalid because it purported to extinguish native title to land in Western Australia and replace it with less-valuable traditional usage rights. The Court was unanimous in its view that protection against racially discriminatory legislation of this sort had been accorded to native title by the 1975 Act because it conferred 'equality of enjoyment of the human rights to own and inherit property' on persons of particular races in Australia, as provided by article 5 of the International Convention on the Elimination of All Forms of Racial Discrimination.[56] Section 10 thus allowed 'protected persons security in the enjoyment of their title to property to the same extent as the holders of titles granted by the Crown are secure in the enjoyment of their titles.'[57]

In New Zealand, of course, there is no federal system and no Racial Discrimination Act that can invalidate discriminatory legislation like the state statutes that were struck down in the *Mabo (No 1)* and *Western Australia* cases.[58] But the point is that those decisions acknowledged the racially discriminatory nature of legislation that treats indigenous land rights based on traditional laws and customs less favourably than land rights derived from Crown grant. As we have seen, this is exactly what the FSA does. Moreover, the Australian cases reveal that this kind of discrimination violates article 5 of the International

---

55. *Western Australia v The Commonwealth* (1995) 128 ALR 1.
56. *Western Australia v The Commonwealth*, above n 55, 24 Mason CJ, Brennan, Deane, Toohey, Gaudron and McHugh JJ. Dawson J delivered a short, concurring judgment.
57. *Western Australia v The Commonwealth*, above n 55, 24 Mason CJ, Brennan, Deane, Toohey, Gaudron and McHugh JJ.
58. The New Zealand Bill of Rights Act 1990 does acknowledge the right to freedom from racial and other forms of discrimination (section 19) as well as the cultural rights of minorities (section 20), but those rights are not constitutionally protected and so can be overridden by Parliament: for discussion of whether the FSA violates the Bill of Rights, see Bennion, Birdling and Paton, above n 48, 81–94.

Convention on the Elimination of All Forms of Racial Discrimination, and thus support the CERD decision to the same effect. One would think that the New Zealand Government would not want to be viewed in the eyes of the world as being guilty of this kind of racial discrimination.

IV Statutory Adoption of the Most Criticised Aspects of Canadian and Australian Law on Indigenous Land Rights

I now want to focus on the provisions in the FSA that legislatively adopt two of the most doctrinally flawed and heavily criticised aspects of the law on indigenous land rights in Canada and Australia, namely the integral to the distinctive culture test and the requirement of substantial maintenance of the connection with the land in accordance with traditional laws and customs. As we have seen, similar requirements have been included in section 50(1)(b) for the establishment in the Māori Land Court of customary rights to engage in activities, uses or practices in relation to the foreshore or seabed.

A THE 'INTEGRAL' REQUIREMENT

Section 50(1)(b) provides in part that, for the Māori Land Court to make a customary rights order, it must be satisfied that the activity, use or practice for which the order is sought 'is, and has been since 1840, integral to tikanga Māori.' This requirement imposes a major change on the common law position respecting Māori customary rights to the foreshore and seabed that was propounded in *Ngati Apa*. As we have seen, in that case the Court of Appeal expressed the view that any Māori rights based on tikanga Māori that were in existence at the time of Crown acquisition of sovereignty in 1840 continued and became enforceable in common law courts, because the doctrine of continuity has been accepted and applied in both British imperial law and international law.[59] By limiting the application of the doctrine of continuity in this context to Māori customary rights derived from activities, uses and practices that were *integral* to tikanga Māori, the FSA effectively extinguished any customary right *not* integral thereto in 1840 and henceforth. Why has this important change been imposed by Parliament?

While the simple answer is that the change is meant to limit Māori rights, the Government's 'Explanatory Note: General Policy Statement'[60] on the Foreshore and Seabed Bill does not provide any justification for this change. It is nonetheless fairly obvious that the source of the limitation is Canadian jurisprudence, specifically the decision of the Supreme Court of Canada in

---
59. See text accompanying nn 4–21 above.
60. Foreshore and Seabed Bill 2004, Explanatory Note.

Van der Peet.⁶¹ In his majority judgment in that case, Lamer CJ formulated a test for the identification of aboriginal rights (apart from title)⁶² for the purposes of section 35(1) of the Canadian Constitution Act 1982, which recognises and affirms the 'existing aboriginal and treaty rights of the aboriginal peoples of Canada.' To establish a right to engage in an activity such as fishing, aboriginal claimants must prove that the activity was 'an element of a practice, custom or tradition integral to [their] distinctive culture' at the time of contact with Europeans.⁶³ Elaborating on the meaning of 'integral' in this context, the Chief Justice said:⁶⁴

> To satisfy the integral to a distinctive culture test the aboriginal claimant must do more than demonstrate that a practice, custom or tradition was an aspect of, or took place in, the aboriginal society of which he or she is a part. The claimant must demonstrate that the practice, custom or tradition was a central and significant part of the society's distinctive culture. He or she must demonstrate, in other words, that the practice, custom or tradition was one of the things which made the culture of the society distinctive – that it was one of the things that truly *made the society what it was*.

After linking aboriginal rights to the aboriginal peoples' prior occupation of Canada, Lamer CJ continued:⁶⁵

> To recognize and affirm the prior occupation of Canada by distinctive aboriginal societies it is *to what makes those societies distinctive* that the court must look in identifying aboriginal rights. The court cannot look at those aspects of the aboriginal society that are true of every human society (e.g., eating to survive), nor can it look at those aspects of the aboriginal society that are only incidental or occasional to that society; the court must look instead to the defining and central attributes of the aboriginal society in question. It is only by focusing on the aspects of the aboriginal society that make that society distinctive that the definition of aboriginal rights will accomplish the purpose underlying s.35(1).

The integral to the distinctive culture test articulated by Lamer CJ is therefore related to the purpose behind section 35(1), which he said was placed in the Constitution in 1982 to:⁶⁶

---

61. *Van der Peet*, above n 2.
62. In Canada, aboriginal title depends on proof of exclusive occupation of land at the time of Crown assertion of sovereignty: see *Delgamuukw*, above n 13; *R v Marshall, R v Bernard*, [2005] 2 SCR 220 (*Marshall/Bernard*).
63. *Van der Peet*, above n 2, para 46.
64. *Van der Peet*, above n 2, para 55 (emphasis in original).
65. *Van der Peet*, above n 2, para 56 (emphasis in original).
66. *Van der Peet*, above n 2, para 31.

... provide the constitutional framework through which the fact that aboriginals lived on the land in distinctive societies, with their own practices, traditions and cultures, is acknowledged and reconciled with the sovereignty of the Crown. The substantive rights which fall within the provision must be defined in light of this purpose; the aboriginal rights recognized and affirmed by s.35(1) must be directed towards the reconciliation of the pre-existence of aboriginal societies with the sovereignty of the Crown.

It is therefore apparent that Lamer CJ formulated the integral to the distinctive culture test in order give effect to his understanding of the purpose behind section 35(1). This is indicated even more clearly by his comments on the meaning of the words 'aboriginal' and 'rights' in this provision: [67]

> The task of this Court is to define aboriginal rights in a manner which recognizes that aboriginal rights are *rights* but which does so without losing sight of the fact that they are rights held by aboriginal people because they are *aboriginal*. The Court must neither lose sight of the generalized constitutional status of what s.35(1) protects, nor can it ignore the necessary specificity which comes from granting special constitutional protection to one part of Canadian society. The Court must define the scope of s.35(1) in a way which captures *both* the aboriginal and the rights in aboriginal rights.

In seeking to explain why only practices, customs and traditions integral to distinctive aboriginal societies are included in section 35(1), I think the key words in this passage are the Chief Justice's admonition that the Court cannot 'ignore *the necessary specificity* which comes from granting special constitutional protection to one part of Canadian society.'[68] The constitutional protection accorded to aboriginal rights in 1982 was therefore an important factor leading him to limit them to integral elements of aboriginal societies because this provided the specificity he thought necessary in this context.

In so doing, however, Lamer CJ created a doctrinally flawed test for aboriginal rights. We have seen that the generally accepted rule of British imperial and international law is that the rights held by the inhabitants of a territory continue after Crown acquisition of sovereignty in the absence of expropriation by act of state.[69] The Supreme Court's integral to the distinctive culture test violates this received doctrine of continuity in two ways.

First, it distinguishes between integral practices, customs and traditions and less important, or incidental, ones by mandating that only the former give rise to aboriginal rights; the latter do not. So what happened to incidental rights

---

67. *Van der Peet*, above n 2, para 20 (emphasis in original).
68. *Van der Peet,* above n 2, para 20 (emphasis added).
69. See authorities cited above nn 13–14.

that the aboriginal peoples had under their own legal systems and that should have been maintained by the doctrine of continuity, but that did not receive constitutional protection in 1982 because they did not meet the integral to the distinctive culture test? Surely those rights did not cease to exist in 1982, as it is clear that section 35(1) was intended to enhance rather than restrict the rights of the aboriginal peoples.[70] This may mean that there are now two categories of aboriginal rights in Canada, namely rights protected by section 35(1) because they meet the integral test, and rights that are not so protected because they do not.[71] But so far the Supreme Court of Canada has not acknowledged this possibility.

The second way the integral to the distinctive culture test violates the doctrine of continuity is by adopting the date of contact with Europeans rather than the date of Crown sovereignty (except where aboriginal title and Métis rights are concerned)[72] as the relevant time for determining the existence of those rights. The rationale Lamer CJ provided for choosing the date of contact was that 'it is the fact that distinctive aboriginal societies lived on the land prior to the arrival of Europeans that underlies the rights protected by s.35(1).'[73] Accordingly, practices, customs or traditions arising 'solely as a response to European influences' do not qualify for recognition as aboriginal rights.[74] But under the doctrine of continuity, the fact that European influences led to creation of a right should not matter, as long as the right was part of the aboriginal legal system at the time of Crown acquisition of sovereignty. Adoption of the contact time frame therefore appears to be another means by which the Chief Justice limited the aboriginal rights that received constitutional protection and made them conform with his conception of aboriginality based on the nature of aboriginal societies before the arrival of Europeans.[75]

The integral to the distinctive culture test has been subjected to severe academic criticism.[76] While detailed review of the arguments made against

---

70. See *R v Sparrow* [1990] 1 SCR 1075; *Van der Peet*, above n 2, para 28; *Mitchell v MNR* [2001] 1 SCR 911, para 11 (*Mitchell*).
71. See Michael Halewood 'Common Law Aboriginal Knowledge Protection Rights: Recognizing the Rights of Aboriginal Peoples in Canada to Prohibit the Use and Dissemination of Elements of their Knowledge' (D Jur dissertation, Osgoode Hall Law School, York University, Toronto, 2005) 200–244; Walters, above n 9.
72. See above n 30.
73. *Van der Peet*, above n 2, para 60.
74. *Van der Peet*, above n 2, para 73.
75. Note that this aspect of his judgment was severely criticized by McLachlin J (as she then was) and L'Heureux-Dubé J in their dissenting opinions in *Van der Peet*.
76. For example see John Borrows 'Frozen Rights in Canada: Constitutional Interpretation and the Trickster' (1997) 22 Am Indian L Rev 37; Russel Lawrence Barsh and James Youngblood Henderson 'The Supreme Court's *Van der Peet* Trilogy: Naive Imperialism and Ropes of Sand' (1997) 42 McGill LJ 993; Bradford W Morse 'Permafrost Rights: Aboriginal Self-Government and the Supreme Court

it cannot be undertaken here, it is worth mentioning a couple of the major criticisms. Primary among these is that the test treats aboriginal societies as relics of the past by limiting aboriginal rights to pre-contact practices, customs and traditions. This approach is inconsistent with the dynamic nature of human cultures generally and aboriginal cultures in particular, and does not allow for sufficient adaptation to meet changing conditions, especially the massive changes necessitated by European colonisation. In addition, the test requires judges to distinguish between integral and incidental aspects of an aboriginal society in the distant past by identifying features that, in Lamer CJ's words, 'truly *made the society what it was*.'[77] Displaying some awareness of the difficulty of applying this test, the Chief Justice provided the following advice: 'A practical way of thinking about this problem is to ask whether, without this practice, custom or tradition, the culture in question would be fundamentally altered or other than what it is. One must ask, to put the question affirmatively, whether or not a practice, custom or tradition is a defining feature of the culture in question.'[78]

With all due respect, I do not see how this makes the task of judges any easier, as the aspects of a society – even one's own society – that are fundamental or defining features are surely matters of opinion that will depend in part on the circumstances and point of view of the person providing the opinion. To ask judges to make this kind of evaluation of societies to which they generally do not belong and in relation to practices, customs and traditions up to 400 years ago when relevant contact with Europeans began in Canada places them in the awkward position of having to make decisions that are bound to be somewhat subjective and arbitrary.

In its recent decision in *R v Sappier; R v Gray*,[79] the Supreme Court of Canada reconsidered the integral to the distinctive culture test in the context of an aboriginal right to harvest wood for domestic purposes. The Court acknowledged that strict interpretation and application of the test can be problematic. Bastarache J, writing for the Court, observed that the 'notion that the pre-contact practice must be a "defining feature" of the aboriginal society, such that the culture would be "fundamentally altered" without it, has … served in some cases to create artificial barriers to the recognition and affirmation of aboriginal rights.'[80] He also warned against 'reducing an entire people's culture to specific anthropological curiosities and, potentially,

---

in *R. v. Pamajewon*' (1997) 42 McGill LJ 1011; Chilwin Chienhan Cheng 'Touring the Museum: A Comment on *R. v. Van der Peet*' (1997) 55 U of T Fac of L Rev 419; Catherine Bell 'New Directions in the Law of Aboriginal Rights' (1998) 77 Can Bar Rev 36, 44–50.
77. *Van der Peet*, above n 2, para 55 (emphasis in original).
78. *Van der Peet*, above n 2, para 59.
79. *R. v Sappier; R. v Gray* [2007] 1 CNLR 359 (*Sappier;Gray*).
80. *Sappier; Gray*, above n 79, para 41.

racialized aboriginal stereotypes.'[81] Instead, he said the Court's task is to inquire 'into the pre-contact way of life of a particular aboriginal community, including their means of survival, their socialization methods, their legal systems, and, potentially, their trading habits.'[82] But while Bastarache J obviously intended to soften the application of the test, he affirmed that '[s]ection 35 seeks to protect *integral* elements of the way of life of these aboriginal societies.'[83] He also accepted that the purpose of section 35 is to reconcile the pre-existence of aboriginal societies with the sovereignty of the Crown, and that specificity is necessary in identifying and defining aboriginal rights because they have been accorded constitutional protection.[84]

Returning to the introduction by section 50(1)(b) of the FSA of an integral requirement for Māori customary rights, this statutory alteration of the common law of New Zealand as expressed by the Court of Appeal in *Ngati Apa* suffers from some of the same defects as the integral to the distinctive culture test created by the Supreme Court in *Van der Peet*. The integral requirement, like the *Van der Peet* test, alters the doctrine of continuity so that only those aspects of tikanga Māori that meet the requirement are capable of recognition by the Māori Land Court. Customary rights and usages that do not meet the requirement are unenforceable and so are effectively extinguished, without compensation. As far as I am aware, no rationale has been provided for this limitation, unlike in Canada where the Supreme Court explained that specificity of definition in the context of section 35(1) rights was necessitated by the fact that the special rights of the aboriginal peoples had received constitutional protection. That explanation has no application in New Zealand, where Māori rights are not constitutionally protected. Moreover, we have seen that it is unclear in Canada whether rights that should have continued after Crown acquisition of sovereignty but that do not meet the integral to the distinctive culture test are nonetheless enforceable as legal (but not constitutional) rights. In New Zealand, on the other hand, Māori customary rights that are not integral to tikanga Māori have been effectively extinguished by the FSA, in violation of the doctrine of continuity and both customary and conventional international law.[85]

Given these important differences between the Canadian and New Zealand situations, I think it would be regrettable and inappropriate for Canadian

---

81. *Sappier; Gray*, above n 79, para 46.
82. *Sappier; Gray*, above n 79, para 45.
83. *Sappier; Gray*, above n 79, para 40 (emphasis added).
84. *Sappier; Gray*, above n 79, paras 22, 42.
85. The authorities cited above n 14 regard the doctrine of continuity to be part of customary international law. And as we have seen, discriminatory treatment of property rights violates the Convention on the Elimination of All Forms of Racial Discrimination: see text accompanying nn 50–57 above.

jurisprudence on the integral to the distinctive culture test to be imported into section 50(1)(b) of the FSA. Instead, the Māori Land Court should interpret the word 'integral' in a way that is appropriate for New Zealand and tikanga Māori. In my opinion, a major consideration in this context should be the interpretive rule that statutes should be construed as far as possible to conform to international law.[86] Given that extinguishment of Māori customary rights without compensation is a violation of international law, the Māori Land Court should construe 'integral' to the extent possible to preserve those rights.[87] The same approach is mandated by the common law rule that statutes are to be interpreted as much as possible to preserve vested rights, especially property rights.[88] The Court could use these rules of statutory interpretation to decide that most Māori activities, uses or practices in relation to the foreshore and seabed are integral to tikanga Māori, excluding only those activities, uses and practices that are truly of little importance.

B The 'Substantially Uninterrupted' Requirement

I am now going to turn to the second problematic requirement in section 50(1)(b) that I want to discuss, namely that the activity, use or practice for which a customary rights order is sought 'has been carried on, exercised, or followed in accordance with tikanga Māori in a substantially uninterrupted manner since 1840, in the area of the public foreshore and seabed specified in the application', and continues to be so engaged in.[89] Like the integral to the distinctive culture element, this requirement was not part of the common law articulated by the Court of Appeal in *Ngati Apa*. But unlike the integral element, which appears to have been inappropriately borrowed from Canadian jurisprudence, the requirement of substantially uninterrupted maintenance of the activity, use or practice probably comes from Australian jurisprudence.

The requirement in Australia that a substantial connection with the land be maintained originated in *Mabo (No 2)*, where Brennan J said:[90]

> Where a clan or group has continued to acknowledge the laws and (so far as practicable) to observe the customs based on the traditions of that clan or

---

86. See *New Zealand Air Line Pilots Association v Attorney-General* [1997] 3 NZLR 269 (CA); *Quilter v Attorney-General* [1998] 1 NZLR 523 (CA); *Sellers v Maritime Safety Inspector* [1999] 2 NZLR 44 (CA).
87. See C Charters 'Developments in Indigenous Peoples' Land Rights under International Law and their Domestic Implications' [2005] 21 NZULR 512.
88. For example see *Colonial Sugar Refining Co v Melbourne Harbour Trust Commissioners* (1927) 38 CLR 547, 559 (PC); *Attorney-General for Canada v Hallet and Carey Ltd* [1952] AC 427, 450 (PC); *Graham v Attorney-General* [1966] NZLR 937, 942 (SC); *Brader v Ministry of Transport* [1981] 1 NZLR 73, 85 (CA); *Colet v R* [1981] 1 SCR 2, 10.
89. See text following n 42 above.
90. *Mabo (No 2)*, above n 3, 59–60.

group, whereby their traditional connection with the land has been substantially maintained, the traditional community title of that clan or group can be said to remain in existence. The common law can, by reference to the traditional laws and customs of an indigenous people, identify and protect the native rights and interests to which they give rise. However, when the tide of history has washed away any real acknowledgment of traditional law and any real observance of traditional customs, the foundation of native title has disappeared. A native title which has ceased with the abandoning of laws and customs based on tradition cannot be revived for contemporary recognition.

In *Yorta Yorta*,[91] the leading Australian case on this matter, a majority of the High Court held that this requirement of substantial maintenance of a connection with the land through traditional laws and customs is included in the definition of native title in section 223(1) of the NTA.[92] As the majority accepted the trial judge's factual findings that 'the forebears of the claimants had ceased to occupy their lands in accordance with traditional laws and customs and that there was no evidence that they continued to acknowledge and observe those laws and customs', they concluded that the Yorta Yorta had lost their native title.[93]

The *Yorta Yorta* decision has been severely criticised.[94] One complaint is over

---

91. *Yorta Yorta*, above n 3.
92. NTA, above n 24. Section 223(1), as amended by the Native Title Amendment Act 1998 (Cth), defines 'native title' and 'native title rights and interests' as 'the communal, group or individual rights and interests of Aboriginal peoples or Torres Strait Islanders in relation to land or waters, where: (a) the rights and interests are possessed under the traditional laws acknowledged, and the traditional customs observed, by the Aboriginal peoples or Torres Strait Islanders; and (b) the Aboriginal peoples or Torres Strait Islanders, by those laws and customs, have a connection with the land or waters; and (c) the rights and interests are recognised by the common law of Australia.'
93. *Yorta Yorta*, above n 3, para 96 Gleeson CJ, Gummow and Hayne JJ. McHugh and Callinan JJ wrote concurring judgments. Gaudron and Kirby JJ dissented.
94. For example see Peter Poynton 'Is *Yorta Yorta* Applicable in Queensland?' (2002–2003) 9 JCULR Special Issue 252; Greg McIntyre 'Native Rights After *Yorta Yorta*' (2002–2003) 9 JCULR Special Issue 268; Noel Pearson 'The High Court's Abandonment of "the Time-Honoured Methodology of the Common Law" in *Mirriuwung Gajerrong* and *Yorta Yorta*' (2003) 8:2 AILR 1; Richard Bartlett 'An Obsession with Traditional Laws and Customs Creates Difficulty Establishing Native Title Claims in the South: *Yorta Yorta*' (2003) 31 WA L Rev 35; David Lavery 'A Greater Sense of Tradition: The Implications of the Normative System Principles in *Yorta Yorta* for Native Title Determination Applications' (2003) 10 E Law. Murdoch University Electronic Journal of Law website <http://www.murdoch.edu.au/elaw> (last accessed 20 August 2005); Shaunnagh Dorsett and Shaun McVeigh 'An Essay on Jurisdiction, Jurisprudence, and Authority: The High Court of Australia in *Yorta Yorta* (2001)' (2005) 56 Northern Ireland LQ 1; Peter Seidel 'Native Title: The Struggle for Justice for the Yorta Yorta Nation' (2004) 29:2 Alt LJ 70; Ben Golder 'Law, History, Colonialism: An Orientalist Reading of Australian Native Title Law' (2004) 9 Deakin L Rev 41; Kirsten Anker 'Law in the Present Tense: Tradition and Cultural Continuity in *Members of the Yorta Yorta Aboriginal Community v Victoria*' (2004) 28 Mel U L Rev 1; Young, above n 18. Compare McHugh's Brief, above n 23, paras 64–72, where the Australian approach to continuing connection with the land appears to be accepted, with the qualification that Kirby J's more generous

the strictness of the test applied for maintenance of the traditional connection with the land, especially in circumstances like those in the case where the aboriginal occupants were displaced by the influx of British settlers.[95] Another is over the Court's rigid adherence to a normative approach to traditional laws and customs.[96] The Court has also been criticised for accepting the comparative weight given by the trial judge to a European squatter's written observations on aboriginal practices and customs in the nineteenth century, as against the much lesser weight given to the oral traditions of the Yorta Yorta themselves. In addition to these valid criticisms, an even more fundamental problem with the Court's approach is that it is difficult to reconcile with the doctrine of continuity (on which the High Court has based native title rights), especially when compared with the common law's treatment of customary rights in England. The Court's approach is also inconsistent with Canadian jurisprudence on aboriginal rights.

We have seen that the doctrine of continuity provides for the continuation of rights held under pre-existing laws and customs after acquisition of sovereignty by the Crown.[97] In a passage from *Fejo v Northern Territory* quoted by Gleeson CJ, Gummow and Hayne JJ in *Yorta Yorta*,[98] six members of the High Court said this:[99]

> Native title has its origin in the traditional laws acknowledged and the customs observed by the indigenous people who possess the native title. Native title is neither an institution of the common law nor a form of common law tenure but it is recognised by the common law. There is, therefore, an intersection of traditional laws and customs with the common law.

In this passage, the Court in *Fejo* relied in turn on Brennan J's judgment in *Mabo (No 2)*,[100] relevant parts of which were incorporated into the statutory definition of native title in section 223(1) of the NTA that was interpreted and applied in *Yorta Yorta*. As affirmed in *Yorta Yorta*, in Australia native title consists of rights and interests that existed in the normative systems of laws and customs of the Aboriginal peoples and Torres Strait Islanders prior to Crown acquisition of sovereignty and that were recognised thereafter by the

---

approach to the matter in *Yorta Yorta* might be preferable to the majority's approach. McHugh did not acknowledge the very different use of the concept of continuity by Canadian courts, discussed below in the text accompanying nn 102–133.
95. See also Shaunnagh Dorsett's chapter in this book, 59–82.
96. See text accompanying nn 24–32 above. See also 'Relevance of Traditional Laws', above n 24, criticizing this aspect of Australian case law prior to the High Court's decision in *Yorta Yorta*.
97. See above n 9 and accompanying text.
98. *Yorta Yorta*, above n 3, para 31.
99. *Fejo v Northern Territory* (1998) 195 CLR 96, 128 Gleeson CJ, Gaudron, McHugh, Gummow, Hayne and Callinan JJ (footnotes omitted).
100. *Mabo (No 2)*, above n 3, 58–61.

common law.

Native title rights and interests have a lot in common with customary rights in relation to land in England.[101] Both arise from normative systems outside the common law that were developed through custom and usage by a community in a particular geographical area. Both have to be proven by evidence because their existence outside the common law means that courts cannot take judicial notice of them. Once proven, however, they are enforceable by common law courts. Both have to be shown to have been in existence at a specified time: for native-title rights and interests, at the date of Crown acquisition of sovereignty, and for customary rights in England, 1189 (though proof that a custom existed as far back as living memory extends raises a presumption that it existed in 1189). But on the issue of continuation of the rights, there is a significant divergence between Australian law on native title and English law on custom.

We have seen that in Australia native-title rights and interests can be lost if the holders of them do not maintain their connection with the land in accordance with their traditional laws and customs. This cannot happen to customary rights in England. On the contrary, continued observance of a custom through usage is not required for the rights it supports to be maintained. This was illustrated by Lord Denman CJ's observation in *Scales v Key* in 1840 that the jury's finding 'that the custom had existed till 1689, was the same in effect as if they had found that it had existed till last week, unless something appeared to shew that it had been legally abolished.'[102] In *Re Yateley Common*, Foster J held that abandonment of a customary right to a common cannot be presumed from non-user:[103]

> A right of common is a legal right, and it is exceedingly difficult to prove that a person having such a legal right has abandoned it. Non-user, if the owner of the right has no reason to exercise it, requires something more than an immense length of time of non-user. It is essential that it is proved to the court's satisfaction that the owner of the legal right has abandoned the right – in the sense that he not only has not used it but intends never to use it again. The onus lies fairly and squarely on those who assert that the right has been abandoned.

Moreover, given that customary rights are communal rather than individual and extend beyond the lifetimes of the current members of the community,

---

101. On custom in England, see Carleton Kemp Allen *Law in the Making* (7 ed, Clarendon Press, Oxford, 1964) 129–146; *Halsbury's Laws of England* (4 ed reissue, Butterworths, London, 1998) Vol 12(1), paras 601–649.
102. *Scales v Key* (1840) 11 Ad & E 819 (QB) 825–826. See also *Heath v Deane* [1905] 2 Ch 86, 93–94; *New Windsor Corporation v Mellor* [1975] 3 All ER 44 (CA) 50–51 Lord Denning MR, 53 Browne LJ.
103. *Re Yateley Common* [1977] 1 All ER 505 (Ch) 510.

those members do not even have the authority to waive or abandon the rights. In *Wyld v Silver*, Lord Denning MR put it this way in relation to a right to hold a fair:[104]

> I know of no way in which the inhabitants of a parish can lose a right of this kind once they have acquired it except by Act of Parliament. Mere disuse will not do. And I do not see how they can waive it or abandon it. No one or more of the inhabitants can waive or abandon it on behalf of the others. Nor can all the present inhabitants waive or abandon it on behalf of future generations.

So extinguishment of a customary right in England will occur only if the custom is expressly abolished by or is clearly inconsistent with a statute.[105]

Why, one might ask, should native rights and interests in Australia be treated less favourably than customary rights in England in this regard? The fact that native rights and interests pre-date Crown sovereignty whereas customary rights do not does not appear to be a ground for making them more vulnerable to loss, especially as native rights and interests enjoy international as well as common law protection.[106] Nor can I think of any principle of justice that would favour customary rights in England. Moreover, the Australian approach is rendered even more questionable when compared with the approach of the Supreme Court of Canada to the issue of continuity of aboriginal rights.

The issue of continuity has come up in Canada in relation to both aboriginal rights to natural resources such as fish and aboriginal title to land.[107] We have seen that Lamer CJ, in *Van der Peet*,[108] decided that aboriginal rights (apart from title to land) depend on proof of a practice, custom or tradition integral to the distinctive culture of the aboriginal group claiming the right at the time of contact with Europeans. Acknowledging how difficult this might be, the Chief Justice said that aboriginal claimants can rely on post-contact practices, customs and traditions as long as it can be shown that they are rooted in the pre-contact society of the aboriginal community.[109] He then cited Brennan J's

---

104. *Wyld v Silver* [1963] 1 Ch 243 (CA), 255–256.
105. *Halsbury's Laws of England*, above n 101, para 646. Note that in Canada as well, in *Re Tucktoo and Kitchooalik* (1972) 27 DLR (3d) 225 (NWTTC), affirmed *Re Kitchooalik and Tucktoo* (1972) 28 DLR (3d) 483 (NWTCA), Morrow J held that the rule that customs can be abolished only by statute applies to aboriginal customs relating to adoption, and that for abolition to occur the legislation would have to be either repugnant to those customs, or directly or by implication intended to abolish them.
106. See above nn 13–14, 52–57, and accompanying text. See also 'Racial Discrimination and Unilateral Extinguishment of Native Title', above n 52.
107. For more detailed discussion, see Kent McNeil 'Continuity of Aboriginal Rights' in Wilkins, above n 9, 127–150, from which the present analysis borrows.
108. *Van der Peet*, above n 2.
109. *Van der Peet*, above n 2, para 62.

'tide of history' *dictum* from *Mabo (No 2)* (quoted above),[110] and continued: [111]

> The relevance of this observation [in *Mabo (No 2)*] for identifying the rights in s.35(1) *lies not in its assertion of the effect of the disappearance of a practice, custom or tradition on an aboriginal claim (I take no position on that matter)*, but rather in its suggestion of the importance of considering the continuity in the practices, customs and traditions of aboriginal communities in assessing claims to aboriginal rights. It is precisely those present practices, customs and traditions which can be identified as having continuity with the practices, customs and traditions that existed prior to contact that will be the basis for the identification and definition of aboriginal rights under s.35(1). Where an aboriginal community can demonstrate that a particular practice, custom or tradition is integral to its distinctive culture today, and that this practice, custom or tradition has continuity with the practices, customs and traditions of pre-contact times, that community will have demonstrated that the practice, custom or tradition is an aboriginal right for the purposes of s.35(1).

From this passage, it appears that continuity operates *backward* where an aboriginal community relies on a post-contact practice, custom or tradition as proof of an aboriginal right. In that situation, evidence is required to connect that practice, custom or tradition with a corresponding practice, custom or tradition in the pre-contact aboriginal society. Unlike the majority of the High Court in *Yorta Yorta*, Lamer CJ did not require proof of continuity *forward* in situations where there is sufficient evidence of the pre-contact practice, custom or tradition itself.[112] Moreover, he expressly refrained from taking a position on Brennan J's *dictum* that aboriginal rights can be lost through the disappearance of traditional laws and customs.

Use of a post-contact practice, custom or tradition to prove an aboriginal right in Canada is illustrated by the Supreme Court's decision in *R v Gladstone* (*Gladstone*),[113] in which a right to collect and sell herring spawn on kelp in commercial quantities was established. The evidence that led a majority of the Court to accept that the Heiltsuk Nation had traded herring spawn on a commercial scale before contact with Europeans consisted of an entry in Alexander Mackenzie's journal in 1793, an entry by Dr William Tolmie (a fur trader) in his journal in 1834, and testimony by Dr Barbara Lane (an expert witness). In his majority judgment, Lamer CJ said that '[t]he evidence presented

---

110. See text accompanying n 90 above (Lamer CJ quoted the last two sentences from this passage).
111. *Van der Peet*, above n 2, para 63 (emphasis added).
112. Note that in this situation it would of course be necessary to show that the present-day activity came within the scope of the right, but even if it did not that would not invalidate the right itself; it would simply mean that the right as proven could not be relied upon to protect the activity in question.
113. *R v Gladstone* [1996] 2 SCR 723.

in this case ... is precisely the type of evidence which satisfies this [continuity] requirement', as described in *Van der Peet*.[114] He elaborated as follows:[115]

> The evidence of Dr. Lane, and the diary of Dr. Tolmie, point to trade of herring spawn on kelp in 'tons'. *While this evidence relates to trade post-contact, the diary of Alexander Mackenzie provides the link with pre-contact times*; in essence, the sum of the evidence supports the claim of the appellants that commercial trade in herring spawn on kelp was an integral part of the distinctive culture of the Heiltsuk prior to contact.

Lamer CJ's decision in *Gladstone* therefore affirms that the purpose of the continuity doctrine in this context is to permit evidence of post-contact practices, customs and traditions to be used to prove pre-contact practices, customs and traditions. Unlike what was required of the Yorta Yorta in Australia, the Heiltsuk did not have to prove substantial maintenance of their practice of trade in herring spawn from the time of contact to the present.

The Supreme Court took a similar approach to continuity in its decision on aboriginal title in *Delgamuukw*, where Lamer CJ summarised the requirements for proof of aboriginal title in these terms:[116]

> In order to make out a claim for aboriginal title, the aboriginal group asserting title must satisfy the following criteria: (i) the land must have been occupied prior to sovereignty, (ii) if present occupation is relied on as proof of occupation pre-sovereignty, there must be a continuity between present and pre-sovereignty occupation, and (iii) at sovereignty, that occupation must have been exclusive.

The second requirement, relating to continuity, need be met only 'if present occupation is relied on.' So in situations where aboriginal claimants are able to meet the other two requirements by direct proof of exclusive occupation at the time the Crown asserted sovereignty, without relying on present occupation, there should be no need to prove continuity in the sense that the occupation has been substantially maintained since then.

This interpretation is confirmed by Lamer CJ's explanation of the second requirement. Referring to his judgment in *Van der Peet*,[117] he said that he had acknowledged in that case that:[118]

> ... it would be 'next to impossible' (at para. 62) for an aboriginal group to provide

---

114. *R v Gladstone*, above n 113 para 28.
115. *R v Gladstone*, above n 113, para 28 (emphasis added).
116. *Delgamuukw*, above n 13, para 143.
117. *Van der Peet*, above n 2.
118. *Delgamuukw*, above n 13, para 152 (emphasis in original). See also paras 83, 101. Note that La Forest J, concurring in result, took an even more flexible approach to continuity where present occupation is relied upon. In his view, 'continuity may still exist where the present occupation of one area is connected to the pre-sovereignty occupation of another area': *Delgamuukw*, above n 13, para 197.

conclusive evidence of its pre-contact practices, customs and traditions. What would suffice instead was evidence of post-contact practices, which was 'directed at demonstrating which aspects of the aboriginal community and society have their origins pre-contact' (at para. 62). The same concern, and the same solution, arises with respect to the proof of occupation in claims for aboriginal title, although there is a difference in the time for determination of title. Conclusive evidence of pre-sovereignty occupation may be difficult to come by. Instead, an aboriginal community may provide evidence of present occupation as proof of pre-sovereignty occupation in support of a claim to aboriginal title. What is required, in addition, is a *continuity* between present and pre-sovereignty occupation, because the relevant time for the determination of aboriginal title is at the time before sovereignty.

This passage is consistent with our analysis of *Van der Peet*, and illustrates once again why Lamer CJ introduced the concept of continuity into aboriginal-rights jurisprudence. His evident intention was to make proof of aboriginal rights, including title, *easier* by permitting evidence of post-contact practices, customs and traditions or post-sovereignty occupation to be presented and relied upon. He did not intend to make proof of aboriginal rights and title *harder* by imposing a requirement of continuity in cases where sufficient direct evidence of the pre-contact practices, customs and traditions or pre-sovereignty occupation is available.

In *Delgamuukw*, Lamer CJ went on to say that 'there is no need to establish "an unbroken chain of continuity" (*Van der Peet*) between present and prior occupation', especially because '[t]o impose the requirement of continuity too strictly would risk "undermining the very purpose of s.35(1) [of the Constitution Act, 1982] by perpetuating the historical injustice suffered by aboriginal peoples at the hands of colonizers who failed to respect" aboriginal rights to land (*Côté, supra*, at para. 53).'[119]

The 'historical injustice' he was anxious to avoid was precisely the kind of injustice suffered by the Yorta Yorta in Australia, who had been dispossessed by European settlers and who lost their connection with the land as a result. Lamer CJ also made clear that 'the fact that the nature of occupation has changed would not ordinarily preclude a claim for aboriginal title, as long as a substantial connection between the people and the land is maintained.'[120] Taken out of context, a statement like this might be interpreted to mean that there is a general requirement of continuity of occupation for aboriginal title to be maintained. However, given that he placed this entire discussion of continuity under the heading '*[i]f present occupation is relied on as proof of occupation pre-*

---

119. *Delgamuukw*, above n 13, para 153, citing *R v Côté* [1996] 3 SCR 139.
120. *Delgamuukw*, above n 13, para 154.

sovereignty, there must be a continuity between present and pre-sovereignty occupation',[121] it is apparent that the Chief Justice, with the explicit intention of making proof of aboriginal title easier, was limiting the application of the concept of continuity to situations where aboriginal claimants rely on present occupation.

This interpretation of the *Delgamuukw* decision was confirmed by the Nova Scotia Court of Appeal in *R v Marshall* (*Marshall*),[122] involving a claim by Mi'kmaq Indians in Nova Scotia to a treaty right and an aboriginal-title right to cut and sell timber. On the issue of continuity, the appellants argued that aboriginal title crystallised at the time of Crown sovereignty, and that continuity of occupation is relevant only where present occupation is relied upon to establish the existence of the title at that time. The Crown, on the other hand, argued that, in addition to proving exclusive occupation at the time of Crown sovereignty, the claimants had to show a continuing substantial connection with the land up to the present.

Cromwell JA analysed this matter in detail.[123] He reviewed what had been said about continuity in *Van der Peet*, *Gladstone*, *Delgamuukw*, and other Canadian cases, and referred to the passage from Brennan J's judgment in *Mabo (No 2)* that introduced the substantial connection requirement into Australian law.[124] He recognised that the Supreme Court of Canada has given three different meanings to the concept of continuity:[125]

> [F]irst, whether the disappearance of a practice, custom or tradition prevents a contemporary claim seeking to revive it, a question on which the Court took no position [in *Van der Peet*];[126] second, the facilitation of proof of a pre-contact practice, custom or tradition by showing sufficient continuity from a present practice back to the time of contact; third, a concept similar to the logical evolution of treaty rights which affirms contemporary practice provided that it is sufficiently anchored in pre-contact practice, custom or tradition. Continuity is seen as a way *to facilitate proof* of pre-contact customs, practices and traditions and allowing these to be recognized in their present forms.

Cromwell JA then pointed out that the 'substantial connection' language in *Mabo (No 2)* has been relied upon by the Supreme Court, not in the context of the ongoing validity of native title in which Brennan J used it, but in situations

---

121. *Delgamuukw*, above n 13, before para 152 (underlining removed, italics added).
122. *R v Marshall* [2004] 1 CNLR 211.
123. Cromwell JA's judgment was concurred in by Oland JA. Saunders JA delivered a judgment concurring in result, in which he agreed with Cromwell JA on the aboriginal title issue but expressed different views on the matter of treaty rights.
124. See text accompanying n 90 above.
125. *Marshall*, above n 122, para 177 (emphasis added).
126. See quotation accompanying n 111 above.

where present occupation is relied upon to prove aboriginal title at the time of Crown sovereignty. He concluded:[127]

> [C]ontinuity of occupation from sovereignty to the present is not part of the test for Aboriginal title if exclusive occupation at sovereignty is established by direct evidence of occupation before and at the time of sovereignty. This view is consistent with the basic principle underpinning *Delgamuukw* that title crystalizes at that time. It also responds to the concern that requiring continuity of occupation after sovereignty would undermine the purpose of s.35 [of the Constitution Act, 1982] by giving effect to displacement of Aboriginals by Europeans as a result of post-sovereignty indifference to Aboriginal rights.

The decision of the Nova Scotia Court of Appeal in *Marshall* to order a new trial was overturned by the Supreme Court of Canada and the convictions of the appellants were restored.[128] However, while expressing some disagreement with Cromwell JA on the test for the exclusive occupation necessary to establish aboriginal title, McLachlin CJ did not contradict him in her brief discussion of the issue of continuity. She said this:[129]

> The third sub-issue is continuity. The requirement of continuity in its most basic sense simply means that claimants must establish they are right holders. Modern-day claimants must establish a connection with the pre-sovereignty group upon whose practices they rely to assert title or claim to a more restricted aboriginal right. The right is based on pre-sovereignty aboriginal practices. To claim it, a modern people must show that the right is the descendant of those practices. Continuity may also be raised in this sense. To claim title, the group's connection with the land must be shown, to have been 'of a central significance to their distinctive culture': *Adams*, at para. 26. If the group has 'maintained a substantial connection' with the land since sovereignty, this establishes the required 'central significance': *Delgamuukw, per* Lamer C.J., at paras. 150–51.

In this passage, McLachlin CJ explained that the concept of continuity applies to aboriginal title claims so as to require a connection between the aboriginal group claiming title today and the group occupying the land at the time of Crown sovereignty. Subject to the possibility envisaged by La Forest J in his

---

127. *Marshall*, above n 122, para 181. See also *R v Bernard* [2003] 4 CNLR 48 (NBCA) (reversed on other grounds in *Marshall/Bernard*, above n 62), para 58, where Daigle JA said that the 'requirement of continuity only applies in cases where present occupation is relied on as proof of pre-sovereignty occupation.'
128. *Marshall/Bernard*, above n 62.
129. *Marshall/Bernard*, above n 62, para 67, citing *R v Adams* [1996] 3 SCR 101 and *Delgamuukw*, above n 13. McLachlin CJ delivered the judgment of herself, Major, Bastarache, Abella and Charron JJ. LeBel and Fish JJ, concurring in result, did not discuss continuity.

concurring judgment in *Delgamuukw* of aboriginal title being transferred from one aboriginal group to another,[130] this is probably uncontroversial. In speaking of rights being descendants of pre-sovereignty aboriginal practices, the Chief Justice may also have meant that there has to be a sufficient connection between the historical practice upon which the right is based and the modern-day right being claimed.[131] This makes sense in the context of an aboriginal right less than title that is based on a pre-contact practice, custom or tradition (for example, a practice giving rise to a right to hunt for food would be unlikely to support a modern-day right to conduct ecotours). But I fail to understand why such a connection between a traditional practice and a present-day right would be necessary in the aboriginal title context, as we know from *Delgamuukw* that aboriginal titleholders have 'the right to exclusive use and occupation of the land held pursuant to that title for a variety of purposes, *which need not be aspects of those aboriginal practices, customs and traditions which are integral to distinctive aboriginal cultures.*'[132] A more consistent interpretation in the title context of McLachlin CJ's statement that rights are descendants of pre-sovereignty practices would therefore be to regard it as an expression of her view that there has to be a connection between the community whose practices amounted to exclusive occupation at the time of Crown sovereignty and the community claiming aboriginal title today.[133]

In the above passage, McLachlin CJ also related continuity to statements in *Adams* and *Delgamuukw* that the occupation of land must be of 'central significance' to the claimant group's distinctive culture, and that maintenance of a substantial connection with the land since sovereignty establishes this. In *Delgamuukw*, Lamer CJ explained that, although central significance:[134]

> ... remains a crucial part of the test for aboriginal rights, given the occupancy requirement in the test for aboriginal title, I cannot imagine a situation where this requirement would actually serve to limit or preclude a title claim. The

---

130. *Delgamuukw*, above n 13, para 198. See also 'Self-Government and the Inalienability of Aboriginal Title', above n 31, 501–502.
131. See above n 111. See also *Sappier/Gray*, above n 79, paras 48–49.
132. *Delgamuukw*, above n 13, para 117 Lamer CJ (emphasis added). This, however, is subject to an inherent limit preventing uses that are irreconcilable with the attachment to the land giving rise to the aboriginal title: paras 125–132. For critical commentary on this limit, see Kent McNeil 'The Post-*Delgamuukw* Nature and Content of Aboriginal Title' in *Emerging Justice?*, above n 24, 102, 116–122.
133. This interpretation is supported by her summation of the requirements for aboriginal title, where all she said in relation to continuity was that it 'is required, in the sense of showing the group's descent from the pre-sovereignty group whose practices are relied on for the right': *Marshall/Bernard*, above n 62, para 70. No further explanation of continuity was given in her judgment, as her conclusion that aboriginal title had not been established on the facts made it 'unnecessary to consider continuity issues relating to the sites claimed': para 84.
134. *Delgamuukw*, above n 13, para 151 (emphasis added).

requirement exists for rights short of title because it is necessary to distinguish between those practices which were central to the culture of the claimants and those which were more incidental. However, in the case of title, it would seem clear that any land that was occupied pre-sovereignty, and which the parties have maintained a substantial connection with since then, is sufficiently important to be of central significance to the culture of the claimants. *As a result, I do not think it is necessary to include explicitly this element as part of the test for Aboriginal title.*

Moreover, at another place in his judgment Lamer CJ distinguished the *Van der Peet* test for aboriginal rights generally from the test for aboriginal title by stating clearly that, in the case of title, 'the requirement that the land be integral to the distinctive culture of the claimants is subsumed by the requirement of occupancy.'[135] As the time for proof of that occupancy is Crown assertion of sovereignty, it would be logically inconsistent to make proof of post-sovereignty occupation necessary to show that the occupation at sovereignty was of central significance to the aboriginal culture.[136] Instead, in referring in the passage above to maintenance of a substantial connection with the land, I think the Chief Justice intended to reinforce his point that post-sovereignty occupation can *also* be relied upon to prove title at sovereignty if sufficient continuity back to the time of sovereignty can be shown.[137]

To sum up, in Canadian aboriginal rights and title law the concept of continuity has been used in more than one sense. First, it means that there has to be a connection between the aboriginal group claiming the right or title today and the historical aboriginal group whose practice, custom or tradition or whose occupation of land provides the basis for the right or title.[138] Second, continuity also means that, in the case of an aboriginal right not amounting to title, the present-day activity has to come within the scope of the right derived from the historical practice, custom or tradition.[139] Third, where evidence of

---

135. *Delgamuukw*, above n 13, para 142.
136. Cromwell JA made a similar observation in *Marshall*, above n 122, para 164, quoting from *Delgamuukw*, above n 13: 'I find it difficult to reconcile this statement [by Lamer CJ in the penultimate sentence of the quotation accompanying n 134 above] with the earlier one to the effect that, in title cases, the "integral to the distinctive culture test" is "...subsumed by the requirement of occupancy..." (para 142). In one case, occupancy at sovereignty is enough, whereas in the other, occupancy plus ongoing substantial connection is required. Moreover, any requirement for ongoing substantial connection with the land seems at odds with the purpose of s.35(1) [of the Constitution Act, 1982] because insisting on post-sovereignty continuity would tend to "...perpetuat[e] the historical injustice suffered by aboriginal peoples at the hands of colonizers who failed to respect aboriginal rights to land": para. 153.'
137. See text accompanying nn 116–121 above.
138. See also *Powley*, above n 30, involving Métis hunting rights, where the Court found a sufficient connection between the historical and contemporary Métis communities.
139. For an example of a case where the present-day activity was held not to fall within the scope of the right, see *Mitchell*, above n 70.

post-contact practices, customs or traditions, or present occupation of land, is relied upon as proof of aboriginal rights or title, there has to be a connection back to the aboriginal society's practices, customs or traditions at the time of European contact or to their exclusive occupation at the time of Crown assertion of sovereignty. This third use of continuity is intended to help overcome the onerous burden faced by aboriginal claimants in proving rights on the basis of practices, customs and traditions or occupation of land a long time in the past. Canadian courts have, however, explicitly avoided imposing the kind of continuity requirement articulated by Brennan J in *Mabo (No 2)* and applied by the majority of the High Court through their interpretation of section 223(1) of the NTA in *Yorta Yorta*, whereby a substantial connection with the land in accordance with traditional laws and customs has to be maintained after Crown sovereignty. In my opinion, the Australian approach to this matter is partly due to a misguided attempt to identify specific normative rules in pre-sovereignty indigenous societies, in contrast to the Canadian approach of basing aboriginal rights on more broadly conceived practices, customs and traditions, and aboriginal title on factual occupation of land.[140]

In New Zealand, we have seen that the approach taken to Māori customary rights by the Court of Appeal in *Ngati Apa* is much closer to the Canadian than the Australian approach.[141] Those rights, both at common law and by statutory definition, are based on tikanga Māori, which includes Māori custom, practice and usage.[142] Consistently with the common law's treatment of custom in England and with the Supreme Court's pronouncements on aboriginal rights and title in Canada, they should continue until either converted into common law interests by the Māori (formerly Native) Land Court or extinguished by clear and plain legislation.[143] But what the FSA has done through section 50(1)(b) is make the legal enforceability of Māori customary rights depend on

---

140. 'Relevance of Traditional Laws', above n 24. See also Young, above n 18; and Anker, Bartlett, and Lavery, all above n 94.
141. See text accompanying nn 22–32 above.
142. See above nn 6, 26–28, and accompanying text.
143. This is the approach taken in *Ngati Apa*, above n 1. Note that it is also consistent with the common law's treatment of property rights generally, which continue until given up by a recognised method such as gift, sale or abandonment: *Moffat v Kazana* [1969] 2 QB 152, 156. For abandonment to occur, a clear intention to abandon must be shown: *Williams v Phillips* (1957) 41 Cr App R 5 (UK Div Ct); *Simpson v Gowers* (1981) 32 OR (2d) 385 (CA). See also *Ward v Ward* (1852) 7 Ex 838, 839; *Swan v Sinclair* [1924] 1 Ch.254 (CA), affirmed [1925] AC 227 (HL); *Gotobed v Pridmore* (1970) 115 Sol Jo 78 (CA). In *Tehidy Minerals Ltd v Norman* [1971] 2 QB 528, 553 (CA), Buckley LJ said: 'Abandonment of an easement or of a profit à prendre can only, we think, be treated as having taken place where the person entitled to it has demonstrated a fixed intention never at any time thereafter to assert the right himself or to attempt to transmit it to anyone else.' Nor can rights in relation to natural resources be lost by non-user. For example, mere failure to exercise a riparian right to use water, for however long, does not result in loss of the right at common law: see *Sampson v Hoddinott* (1857) 1 CB (NS) 590, 611 (CP), affirmed 3 CB (NS) 596 (Ex Ch).

substantially continuous engagement in an activity, use or practice in the relevant area of the foreshore or seabed in accordance with tikanga Māori.[144] A version of the heavily criticised *Yorta Yorta* requirement of continuing connection with the land in accordance with traditional laws and customs has thus been legislatively introduced into New Zealand law, without the common law support for this requirement that was found in Australia in Brennan J's judgment in *Mabo (No 2)* before its legislative adoption by section 223(1) of the NTA (as interpreted in *Yorta Yorta*). But as with the integral requirement that was also introduced into New Zealand law by section 50(1)(b), apart from statutory amendment the best that can be hoped for is that the Māori Land Court will limit the impact of the substantially uninterrupted requirement by applying established principles of statutory interpretation that favour conformity with international law and preservation of vested rights.[145]

V Conclusion

We have seen that the Court of Appeal in *Ngati Apa* distinguished between sovereignty and property and applied the doctrine of continuity to hold that Māori customary land rights, broadly defined by tikanga Māori, continued after Crown acquisition of sovereignty in 1840 and became enforceable in New Zealand courts thereafter. These rights include any unextinguished rights to the foreshore and seabed. In so doing, the Court resolved the uncertainty on these matters arising from controversial decisions such as *Wi Parata*[146] and *In re the Ninety-Mile Beach*,[147] and confirmed that New Zealand law is generally consistent with the law in other Commonwealth jurisdictions in this regard.[148] The Court nonetheless avoided introducing problematic specific aspects of the jurisprudence on indigenous rights from elsewhere, especially the Canadian integral to the distinctive culture test and the Australian requirement of a substantial maintenance of a connection with the land in accordance with traditional laws and customs. As discussed in this chapter, those aspects of indigenous-rights law, which arose in part from judicial perceptions of the circumstances in Canada and Australia, are doctrinally flawed and have been subjected to severe criticism. I therefore think the New Zealand Court of Appeal was right to avoid them.

Unfortunately, the New Zealand Parliament has not shown the same respect

---

144. Section 50(1)(b) is quoted in the text following n 42 above.
145. See above nn 86–88 and accompanying text.
146. *Wi Parata*, above n 4.
147. *In re the Ninety-Mile Beach*, above n 8.
148. See the 1847 decision of the New Zealand Supreme Court in *Symonds*, above n 31.

for either Māori rights or common law doctrine. Nor has it demonstrated a commitment to racial equality and the international human-rights obligations of New Zealand. Instead, it used its legislative authority to enact the FSA and extinguish most Māori rights to the foreshore and seabed, while leaving freehold interests thereto untouched. This violates common law principles and international law. Moreover, the FSA has subjected remaining Māori rights to those coastal areas to versions of both the Canadian integral to the distinctive culture test and the Australian continuing connection test, and placed the burden of meeting those tests on Māori claimants. While the express purpose for all this is 'to *preserve* the public foreshore and seabed in perpetuity as the common heritage of all New Zealanders',[149] the reality is otherwise: the goal is to *take away* Māori rights because that is perceived as beneficial to New Zealanders generally. In other words, the *interests* of the Pākehā majority take precedence over the *rights* of the Māori minority.

It might be argued that, given the reaction by segments of the public to the *Ngati Apa* decision, the FSA was necessary to preserve social peace and harmony. If so, that is a sad reflection on modern New Zealand society, which has a reputation for tolerance and respect for the rule of law. This kind of argument also reveals a lack of appreciation of the significance of the *Ngati Apa* decision itself. The Court of Appeal decided that Māori customary rights to the foreshore and seabed could exist as a matter of law, and so the Māori Land Court had jurisdiction to hear claims thereto. The Court of Appeal did not decide that any such rights actually exist, as they would still have to be proven in accordance with tikanga Māori to the satisfaction of the Māori Land Court, and could have been extinguished in specific instances. The judges were careful to point this out.[150] Gault P, in reference to the actual claim to the foreshore and seabed in the Marlborough Sounds, even said he had 'real reservations about the ability for the appellants to establish that which they claim.'[151] In light of this,[152] concerns that Māori would be able to establish exclusive rights over extensive areas of the foreshore and seabed were at best exaggerated, and at worst fear-mongering. Moreover, one can question whether there was any real reason to think that the Māori who were successful in establishing such rights would exclude the public from access

---

149. FSA, s 3 (emphasis added). See Part III The Political Reaction: The Foreshore and Seabed Act 2004.
150. *Ngati Apa*, above n 1, paras 8–12, 57–58 Elias CJ, 93, 106, 112, 125 Gault P, 129, 150, 181–182 Keith and Anderson JJ, 186, 216 Tipping J.
151. *Ngati Apa*, above n 1, para 106.
152. Significantly, Prime Minister Helen Clark and Attorney-General Margaret Wilson acknowledged the narrow ambit of the decision in a press release the day after it was handed down, but soon after the Government announced an intention to take a legislative approach: see Bennion, Birdling and Paton, above n 48, i.

to beaches and other sites, other than in exceptional circumstances where such access would cause environmental or cultural harm.[153] Such fears seem inconsistent with a long history of Māori generosity and willingness to share with those who have come to live in New Zealand more recently.[154]

I am therefore of the opinion that the legislative response to the *Ngati Apa* decision was unduly hasty and unnecessary. Rather than give in to political pressure from some quarters, it would have been preferable for the Government to bide its time and see what impact the decision would eventually have on the ground, and negotiate settlements with Māori where circumstances warranted.[155] This would have been in keeping with the common law tradition of having property rights determined in accordance with historical claims. Moreover, it might even have enhanced Māori confidence in parliamentary democracy, and would have avoided tarnishing New Zealand's reputation in the international community. As for the political pressure, a more appropriate response would have been a public education campaign explaining the bases of Māori rights to New Zealanders and providing them with a realistic appraisal of the potential impact of the *Ngati Apa* decision. All too often, opposition to indigenous rights is based on misinformation and prejudice, rather than on facts and informed understanding.

---

153. See Waitangi Tribunal Report, above n 6, 121.
154. 'Tikanga Māori involves the application of the important ethic of hospitality and generosity (manaakitanga) to the foreshore and seabed situation': Waitangi Tribunal Report, above n 6, 121. For example, public access to the Māori-owned beach at Ōrākei near Auckland has been assured by an agreement negotiated with the Ngāti Whātua, see Waitangi Tribunal Report, above n 6, 142–43; Bennion, Birdling and Paton, above n 48, 5.
155. See Waitangi Tribunal Report, above n 6, 138–141.

The Foreshore and Seabed Legislation: Resource- and Marine-Management Issues

Catherine Iorns Magallanes[*]

I Introduction

As the foreshore and seabed legislation concerns the coastal marine area, a key element of the legislative package is the interface between the new provisions and the existing legal regime governing the coastal marine area.[1] This chapter focuses on that interface. First, it explains the existing resource management regime and its provision for Māori interests. Second, it examines the resource management origins of the original dispute which led to the foreshore and seabed legislative package: namely the tussle over marine-farming permits and reform of the permitting regime. Third, it describes the evolution of the resource management provisions in the foreshore and seabed legislation. Finally, it comments on selected aspects of those provisions, primarily from the perspective of environmental protection, but also in terms of the Treaty of Waitangi partnership in resource management decision making.

II Resource Management Act 1991

The Resource Management Act 1991 (RMA) is the primary legislation governing resource use and development in New Zealand, both on land and in the coastal marine area (that is, including the foreshore and seabed). When it came into force it repealed all previous planning and environmental protection

---

[*] Senior Lecturer, Faculty of Law, Victoria University of Wellington.
[1] References to the foreshore and seabed legislation, or the legislative package, are to both the Foreshore and Seabed Act 2004 and to the Resource Management (Foreshore and Seabed) Amendment Act 2004. Where only one Act is referred to, it is referred to by name.

legislation and many aspects of other resource-use legislation, affecting over fifty statutes in all.

The purpose of the RMA is to 'promote the sustainable management of natural and physical resources.'[2] This requires that people and communities are able to provide for their social, economic and cultural well-being while also (among other things) 'avoiding, remedying, or mitigating any adverse effects of activities on the environment.'[3] Any activity on land or in the coastal marine area must either be approved in advance in an approved plan or by a resource consent issued by a proper consent authority (a regional, district or city council, or the Department of Conservation, depending on the area or activity, or both). Local councils are responsible for managing resources in the area and thus the development of plans and issuing of resource consents. Those undertaking resource activities pursuant to plans or consents are responsible for 'avoiding, remedying, or mitigating' their environmental effects.

The RMA provides procedural and substantive guidance to authorities making decisions on resources and carrying out their functions and duties under the Act. For example, the RMA provides for matters of national importance which must be recognised and provided for,[4] other matters which must be paid particular regard to,[5] and matters to take into account.[6] Matters of national importance relevant to this chapter include the preservation of the coastal environment – including the coastal marine area – and the relationship of Māori and their culture and traditions with their ancestral lands, water, sites, sacred sites, and other taonga. Matters that authorities must have particular regard to include kaitiakitanga (Māori guardianship).[7] The principles of the Treaty of Waitangi must be taken into account, which includes a duty of the Crown to actively protect Māori interests.[8]

The Crown has delegated its responsibility in the area of resource management to consent authorities. These authorities, while not partners to the Treaty of Waitangi, have thus assumed the Crown's responsibility to take Treaty of Waitangi matters into account as well as to ensure that the processes – especially consultation pursuant to the duty to enable Māori to make informed decisions – enable the recognition and provision for the relevant

---

2. See Resource Management Act, s 5. 'Promote' is a positive duty and requires affirmative steps be taken to ensure sustainable management.
3. See RMA, s 5(2).
4. See RMA, s 6.
5. See RMA, s 7.
6. See RMA, s 8.
7. 'Kaitiakitanga' has been specifically defined in the Act (RMA, s 2(1)) as 'the exercise of guardianship by the tangata whenua of an area in accordance with tikanga Maori in relation to natural and physical resources; and includes the ethic of stewardship.'
8. There is extensive case law providing guidance on the effect of these different provisions on decision making procedures and results.

matters of national importance.

The RMA contains particular consultation requirements whereby iwi must be consulted by the relevant authorities preparing plans covering lands of tribal interest.[9] In addition, iwi have the power to prepare iwi management plans which identify the special interests iwi may have in an area. For example, an iwi may identify a particular relationship with specific waters, mountains, spiritually significant sites or burial grounds, or both. Under the RMA, authorities must 'take account of' such iwi planning documents.[10]

While inclusion of these references to Māori interests is certainly a vast improvement on the previous resource management legislation, they are not sufficiently strong to guarantee that Māori interests will be protected. Māori interests are only some of several matters which must be provided for, and decision makers are certainly not required to act in conformity with the Treaty of Waitangi. On many occasions, while Māori interests have been taken into account and/or paid particular regard to, they have not been upheld in the final decision and have instead been outweighed by other considerations also provided for in the Act. This is particularly the case in respect of individual resource consents affecting Māori interests, such that Māori have repeatedly been denied substantive protection of their interests, even while the RMA has been followed and its requirements upheld.[11]

Notably, Māori land is not exempt from the provisions of the RMA. The regulation of the uses of Māori land for the purposes of sustainable management and environmental protection is considered to be an exercise of the Crown's Treaty of Waitangi right to govern, delegated through the RMA to local authorities.[12] Land that is not designated Māori land, but in respect of which Māori have historically had a special interest, is also managed under the RMA according to the considerations mentioned above. Thus Māori must apply for

---

9. While the RMA has general requirements to notify and consult publicly in respect of both plans in general and resource consents in particular, there is a greater duty on consent authorities to actively investigate whether the issue concerns Māori more than other people. This duty can stem from the requirements in sections 6, 7, and/or 8 described above.
10. The original RMA merely stated that authorities must 'have regard to' such documents; this was amended in 2003.
11. Indeed, the Waitangi Tribunal has described the RMA as 'fatally flawed' because decision makers are not required to act in conformity with the Treaty (*Ngawha Geothermal Resource Report 1993: Wai 304* (Brooker & Friend, Wellington, 1993) para 7.7.9). At para 8.5.2, the Tribunal recommended 'that an appropriate amendment be made to the Resource Management Act 1991 providing that ... all persons exercising functions and powers under it, in relation to management the use, development and protection of natural and physical resources, shall act in a manner that is consistent with the principles of the Treaty of Waitangi.' The Government has not implemented this recommendation. The Parliamentary Commissioner for the Environment has also criticised the protection of Māori interests by local authorities in: Parliamentary Commissioner for the Environment *Kaitiakitanga and Local Government: Tangata Whenua Participation in Environmental Management* (Wellington, 1998).
12. See, for example, *Minister of Conservation v Southland District Council* (19 April 2001) EC AK A39/2001.

resource consents to use land for activities – even traditional activities – in the same way that others must do so. Such applications are evaluated according to the same criteria as other applications, such that Māori interests may still be outweighed by other considerations provided for in the RMA.

The RMA includes the potential for iwi to exercise powers under the RMA, including the power to grant resource consents, for example, in respect of lands in which they may have a special interest. This may be achieved through delegation from existing consent authorities, following a process which includes broad public consultation.[13] However, this potential has never been realised: no such powers have been delegated to iwi since the passage of the RMA.

In summary, Māori interests have been singled out for special attention in the RMA and are specifically provided for in several places, from the process of decision making to substantive outcomes. But there is no guarantee that they will be upheld in any final decision, either on the adoption of a planning document or decision on a resource consent. It was this lack of protection of Māori interests in respect of marine-farming decisions in the Marlborough Sounds that sparked the decision of iwi to apply to the Māori Land Court for a declaration of customary title over the foreshore and seabed and which in turn led to the Court of Appeal *Attorney-General v Ngati Apa (Ngati Apa)*[14] decision and the subsequent foreshore and seabed legislation.

III Marine Farming

Before the 1991 Resource Management Act, the Marine Farming Act 1971 was the primary legislation governing the establishment of marine farms around the New Zealand coastline. In this 1971 legislation Māori interests were not referred to and marine areas were gazetted for farming without reference to any customary activities which Māori had exercised – or were still exercising – in the coastal marine area. Licences and leases under the 1971 Marine Farming Act could contain rights of renewal and thus effectively last for more than forty years.

Under the RMA, decision making on the granting of marine-farming permits was devolved to regional and local consent authorities. The RMA allowed existing licences to continue under the new regime, but removed the rights of renewal. Under the new regime, marine farmers must obtain two permits: a coastal permit, under the RMA, to occupy coastal marine space, and a marine-farming licence from the Minister of Fisheries, to grow and

---

13. See RMA, s 33.
14. *Attorney-General v Ngati Apa* [2003] 3 NZLR 643 (CA).

harvest marine life.[15] Applications for coastal permits must be handled on a 'first come, first served' basis.[16] Only those with coastal permits may apply for a marine-farming licence.[17] Coastal permits last for up to thirty-five years but have no right of renewal.[18]

As soon as the RMA came into force, a 'gold rush' of applications were made to the Marlborough District Council for marine-farming permits in the Marlborough Sounds. In many areas there were competing applications covering the same space, and many applications covered marine areas currently being customarily used by Māori. The Marlborough District Council proceeded to decide upon applications and issue permits; the marine-farming industry began to take off in the Marlborough Sounds; and space suitable for marine farming became increasingly in short supply.

Iwi were involved with the permit application process, both as objectors to some applications and as applicants in others. Because of the several references to the protection of Māori interests in the RMA, Māori expected much better protection of their interests in the coastal marine area than before. Unfortunately, their success rates as both objectors and applicants were low. In some areas outside the Marlborough Sounds, iwi were able to be involved extensively in aquaculture and marine farming. For example, Te Ātiawa Manawhenua ki te Tau Ihu Trust, through its corporate subsidiary Totaranui Ltd, has extensive interests in Tasman Bay and Golden Bay; as does Ngāti Tama ki te Tau Ihu.[19] However, in other areas, iwi had a much lower success rate and felt excluded from the increasing marine-farm developments.

In relation to the Marlborough Sounds, local iwi felt that their interests had been ignored in respect of coastal permit decisions made by the Marlborough District Council. For example, in the early 1990s Ngāti Tama is reported to have made at least thirty-five applications for marine-farming licences in the Marlborough Sounds, of which none were granted.[20] Iwi also failed in

---

15. Fisheries Act 1983; now Fisheries Act 1996. The Fisheries permit considers matters relating to the management of fisheries and effect on marine life of the proposed marine farm. This requirement for two permits arose in 1993 as a result of the Resource Management Amendment Act 1993. Note that, while the present tense is used in describing the regime, it has since been altered by the aquaculture reforms, adopted in December 2004; described below n 39 and accompanying text.
16. *Fleetwing Farms Ltd v Marlborough District Council* [1997] NZRMA 385 (CA).
17. Unless the relevant plan already permits marine farming.
18. RMA, s 123(c).
19. Waitangi Tribunal *Ahu Moana: The Aquaculture and Marine Farming Report: Wai 953* (Legislation Direct, Wellington, 2002) 11, para 2.1.3.
20. See, for example, Fisheries and Other Sea-Related Legislation Committee 'Foreshore and Seabed Bill' [2004] AJHR I 22C 379, 10. The Report notes that Ngāti Tama told the Select Committee that no reasons were provided about why their applications had failed, plus that 'Maori applicants were approached by others for copies of their applications' and that 'the same applications were lodged in other names and licences were granted.' *Ahu Moana*, above n 19.

opposing other applications on the grounds of customary usage.[21] Some iwi were successful in gaining marine-farming permits, even in Marlborough. However, they were outnumbered significantly by successful non-Māori applicants. For example, in the period 1991–1996 only one application from an iwi trust for marine-farm space in the Marlborough Sounds was successful[22] while in one year alone – 1996 – ten permits were granted to non-Māori applicants.[23] Most importantly, much of the non-Māori marine farming was taking place in areas that had customarily been used by Māori, even while Māori were unsuccessful at gaining coastal permits in their own traditional areas.[24] These customary uses were thus being nudged out by marine-farming structures – anchored to the seabed – without any kind of redress or compensation. And this was occurring despite the relative sensitivity of the RMA to Māori interests.

Because of the 'gold rush', the Government imposed a moratorium on the granting of marine-farming applications from 1996 to 1999. The Government and Marlborough District Council sought time to consider how best to evaluate applications and allocate coastal marine space.[25] There were

---

21. Grant Powell, one of the lawyers involved in the Marlborough Sounds court case, states that 'Marlborough iwi had a 100 per cent failure record in opposing applications for marine farming on customary grounds.' Grant Powell, Powell Webber & Associates 'A Few Thoughts on Foreshore and Seabed'. <http://www.arena.org.nz> (last accessed 1 April 2005).

    For some evidence for Grant Powell's statement, see, for example, the summary provided by the Marlborough District Council, 'Marlborough District Council Decisions on Marine Farm Applications in the Marlborough Sounds Identified by Te Ohu Kaimoana: Information Provided to Tariana Turia, MP', 28 October 2004. It includes ten applications, all decided in 1996, which were made by non-Māori but objected to by various Māori bodies, primarily for being over ancestral lands but also for interfering with other activities (such as one application being for a farm in front of a waka landing site). All of these ten applications were granted; none of the objections were upheld by the Marlborough District Council.

22. See the summary provided by the Marlborough District Council, above n 21. Note that this does not include consideration of applications by other Māori corporations, such as Sealord Marine Farms. Multiple applications by Māori corporate bodies have been successful but the total figures are not supplied.

23. See the summary provided by the Marlborough District Council, above n 21.

24. See, for example, the decision in Application U951161 by Ngāti Apa Ki Te Waipounamu Trust. This application was refused and the primary reason given by the Marlborough District Council is as follows:

    1. The Committee took into account the principles of the Treaty of Waitangi, as required by Section 8 of the Resource Management Act, and acknowledged the proximity of Ngati Apa ancestral lands to the proposed site. The Committee also acknowledged that Section 6(e) of the Resource Management Act 1991 requires that the relationship of Maori and their culture and traditions with their ancestral lands, water, waahi tapu and other taonga is a matter of national importance, but was of the opinion that when balanced against Section 6(a) and 6(c), especially the preservation of the natural character of the area for all persons, these were considered to be of overriding importance.

    See the summary provided by the Marlborough District Council, above n 21.

25. For example, litigation establishing that the Marlborough District Council must employ the method 'first come, first served' was decided in 1997. See *Fleetwing Farms Ltd v Marlborough District Council*, above n 16.

suggestions that the Government would consider developing a tendering process for the coastal space.

This lack of iwi success in respect of the protection of their interests, in relation to both their own and non-Māori applications, led to a sense of grievance and frustration. In addition, the suggestion that the Government might consider a tendering process for managing the allocation of coastal space was an aggravating factor, and has been described as 'the last straw.'[26] If a tendering process was implemented then proceeds would go to central or local government, or both. As marine farming was effectively privatising large areas of marine space in the Marlborough Sounds, and as iwi had asserted customary rights over some of this marine space, they felt that they should at least get some of the financial benefit — even if only redress for the extinguishment of their usage rights. But they also wanted the rights recognised so as to be able to continue to exercise them. Thus it was these two factors — the lack of success in the marine-farming applications plus the issue of allocation by tendering — which led to the lodging in 1996 of the Māori Land Court claim for recognition of customary title to areas of the foreshore and seabed in the Marlborough Sounds.[27]

During the moratorium, many things were happening. Māori and non-Māori were busy preparing applications to be lodged when the moratorium lifted.[28] Central Government was considering reform of the aquaculture-permitting regime, in respect of both substance and process. In 1998, an independent review recommended major reform and the then National Government Cabinet agreed to proposals which 'would have significant implications for Maori.'[29] The 1999 Labour Government continued to work on the reform and formally announced it in 2000, releasing a public discussion document. After a brief period of public consultation it announced its reform proposals, including the introduction of another moratorium in 2002 pending their adoption.[30]

---

26. Powell, above n 21.
27. See, for example, Maui John Mitchell (personally and on behalf of Ngāti Tama Manawhenua ki te Tau Ihu Trust, Huria Matenga Wakapuaka Estuary Trust, Wakapuaka Taiāpure Management Committee, and Tāngata Tiaki nō Ngāti Tama) 'Submission to the Fisheries and Other Sea-Related Legislation Committee on the Foreshore and Seabed Bill 2004' 1215, paras 2.1–2.2.3 and appendix A; 'What Led to the Court of Appeal Decision which Sparked the Controversy?' (July 2004) *Wel-com* Wellington, Catholic Online News for the Wellington and Palmerston North Dioceses <http://www.welcome.org.nz> (last accessed 1 April 2005).
28. Indeed, when the moratorium was lifted, in July 1999, the Marlborough District Council received 439 applications for either new farms or extensions to existing farms. It took four years to process these applications. See Marlborough District Council *Marine Farms* <http://www.marlborough.govt.nz> (last accessed 1 April 2005).
29. *Ahu Moana*, above n 19, 17, para 3.1.1. For more detail on the substance and process of this reform see *Ahu Moana*, above n 19, Ch 3 'The Aquaculture Reform Process', 17–28.
30. I note that this moratorium only caught seven of the huge number of applications received by the Marlborough District Council.

Māori objected to several aspects of the aquaculture reform proposals: their substance;[31] the second moratorium;[32] the process through which they had both been developed;[33] and the lack of clarity about the effect of the reform on the 1992 fisheries settlement, on customary fisheries, and on the ongoing foreshore and seabed litigation. A claim was thus made to the Waitangi Tribunal, including for breach of the Treaty of Waitangi in not making specific provision for Māori interests in marine farming in the reform proposals.[34]

In 2002, under urgency and before the Court of Appeal decision in *Ngati Apa*, the Waitangi Tribunal agreed that the aquaculture reform proposals breached the Treaty of Waitangi and needed to adequately provide for Māori interests.[35] This needed to include participation in development of the regime as well as an appropriate share in the resulting fishing interests. It was suggested separately that iwi receive at least 20 per cent of new aquaculture in marine areas, in line with the 1992 fisheries settlement.

The Government did not immediately accept the Waitangi Tribunal's recommendations and deferred negotiation on this issue.[36] However, it appears that *Ngati Apa* provided the impetus for resolving it. In July 2003, soon after the *Ngati Apa* decision, Helen Clark suggested that the two issues could be resolved together;[37] she later announced the policy that Māori hold 20 per cent of all marine-farming space issued since 1992.[38] While this particular provision was controversial among both Māori and non-Māori, the legislation

---

31. The primary substantive difficulties were with the adoption of Aquaculture Management Areas and with the delegation to local authorities of a tendering process for the allocation of coastal marine space.
32. Māori considered that they would be unduly affected by the moratorium because they had a larger proportion of the applications submitted compared with those already granted.
33. Māori had not been given an opportunity to consider the final proposals when they had been substantially revised from those described in the public discussion document and those revisions would significantly affect Māori interests.
34. See *Ahu Moana*, above n 19, 2–5, paras 1.3–1.7 for a description of the parties and the original and amended statements of claim.
35. See Waitangi Tribunal Report, *Ahu Moana*, above n 19, Ch 7 'Findings and Recommendations', 73–77, paras 7.1–7.2.
36. Indeed, the Government apparently attempted to make final the aquaculture legislation with the inclusion of an 'intervention clause' designed to allow it to defer negotiations on providing for Maori interests while allowing for the much-needed reform to go ahead. However, iwi were – not surprisingly – unhappy with this approach. Ruth Berry, Political Reporter 'Secrecy over Seabed Trade-off' (7 July 2003) <http://www.arena.org.nz> (last accessed 8 December 2004).
37. Ruth Berry quotes Prime Minister Helen Clark as saying in a radio interview 'There's enormous interest in the aquaculture legislation [and Marine Reserves Bill] ... and the Court of Appeal decision in a sense brings these issues around those bills to the fore and I think we may be able to resolve a number of things together.' Berry, above n 36.
38. This would be achieved both through the provision of new licences and from the purchase and allocation of existing licences.

implementing this policy was passed in December 2004.[39]

The case that came before the Court of Appeal was not actually about marine-farming space. By the time that it got that far, the only issue was whether the Māori Land Court had jurisdiction to consider customary title claims to the foreshore and seabed. This was a much narrower legal issue, divorced from any facts concerning activities in the Marlborough Sounds. However, I consider that this background is still necessary to keep in mind as they were joined politically, even if not legally.

As further background, also during the 1990s, a new regime was introduced for management of non-commercial Māori customary fishing, with substantial Māori input into and control of the new regime.[40] Iwi in the Marlborough–Nelson area were involved with the negotiation for development of the new regime and are currently using it.[41] For example, they have established tangata kaitiaki/tiaki to authorise customary fishing within their rohe moana, in accordance with tikanga Māori,[42] and Marlborough–Nelson iwi are some

---

39. The Aquaculture Reform Bill was divided into two new Acts (Aquaculture Reform (Repeals and Transitional Provisions); Maori Commercial Aquaculture Claims Settlement) and four Amendment Acts (Te Ture Whenua Maori Amendment (No 3); Biosecurity Amendment; Conservation Amendment; and Fisheries Amendment (No 3)). All of these Acts were assented to on 21 December 2004.

    The legislation implements the announced intended policy of 20 per cent allocation of marine-farming space issued since 1992. While this aspect was a legislated rather than a negotiated settlement, it was explicitly stated to be included 'in direct response to an established grievance as found by the Waitangi Tribunal relating to Maori interests in marine farming.' Primary Production Committee 'Aquaculture Reform Bill' [2004] AJHR I 22C 1173, 17. At the time of the conference where this paper was presented, the Select Committee had just released its report on the Aquaculture Reform Bill, and the Bill was scheduled for its Second Reading. For a detailed explanation of the aquaculture reforms see Camilla Owen's paper in Bronwyn Arthur, Paul McHugh and Camilla Owen *Foreshore and Seabed, Aquaculture Reform and the RMA* (NZLS Continuing Legal Education, Wellington, 2005) 59–90; the Māori claims settlement legislation is explained at pages 74–81.

40. Māori customary fishing rights are recognised but managed. There are three mechanisms under the Fisheries Act 1996 and the customary fishing regulations (the Fisheries (Kaimoana Customary Fishing) Regulations 1998 and the Fisheries (South Island Customary Fishing) Regulations 1999): the establishment of tangata kaitiaki/tiaki to authorise customary fishing within their rohe moana, in accordance with tikanga Māori; the establishment of taiāpure (local fishery in an area of special significance); and the establishment of mātaitai reserves (customary fishing areas where the tangata whenua manage all non-commercial fishing by making bylaws). Note that, while this regime took years to negotiate and implement, the latter two aspects of it have been criticised by the Waitangi Tribunal as not working as intended. For example, the process for establishing taiāpure is 'time- and resource-intensive', its management does not implement rangatiratanga over the fishery, and mātaitai do not effectively affirm customary rights. 'Arguably, the very low level of take-up by hapu Maori speaks for itself.' Waitangi Tribunal *Report on the Crown's Foreshore and Seabed Policy: Wai 1071* (Legislation Direct, Wellington, 2004) 116–7.

41. 'Ngati Tama... in conjunction with the other seven iwi of Te Tau Ihu (and with Ngai Tahu), negotiated the South Island Fisheries Regulations during the late 1990s.' Mitchell, above n 27 para 1.4.1.

42. This is pursuant to the customary fishing regulations, cited above n 40. 'Tangata Katiaki/Tiaki [sic] currently cover practically the whole of the South Island and Tangata Kaitiaki/Tiaki cover much of

of the few to have established a taiāpure fishing area under the regime.[43] However, while negotiations on the new regime began in the early 1990s,[44] these developments were not finalised until after 1996. This presumably added to iwi frustration with the overall management of fisheries in the area.

Government is currently in the process of reviewing other marine-related laws and policies: its oceans policy, marine reserves, the New Zealand Coastal Policy Statement,[45] and the giant RMA.

In summary, there is extensive history of Marlborough iwi exercising customary rights in the coastal and marine area, both in the past and present. Most of those rights are fishing related. This has translated into involvement in some marine-farming activities in the area, but this is only a small amount considering both their historical involvement and the extent of current non-Māori involvement. Plus, it has come at the expense of some customary activities. The Government is reforming much of its marine legislation and policy, including aquaculture, and – as part of that reform – has agreed to resolve the issue about lack of Māori access to marine-farming permits. *Ngati Apa* is about much more than access to marine farming in the Marlborough Sounds, but it was marine farming which provided the primary impetus for initiating the claim before the Court.

IV *Evolution of the Resource Management Amendments*

The Court of Appeal released its *Ngati Apa* decision in June 2003. The Government immediately announced that it would introduce a new regime overriding the decision and in August 2003 released its draft policy (the August Policy).[46] The policy proposals outlined four 'basic principles', including that ownership be in the 'public domain, with the consequence that all New Zealanders are able to enjoy open access and use'[47] but also 'that processes should be established to enable the customary interests of whanau, hapu and iwi in the foreshore and seabed to be acknowledged, and specific rights

---

the North Island.' Ministry of Fisheries *Customary Fishing Rights and Rules* <http://www.fish.govt.nz> (last accessed April 1 2005).

43. One taiāpure was established in 2003 in Delaware Bay, northeast of Nelson, with Ngāti Tama and Ngāti Koata on the management committee (jointly with other non-Māori members). Currently only seven taiāpure have been established nationwide. Only three mātaitai reserves have been established and none are in the Marlborough–Nelson area.
44. This was prompted by the 1992 Maori commercial fisheries settlement and began soon after.
45. These were put on hold in 2003 until the foreshore and seabed and aquaculture reforms were finalised. It is expected to continue in 2005.
46. *The Foreshore and Seabed of New Zealand: Protecting Public Access and Customary Rights: Government Proposals for Consultation* Department of the Prime Minister and Cabinet (Wellington, 2003).
47. *Government Proposals*, above n 46, 16.

identified and protected.'[48] The August Policy noted that the RMA does offer some protection for Māori interests, including decision making and taking 'direct control of certain areas' and even stated that '[t]here are concerns with the effectiveness of some of these mechanisms. For example, many Māori have been dissatisfied with the way in which some local authorities give effect to the requirements of the Resource Management Act.'[49]

One of the options proposed for implementing the principle of protection of Māori interests was the strengthening of the existing system, including strengthening the RMA system. However, the August Policy explicitly did not favour this option and concentrated instead on designing a new system.[50]

In December 2003, after a very quick consultation round (including hui around the country) and a period for development of the Government's response, the Government released official policy statements outlining proposals for legislation (the December Policy).[51] The statements confirmed the Government's intention to legislate as proposed in the August Policy. Interestingly, some changes were made to the proposed treatment of the resource management regime: it would be improved in order to better protect Māori customary rights at the same time as a new system would be devised to recognise them.[52] This had apparently emerged as a 'major issue' during the consultation period over the proposals and, unlike some of the other major concerns, the Government felt able to address this.[53]

The other reference to the RMA regime in the December Policy was that any Māori customary rights recognised would be 'subject to regulation through the Resource Management Act to ensure sustainability.'[54] While the

---

48. *Government Proposals*, above n 46, 27.
49. *Government Proposals*, above n 46, 26.
50. *Government Proposals*, above n 46, 28.
51. See, for example, Hon Dr Michael Cullen 'Government Proposals on Foreshore-Seabed' (17 December 2003) Press Release.
52. See, for example, Dr Michael Cullen's Press Release, above n 51:
    A number of instruments exist now to protect Maori customary rights, including the RMA, the Fisheries Act and the Local Government Act. But these systems do not always or everywhere work as well as they could.
    To address these problems, the government will establish and resource 16 regionally based working groups comprising central government, local government and Maori to reach agreement on how Maori participation in coastal management might be improved.
    Once these agreements are concluded, they will be formally recognised by the Crown so that the commitments in them become legally binding.
53. See, for example, Hon Parekura Horomia 'Consultation Process to Continue' (17 December 2004) Press Release:
    A major issue which emerged during the hui and in the later dialogue with Maori was that the provisions which now exist in the Resource Management Act, the Fisheries Act and the Local Government Act to protect Maori customary rights – including fishing rights – were not working as well as they might…. Often the impediments relate to the resourcing and capacity of local Maori and relevant government agencies to participate effectively. The government would expect these matters to be part of the discussions.
54. See, for example, Dr Michael Cullen's Press Release, above n 51: 'Dr Cullen said the customary rights would be strong rights but subject to regulation through the Resource Management Act to ensure sustainability.' This was also part of the Proposal Paper approved by Cabinet: see Office of

precise parameters for this regulation were still unclear, it was expected that the current standards for regulation of an activity in the RMA would be applied, and that it would be possible to decline or prohibit the exercise of a customary right for reasons of environmental sustainability.[55]

The Government identified its intention to finalise the relevant legislation over summer – including consideration of an anticipated report of the Waitangi Tribunal on the December Policy – and introduce legislation in March 2004.[56] It was also noted that the other significant reviews of laws and policies in respect of the marine environment had been 'put on hold awaiting final policy decisions on foreshore and seabed policy.'[57] Interestingly, the only further comment on the aquaculture reform was that it was 'considered to be a separate issue from foreshore and seabed policy and will therefore be progressed in due course.'[58]

Māori were extremely unhappy with the Government's proposals and lodged a claim with the Waitangi Tribunal that they breached the principles of the Treaty of Waitangi.[59] An urgent hearing was held in late January 2004 and the Tribunal released its report on 4 March.[60]

Many other New Zealanders were also unhappy with the Government's handling of the foreshore and seabed issues. A very vocal majority thought that the Government was moving too slowly in extinguishing any Māori customary ownership rights. Much of this opinion coalesced around the contribution to the debate made by the then Leader of the Opposition in his infamous Orewa address, also in late January 2004. Don Brash was strongly critical of the Government's proposals on the basis that they went too far in

---

the Deputy Prime Minister 'Cabinet Proposal Paper: Foreshore and Seabed: A Framework' (17 December 2003) <http://www.beehive.govt.nz/foreshore> (last accessed 1 April 2005). ('Cabinet Proposal Paper').

55. See, for example, the 'Cabinet Proposal Paper', above n 54, paras 155–161. The change suggested in that Paper to the application of the RMA standards was in respect of who can make the decision, rather than to the standards themselves: that any decision prohibiting or declining a customary activity – particularly one which had been recognised as a right by the Māori Land Court – will have to be taken by central government (for example, the Minister of Conservation, perhaps in consultation with the Minister of Māori Affairs). 'Cabinet Proposal Paper', above n 54, para 160. This was reflected in the final Cabinet decisions. See New Zealand Government *Foreshore and Seabed: A Framework – Government Decisions on the Foreshore and Seabed Framework* paras 65–80. <http://www.beehive.govt.nz> (last accessed 1 April 2005). Cabinet also expressly noted at paragraph 60 that any development of a customary right would be 'subject to the Resource Management Act and other general regulatory controls.'
56. See 'Cabinet Proposal Paper', above n 54, para 292.
57. These were the reviews of the Oceans Policy, Marine Reserves Bill 2002, no 224, and aquaculture reform. See the 'Cabinet Proposal Paper', above n 54, paras 279–284.
58. 'Cabinet Proposal Paper', above n 54, para 284.
59. An application for urgency was accepted by the Tribunal in August 2003, after release of the *Government Proposals*, above n 46. See Waitangi Tribunal *Report on the Crown's Foreshore and Seabed Policy: Wai 1071* (Legislation Direct, Wellington, 2004) appendix 1, 147.
60. *Report on the Crown's Foreshore and Seabed Policy*, above n 59, 148.

according Māori special rights. He argued against 'racial separatism' and was strongly critical of one aspect of the resource management regime proposals: what he labelled as the 'veto' that Māori customary rights holders would have over resource development proposals with an impact on the exercise of their customary rights.[61] Perhaps because of the attention drawn to it in this address, there was a lot of public debate over the 'veto' and what the Government's proposals would mean for the interface between Māori customary rights and the resource management regime.

The next public development in terms of chronology was the release of the Waitangi Tribunal report, with the Tribunal's finding that the Government's policy 'breaches the Treaty of Waitangi in ways that we regard as fundamental and serious.'[62] A primary reason for this finding was the lack of detail provided in the December Policy about the replacement customary rights regime and thus uncertainty entailed in the Government's proposals, when a right of access to the courts was being removed – particularly where the right of access was for the determination of a property right. Aspects explicitly mentioned as contributing to the uncertainty included 'how the interface with the Resource Management Act will be handled' and 'how parts of the policy will work in practice.' The Waitangi Tribunal singled out for criticism the likely achievement of the proposed 'enhanced role in decision making.' The Tribunal suspected that Māori were being promised this when they should have already achieved it under the RMA and the customary fishing regulations regimes.[63]

In its response to the Waitangi Tribunal's report, the Government rejected the finding that its policies breached the Treaty of Waitangi, while noting that it would take account of some of the more constructive suggestions. However, the resource management aspects were not mentioned in the public comment.[64] The implication was that the policy would remain as proposed.[65]

The Foreshore and Seabed Bill (the Bill) was introduced to the House of Representatives on Thursday, 6 May 2004, the day after a 15–20,000 strong hīkoi (march) against its passage arrived at Parliament. Some provisions were significantly different from what was foreshadowed in the August and

---

61. Don Brash, Leader of the Opposition 'Nationhood' (An address to the Orewa Rotary Club, Auckland, 27 January 2004) 10–11. National Party <http://www.national.org.nz> (last accessed 1 April 2005).
62. Judge Carrie Wainwright, to the Minister of Māori Affairs (4 March 2004) Covering letter enclosing the Report in *Report on the Crown's Foreshore and Seabed Policy*, above n 59, ix.
63. *Report on the Crown's Foreshore and Seabed Policy*, above n 59, 122.
64. Hon Dr Michael Cullen 'Waitangi Tribunal Report Disappointing' (8 March 2004) Press Release.
65. See also Dr Michael Cullen's statement, 'Waitangi Tribunal Report Disappointing' above n 64:
    > It is ironic that the major opposition parties are attacking the government for leaning too much towards Maori while some Maori and the Tribunal are saying the exact opposite. Perhaps that might suggest to a fair and independent observer that the government has it about right.

December policies, which had been subjected to Waitangi Tribunal scrutiny. For example, in response to the criticism by the Waitangi Tribunal of the denial of access to the court system for determination of customary titles, a new codified High Court jurisdiction to determine customary titles and/or rights was included in the Bill.[66]

The resource management aspects of the Bill largely followed what had been indicated. For example, what Don Brash referred to as the 'veto' power of Māori customary rights holders was included, as expected. Yet there were also some significant changes which had not been foreshadowed in the previous discussions on policy. A significant change was that Māori customary rights activities would not be subject to the RMA regime in the normal way, as earlier suggested. Instead, they would be exempt from the existing resource consent and compliance procedures, subject to their own separate compliance regime.[67]

The Select Committee received 3946 written submissions on the Bill, of which 94 per cent opposed its passage. Most submissions focused on Crown ownership of the foreshore and seabed and the replacement Māori customary title and rights processes. The submissions which did comment on the resource management provisions objected to them. For example, local authorities were of the opinion that they would undermine sustainable management as well as frustrate development of the foreshore and seabed; network utility operators were concerned that they could affect their investment in infrastructure; and recreational groups were concerned generally.[68] Interestingly, the Green Party did not explicitly address the issue of meeting environmental standards (for example, the exemption from normal resource management regime compliance). The Green Party focused instead on the shortcomings of the Bill surrounding the inclusion of Māori in environmental management and decision making, arguing that the amendments did not go far enough to recognise or enable the exercise of Māori responsibility in such matters.[69] In relation to the resource management provisions, it was this aspect which also most concerned Māori.

The regime introduced by the Bill included three different types of orders: orders from the Māori Land Court for ancestral connection, and/or non-exclusive, non-territorial customary rights; and orders from the High Court for exclusive territorial customary rights.[70] The proposed effect of an ancestral connection order was to 'acknowledge kaitiakitanga and to provide opportunities for more effective participation in decision making processes by

---

66. See Fisheries and Other Sea-Related Legislation Committee, above n 20, 5.
67. These aspects are described in more detail below.
68. See Fisheries and Other Sea-Related Legislation Committee, above n 20, 3–4.
69. See Fisheries and Other Sea-Related Legislation Committee, above n 20, 21–22.
70. These orders are described in more detail in the introductory section in this book.

Māori groups who have traditionally cared for the coastline.'[71] It allowed for the transfer of powers under the RMA to iwi authorities, which is currently available under section 33. It also allowed for holders of ancestral connection orders to be consulted during the preparation of regional coastal plans, policy statements and district plans; and any planning document prepared by the holder of such an order must be 'taken into account' by regional and district councils when preparing their relevant plans. The ancestral connection orders were criticised particularly on the basis that they did not offer much that was not already available under the RMA. It was thus not worth the time and resources to apply for such an order.

The Select Committee could not agree on any changes to the Bill (nor even whether the Bill should be passed) so it was reported back to the House (in November 2004) unmodified. However, the Government found the numbers in Parliament to introduce amendments by Supplementary Order Paper and managed to address some of the concerns identified during the Select Committee process.

A key resource management-related amendment was the removal of ancestral connection orders and a promise to better address more effective consultation with local Māori over the coastal area under the review of the RMA. The Supplementary Order Paper also introduced the capability to establish a Foreshore and Seabed Reserve for those groups holding a territorial customary rights order from the High Court.[72] However, the resource management concerns addressed were solely those concerning Māori participation in resource management decision making; other concerns were not addressed.[73]

V The New Resource Management Provisions

A TERRITORIAL CUSTOMARY RIGHTS ORDERS

Where a group obtains a territorial customary rights order from the High Court, it is also able to obtain a High Court order establishing a reserve over the claimed area.[74] The reserve is to be managed by a board whose functions and membership have been agreed upon by the rights holder, the local regional council and central government.[75] The primary function of the board is the preparation of a management plan, similar to the iwi management plans

---

71. Foreshore and Seabed Bill 2004, Explanatory Note.
72. This is described in more detail in the next section.
73. These are discussed below, particularly those surrounding environmental standards and sustainable management.
74. Under FSA, s 43.
75. FSA, s 41.

prepared under the RMA.[76] Indeed, the plan must be prepared in accordance with Part II of the RMA and be consistent with the New Zealand Coastal Policy Statement.

The importance of the management plan is that regional and local councils must recognise and provide for it in preparing their regional policy statements and/or regional and district plans. Once a new foreshore and seabed management plan has been finalised and lodged with the relevant council, the council must within six months commence a review of the policy statements and plans, and then make any changes necessary in order to recognise and provide for the management plan.[77] As it is likely that any Māori customary activities in the area would be provided for under the management plan, they have the potential to then be protected by the regional and local plans and statements. While they will already be listed as matters of national importance, this provides an additional, reinforcing avenue for protection, perhaps through more specific controls. One author even suggests that the effect may be that greater weight will be given to recognised customary rights over other rights or matters of national importance.[78] Thus, 'although a foreshore and seabed reserve itself could have little real impact, if the board does produce an effective management plan then there is the opportunity for the group which held the territorial customary rights to obtain some significant controls through completely new mechanisms.'[79]

Another potentially important feature is the capability for a board to be delegated or transferred powers under the RMA, for example, including powers to issue resource consents for the area.[80] Why I consider this to be an important feature is that it illustrates the potential for co-management of the resource. In this sense, it provides a better model of partnership in resource management decision making than we have witnessed to date.

The primary drawback to this aspect, from the perspective of the resource management regime, is that a similar power already exists in the RMA in respect of iwi authorities.[81] The amendment extends the range of bodies which can exercise the power, but this may not amount to offering much more than should already be available to those wishing to exercise kaitiakitanga over a

---

76. Under RMA, s 44.
77. RMA, ss 79A, 79B. If there is a dispute over whether any changes are required to recognise and provide for the management plan, the board may refer the dispute to the Environment Court for decision.
78. Bronwyn Arthur 'Rights-Bearers and Rights-Integration' in Bronwyn Arthur, Paul McHugh and Camilla Owen *Foreshore and Seabed Act, the RMA and Aquaculture* (NZLS Continuing Legal Education, Wellington, 2005) 48.
79. Arthur, above n 78, 48.
80. RMA, s 33(2), as inserted by Resource Management (Foreshore & Seabed) Amendment Act 2004 (RM(FS)AA), s 9.
81. RMA, s 3.

foreshore and seabed area. This is because the holder of a territorial customary rights order, and thus the Māori membership of the relevant board, is likely to be the local iwi.[82] They should thus have been able to obtain the delegated RMA powers on their own, without having to establish a foreshore and seabed reserve board (and engage in all the negotiation that that requires).[83] When this criticism was made of the proposed ancestral connection orders, they were dropped from the legislative scheme. It is interesting to see this aspect brought back in, especially as it was brought back in respect of a much more important matter, that is, in respect of redress for loss of territorial rights.

However, as noted above, this delegation of powers has never been exercised in favour of an iwi authority. Some commentators have suggested that this is due to the public input required in order to achieve this,[84] that is, it is subject to (among other things) broad public consultation under the new special consultative procedure set out in the Local Government Act 2002.[85] There is thus the fear that this would be a hindrance to any actual delegation of powers to a foreshore and seabed reserve board. For example, Andrew Erueti suggests that passing such public scrutiny 'is unlikely to happen in the current political environment.'[86]

I note that there is a key difference between the two different types of bodies, and that is their establishment, which could produce a different membership. The boards are established by a High Court order, after scrutiny of its charter, where that charter is reached through agreement between the territorial customary rights holders, the relevant regional council and central government. It is quite possible that the members of the board will not be limited to the territorial customary rights holder. If so, this would be more likely to get a sympathetic public reaction to its exercise of delegated consent powers. But even if the members are substantially the same as the relevant iwi or local Māori authority, the board has the backing of the High Court. I suggest that this would put a politically different light on it in terms of public image and thus in the consultation procedure undertaken before any delegation is agreed upon. It is thus possible that foreshore and seabed boards may find it easier to obtain delegated powers under the RMA than iwi authorities do.

---

82. The legislation refers to 'the applicant group' without specifying that it must be an iwi. I am using 'iwi' for ease of reference only.
83. See FSA, ss 41–42.
84. See, for example, Andrew Erueti '*Ngati Apa* and the Environmental Management of New Zealand's Coastal Marine Area' in Alberto Costi and Yves-Louis Sage (eds) *Droit de l'Environnement dans le Pacifique: Problematiques et Perspectives Croisees/Environmental Law in the Pacific: International and Comparative Perspectives* (NZACL/ALCPP, Wellington, 2005) 235–261, 241. See also, Tom Bennion, Malcolm Birdling, and Rebecca Paton *Making Sense of the Foreshore and Seabed* (Maori Law Review, Wellington, 2004) 72.
85. Local Government Act 2002, s 33(4)(a).
86. Erueti, above n 84, 241.

I stress that this discussion is leaving aside the issue of adequacy of redress for extinguishment of common law native title.[87] The inadequacy is certainly a drawback to the scheme overall. However, in terms of environmental management, the concept of establishing a board, through negotiated agreement between Māori and central and local government, certainly has potential in terms of an approach to the management of the foreshore and seabed based on partnership. In this sense, and in spite of its drawbacks, it can be seen to support the Treaty of Waitangi partnership more than other aspects of the foreshore and seabed legislative package do.

B Customary Rights Orders

Customary rights orders can be obtained either through the Māori Land Court, for Māori,[88] or through the High Court, for non-Māori.[89] They are recognition of rights to engage in activities that were integral to the customary laws of the claimant group in 1840, have continued to be practised since 1840, and remain integral today.[90] Perhaps most importantly, any activities relating to fishing – including gathering live seaweed – are excluded by virtue of the 1992 fisheries settlement.[91] Examples of what kinds of activities might be left once fishing is excluded have included: the right to gather rocks, sand, shells and seaweed from the foreshore; the right to launch waka from the foreshore; and the right to protect access to sites of spiritual significance.[92] It has been derogatorily called the right to gather mud.

As these are activities that have been practised customarily and thus presumably without resource consent under the RMA since 1991, it is fair to assume that we are talking about only such activities that are practised on a scale so as to fall within permitted activities under district plans. We are highly unlikely to be concerned with activities on a scale that would cause adverse environmental effects. Any such activities would presumably have come to the attention of councils earlier and either been required to stop or to obtain a resource consent.

It is perhaps because of this presumably small scale that the Government has felt able to adopt the RMA amendments that it has in relation to customary rights orders. In the initial framework policy document issued by the Government there was no suggestion that customary rights would be exempt from the ordinary requirements under the RMA to obtain resource consents.

---

87. Discussed in Claire Charters' chapter in this book, 143–174.
88. FSA, ss 46, 47.
89. FSA, ss 67, 68.
90. FSA, ss 50, 74 respectively.
91. FSA, ss 49, 79 respectively.
92. See, for example, the list of activities in the 'Cabinet Proposal Paper', above n 54, para 156.

In the new foreshore and seabed amendments to the RMA, the exemption from RMA compliance is a major feature of customary rights orders.

As described above,[93] under the RMA, any activity with adverse environmental effects is prohibited without a resource consent. Indeed, all activities which make any use of the natural resources of the coastal marine area currently require either a resource consent or express permission in a coastal plan. Even where a resource consent has been obtained, every person has a duty to avoid, remedy or mitigate any adverse environmental effects of that activity. However, customary rights orders have been exempted from these requirements.

Under the Resource Management (Foreshore and Seabed) Amendment Act 2004 customary rights orders are given extremely high legal priority:

(i) They are included in section 6 of the RMA as a matter of national importance which must be recognised and provided for in all functions under the RMA.[94] I suggest that this is appropriate: it accords a high priority for Māori customary activities without compromising environmental protection.

(ii) The protection of customary rights orders may be provided for in the New Zealand Coastal Policy Statement.[95] This too is appropriate, for the same reason.

(iii) Other useful aspects include the creation of a public register, so that councils are able to see a list and location of all activities.[96] So is the fact that Māori will not be charged the coastal occupation charges for customary activities which are normally applicable for coastal activities.[97]

(iv) Another feature of the customary rights activities regime is that district plans may not include any rule which would prevent or have a significant adverse effect on a recognised customary activity.[98] If the holder of the customary rights order believes that such a rule exists in the plan, they may apply to the relevant authority and/or the Environment Court for its change.[99] This is another feature that does not pose a particular problem for environmental protection (though I do note below that it has probably not been implemented as well as it might have).

(v) A strong feature is what has been referred to as the 'veto', as discussed above. When other resource consents are applied for, consent authorities must

---

93. See Part II Resource Management Act 1991.
94. RMA, s 6(g), as inserted by RM(FS)AA, s 4.
95. RMA, s 58(gb), as inserted by RM(FS)AA, s 13.
96. FSA, s 92.
97. RMA, s 64A(4A), as inserted by RM(FS)AA, s 16. Note that I am focusing on Māori customary activities; I am ignoring the other category of potential activity orders from the High Court for the purposes of this paper (plus I doubt that many, if any, would meet the stringent criteria, particularly that of having existed since 1840).
98. RMA, s 85A, as inserted by RM(FS)AA, s 21.
99. RMA, s 85B, as inserted by RM(FS)AA, s 21.

consider whether the proposed activity would have any adverse effect on any recognised customary activity. An authority must not grant a resource consent for any activity that will, or is likely to, have a significant adverse effect on a recognised customary activity, unless written approval is given for the proposed activity by the holder of the relevant customary rights order.[100] Most of the adverse comments on these resource management aspects of the Bill focused on the 'veto' right: that Māori would have the capability to frustrate development, and that no group should have that kind of priority over others.[101] That aspect is not my concern here. Indeed, I consider that the so-called 'veto' actually accords an appropriate priority to the customary activities.

(vi) Activities undertaken pursuant to a customary rights order are exempt from the requirements to obtain resource consents, even though the activities are in the coastal marine area.[102] There are some limits or controls on customary activities, but these are not the usual resource management controls. Instead, a whole new Schedule 12 has been inserted to enable the Minister of Conservation to impose any necessary controls. Such controls may be imposed only where an activity has, or may have, a significant adverse effect on the environment (among other things). What is most important about this is, first, the threshold: it requires a significant adverse effect, not merely an adverse effect as under the RMA. Second, controls can only be imposed after an adverse-effects report has been obtained in relation to that activity and after consultation. That is, such controls cannot be imposed in advance, but only after the effects have occurred. The Minister of Conservation has the power to request the relevant regional council to prepare an adverse effects report and recommend whether controls should be imposed.

As an environmental lawyer I disagree with the exemption from RMA compliance and I disagree with the Schedule 12 regime. Instead, I consider that *all* land and the coastal marine area should be governed by the RMA. Restrictions on uses of land made for environmental protection in the public interest is a restriction recognised by the common law as able to be made even over customary title land and resources. This was one restriction recognised by the Chief Justice in her judgment in *Ngati Apa*. She observed that '[t]he management of the coastal marine area under the Resource Management Act may substantially restrict the activities able to be undertaken by those with interests in Māori customary property. That is the case for all owners of foreshore and seabed lands and indeed for all owners of land above the high water mark.'[103]

---

100. RMA, s 107A, as inserted by RM(FS)AA, s 25.
101. For example, see Brash, above n 61 and accompanying text.
102. RMA, s 17A, as inserted by RM(FS)AA, s 5.
103. *Ngati Apa*, above n 14, 76 Elias CJ.

It is likely that the rationale for the exemption adopted is based on the difference in nature between customary rights activities and other resource activities: their source or authorisation (from a court, not local authority) and duration (in perpetuity, not time-limited by resource consent).[104] Hence the statement in the Foreshore and Seabed Cabinet Paper that '[i]t is considered inappropriate for a local authority to take decisions that would overrule the recognition of a customary right by the Māori Land Court.'[105] But even this statement was made in the context of a proposal 'that the Resource Management Act would regulate the way in which the activity was undertaken, in order to ensure sustainability.'[106] This latter aspect has since been modified.

I suggest that the differences outlined do not require the system which has been devised. Consistency in form – in constitutional status – has been chosen over consistency in substance, in the protection offered. The method devised to ensure environmental protection is not within the spirit of the existing regime. The premise of the RMA is precautionary: the effects of an activity are assessed before it is allowed to proceed, and it can only proceed when the risks are deemed acceptable. This new regime has the opposite effect: an activity is allowed to proceed until a significant adverse effect is proven and only then may it be restricted.

As suggested above, it is highly likely that only activities without significant adverse effects are likely to be recognised for the purposes of this legislation. It is thus possible that worry over possible environmental damage is simply not necessary. While a recognised customary activity may have a commercial aspect, it is not possible for it to increase in its scale, extent or frequency after recognition in an order.[107] Indeed, if it does exceed the scale, extent, or frequency specified in the order, then the exemption from the RMA does not apply.[108] But if they are only comparatively minor activities, then the exemption and Schedule 12 regime is arguably unnecessary. It is a bad precedent in terms of environmental principle and I suggest that its aims can be achieved in other ways which are less damaging to the principle.

A possible rationale is that ex-post-facto controls are in fact the most appropriate for this kind of activity. That is because that is how the need for controls is most likely to arise. If a customary activity is recognised by the Court and has not been causing adverse effects beforehand (as this is the only way in which it will have been continuing as a customary activity), then it will only cause significant harm to the environment if something changes. This may be a change caused by the cumulative effects of the activity or, more likely,

---

104. 'Cabinet Proposal Paper', above n 54, para 157.
105. 'Cabinet Proposal Paper', above n 54, para 160.
106. 'Cabinet Proposal Paper', above n 54, para 157.
107. FSA, s 52(3).
108. FSA, s 52(4).

by some other event, such as an environmental change due to the weather or other natural event. In this kind of situation only a procedure focused on regulating an activity after it has been shown to be causing significant harm to the environment may be appropriate. However, this rationale was not part of the formal justification of the measures proposed or those adopted. It gives the appearance that it was a unique decision made for political reasons and thus one not too concerned about (in)consistency with other aspects of the prevailing regime.

If a real concern is Māori control over Māori activities, and avoiding discriminatory treatment and control over customary activities by consent authorities, then I suggest that the issue of decision making and control under the RMA should be addressed – not the establishment of a parallel control system. What should be addressed is the Māori input into RMA decision making in relation to such activities.

An interesting issue is whether this could be another place where the possible delegation of powers under section 33 of the RMA to iwi authorities is relevant. It is possible that, if an iwi is practising customary activities in an area, it may have a close traditional connection with, and even a guardianship role over, the area. Even if the stringent requirements for the proof of a territorial customary right – and thus creation of the reserve – cannot be met, it may still be appropriate that iwi exercise a decision making power over the area. And even if this decision making capability was not appropriate to the situation, there is definitely a greater role that Māori could and should play in the management of an area within which they exercise customary activities. It is a pity that this could not be progressed further before the foreshore and seabed legislative package was adopted.[109]

(vii) A more minor aspect with which I disagree also relates to the Schedule 12 controls: the reporting on the effects of a customary activity. As part of the determination of whether an activity is causing significant harm, regional councils have been given the functions of fact finding and reporting on the activity and its effects. The preparation of an environmental impact assessment of an activity is normally undertaken by an applicant for a resource consent, not by the decision maker on that application. Our existing resource management

---

109. There are other areas besides resource management where iwi hold decision making powers delegated from central government. For example, in respect of Māori child welfare. The Government has supported capacity building among iwi and then the transfer of some decision making powers in relation to the welfare of Māori children. In terms of principle, the standards in the legislation still apply – in this case, the paramountcy of the interests of the child – but Māori are acting as decision makers and exercising control over this extremely important aspect of their current and future self-determination. For more detail, see, for example, Iorns Magallanes 'A New Zealand Case Study: Maori Child Welfare' in Alison Quentin-Baxter (ed) *Recognising the Rights of Indigenous Peoples* (Institute of Policy Studies, Wellington, 1998).

regime allocates a decision making role to councils, not an application role. The Schedule 12 regime reverses this. Further, this role is mixed: both the Minister of Conservation *and* regional councils have this role, with the actions of the regional council being dependent to a large degree on actions of the Minister — indeed, in some cases acting at the direction of the Minister. This is a little unusual and not necessary. While it is comparatively minor compared with the other problems I have with this Act, it is not helpful.[110]

(viii) There are other difficulties with the overlapping and blurring of roles, compared with current processes. For example, the process whereby the holder of a customary rights order seeks change to a rule in a plan that is not consistent with their customary activities. It appears that the holder may bypass the normal processes and go straight to the Environment Court, which could cause confusion in the usual roles and processes.

In summary, the RMA has not worked for Māori as well as it might. But I consider that the solution is not to set up a parallel process of environmental protection for customary rights activities, but to make the Act work better in all circumstances, not just in relation to the very small area of customary rights orders. There should be stronger provisions in terms of joint decision making to better reflect a Treaty of Waitangi partnership in operation. Reforms could have been targeted at that aspect. Instead, in respect of resource management, what was sacrificed on the altar of political negotiation was the consistency and coherency of our environmental protection regime.[111]

I suggest that this sacrifice was a distraction away from the primary issue of Māori control over a wider range of decisions — and a range of decisions that are much more significant than those pertaining to the very narrow range of customary rights covered by the foreshore and seabed legislative package. Thus, while many aspects create the impression that there is strong protection for customary rights — especially the setting up of a parallel system outside normal legislative controls — there is not. It would have been stronger and more permanent to adopt rights on the basis of title rather than usage. Despite its appearances, I therefore suggest that it is really part of a move away from biculturalism and Treaty of Waitangi partnership and toward one of general

---

110. For more detail in argument against this aspect, see, for example, Local Government New Zealand *Submissions of Local Government New Zealand on Foreshore and Seabed Bill* <http://www.lgnz.co.nz> (last accessed 1 April 2005).
111. There have clearly been other sacrifices made for political reasons which affect more than environmental protection. For example, the legislated right of access to the foreshore and seabed (FSA, s 7) takes priority over the protection of wāhi tapu, unless already protected by other legislation. If a customary rights order is made by the Māori Land Court which relates to a wāhi tapu, and the Court finds that the right of access over it is inconsistent with the protection of the wāhi tapu, it is not protected unless the Minister of Conservation and Māori agree that it should be protected and gazette that restriction (FSA, ss 26 and 54). That is, a political assessment is made of its need for protection, not a purely legal assessment.

citizenship. Rights based on title are more permanent and enduring and there is thus more need to provide for them in the longer term. Rights based on usage are more malleable and less enduring, and thus more easily modified in the longer term.

VI Conclusion

This chapter has focused on the interface between environmental protection and the protection of Māori interests in the foreshore and seabed legislation. It suggests that both are wanting. Perhaps what is most interesting – from the perspective of an academic – is the interface between law and politics which has been evident throughout, from the initial application to the Māori Land Court, to the different legislative packages adopted to resolve the twin issues: recognition of customary rights (through the foreshore and seabed legislative package), and Māori access to marine farming (through the aquaculture reforms).

The extinguishment of title in return for the provisions adopted – especially the environmental trade-offs – could perhaps be likened to using a sledgehammer to crack a nut: the tool chosen is unnecessary and it has caused needless collateral damage. It is arguable that less damage would have been done if it had been left to the courts. It is clear that we still need to work toward a stronger Treaty of Waitangi partnership and decision making role in the resource and marine management area, and the Government has stated clear intentions to pursue this. But it appears that what has been pointlessly sacrificed along the way is the integrity and coherency of our environmental protection regime.

Overall, this is clearly an example of legislation driven by political judgment about societal needs – that is, rather than jurisprudential coherency or principle – and thus one which illustrates well how law is a tool of society and social ordering. As society and its perceived needs evolve, perhaps the package can be changed to better suit a future direction based on a stronger Treaty partnership.

Fiduciary Duties to Māori and the Foreshore and Seabed Act 2004: How Does it Compare and What Have Māori Lost?

Claire Charters*

I Introduction

One legal issue arising out of the Court of Appeal's decision in *Attorney-General v Ngati Apa* that drew surprisingly little public or academic scrutiny was this:[1] the potential for the Crown to have been held to fiduciary standards when dealing with Māori interests in the foreshore and seabed.[2] Crown fiduciary duties to Māori deserved more attention. They could have imposed substantial obligations on the Crown to the benefit of Māori; and the Government's foreshore and seabed policy, given effect in the Foreshore and Seabed Act 2004 (FSA), was to legislatively remove any fiduciary duty it owed to Māori.

Perhaps there was little criticism of the Government's fiduciary-duty policy because of the focus on other concerns, such as human rights and Treaty of Waitangi rights, the Government's rejection of the Waitangi Tribunal's report on the foreshore and seabed and the extinguishment of aboriginal title in

---

* Ngāti Whakaue. Senior Lecturer, Faculty of Law, Victoria University of Wellington and PhD Candidate, University of Cambridge. I sincerely thank Karen Jackson, for her comprehensive research assistance, and Jacinta Ruru, who provided insightful comments on an earlier draft of this paper. All errors and omissions remain my own.
1. *Attorney-General v Ngati Apa* [2003] 3 NZLR 643 (CA).
2. Although some did raise the issue of Crown fiduciary duties to Māori in relation to the foreshore and seabed. For example, see Alex Frame 'Submission to the Fisheries and Other Sea-Related Legislation Committee on the Foreshore and Seabed Bill 2004' 1–2. Further, others, such as Nanaia Mahuta, spoke of Crown fiduciary duties to Māori in parliamentary debates on the Foreshore and Seabed Bill. Unfortunately, it seems that Ms Mahuta mistakenly believed the Crown would still be subject to fiduciary duties to Māori under the Foreshore and Seabed Bill. See Nanaia Mahuta (16 November 2004) 621 *NZPD* 17207.

the foreshore and seabed. It may also be more simply explained by general uncertainty surrounding the contours of legally enforceable Crown fiduciary duties to Māori. Irrespective of the reasons for it, the relative silence on fiduciary duties was unfortunate. It enabled the Government to implement harsh policy with little public censure.

One of the principal purposes of this chapter is to make-up for the lack of consideration of potential Crown fiduciary duties to Māori in relation to their interests in the foreshore and seabed, and the FSA's treatment of them. First, I examine how New Zealand's legislative extinguishment of any Crown fiduciary duty to Māori in relation to the foreshore and seabed compares with law on Crown fiduciary duties to First Nations in Canada.

Second, and drawing on Canadian jurisprudence, I hypothesise how the fiduciary-duty doctrine might have applied to Crown dealings with Māori foreshore and seabed interests but for the enactment of the FSA. The purpose here is to quantify what Māori have lost as a result of the FSA's legislative override of the Crown's fiduciary duties. Of course, there are difficulties involved in such a contingent assessment. Any conclusions drawn must be recognised for what they are: an informed guess. Nonetheless, there is good reason to suggest that the potential for legal recognition of Crown fiduciary duties to Māori but for the FSA was strong.

Third, I suggest that a fair government, concerned to ensure that indigenous peoples' rights are protected in New Zealand as well as they are in other countries, would remedy the loss arising from legislative override of Crown fiduciary duties to Māori with redress.

II Fiduciary Duty

A Fiduciary duties

Fiduciary duties are enforceable obligations under equity.[3] While there are some relationships that are presumed to be fiduciary in nature, such as that between trustees and beneficiaries,[4] the courts will also find fiduciary duties in other circumstances. There is no general principle to explain when a relationship attracts fiduciary duties. However, case law suggests there are several indicia relevant in the assessment. They include: an undertaking to act in the interests

---

3. I particularly acknowledge Karen Jackson's research in relation to this section. It forms the basis of these 3 paragraphs.
4. *Keech v Sandford* (1726) Sel Cas T King 61; 25 ER 223. Other relationships in this category include those between: solicitor and client (*Boardman v Phipps* [1967] 2 AC 46 (HL); *Sims v Craig Bell & Bond* [1991] 3 NZLR 83 (CA)); director and company (*Pascoe Ltd v DFC Overseas Investments Ltd* [1994] 3 NZLR 627 (CA)); and partners (*Rama v Millar* [1996] 1 NZLR 527 (PC)).

of another;[5] a relationship of trust and confidence; disadvantage, vulnerability and unequal bargaining power (for example, the test from *Frame v Smith*);[6] and the objective expectations-based principle (exemplified in *LAC Minerals Ltd v International Corona Resources*).[7] The way in which the fiduciary principle is conceptualised will depend on the facts of the case, and courts have tended to leave the concept open. However, commentators suggest that there is growing judicial support for the view that 'a fiduciary is someone who has undertaken to act for or on behalf of another in a particular matter in circumstances which give rise to a relationship of trust and confidence.'[8]

The content of fiduciary obligations will vary according to the particular relationship. However, generally, 'equity mandates a demanding level of propriety of conduct exceeding the tortious standard of care and usually also the standards imposed by contracts.'[9] The standard of conduct required by the fiduciary can be described as 'selfless'.[10] Usually, a fiduciary must act for the beneficiary with undivided loyalty.[11] This means that a fiduciary must not, except with the informed consent of the beneficiary, place herself in a position where there is or may be a real and sensible possibility of a conflict between the duty as a fiduciary and her own interest or duty to a third party.[12] Further, a fiduciary must not make a profit out of her position as a fiduciary, except with the informed consent of the beneficiary.[13] Fiduciary duties can co-exist with other duties owed in tort and contract.

Claims for equitable relief are not subject to a statutory six-year limitation period unless the Court decides that the action should be limited by analogy with the other remedies claimed.[14] However, section 31 of the Limitation Act 1950 allows a claim for equitable relief to be met by the defences of laches (where a remedy is not pursued with due speed) and acquiescence (which includes estoppel and waiver). Equitable remedies (such as an injunction,

---

5. See Mason J in *Hospital Products Ltd v United States Surgical Corporation* (1984) 156 CLR 41, 69 (HCA).
6. *Frame v Smith* (1987) 42 DLR (4th) 81 (SCC). The test is set out on page 99:
   Relationships in which a fiduciary obligation have [sic] been imposed seem to possess three general characteristics:
   (1) The fiduciary has scope for the exercise of some discretion or power.
   (2) The fiduciary can unilaterally exercise that power or discretion so as to affect the beneficiary's legal or practical interests.
   (3) The beneficiary is peculiarly vulnerable to or at the mercy of the fiduciary holding the discretion or power.
7. *LAC Minerals Ltd v International Corona Resources* (1989) 61 DLR (4th) 14 (SCC).
8. John McGhee (ed) *Snell's Equity* (31 ed, Sweet and Maxwell, London, 2005) 148.
9. G E Dal Pont and D R C Chalmers *Equity and Trusts in Australia* (Lawbook Co, Pyrmont, 2004) 83.
10. P D Finn 'The Fiduciary Principle' in T G Youdan (ed) *Equity, Fiduciaries and Trusts* (Carswell, Ontario, 1989) 4.
11. Dal Pont and Chalmers, above n 9, 86; Dr Andrew S Butler (ed) *Equity and Trusts in New Zealand* (Brookers, Wellington, 2003) 344.
12. Dal Pont and Chalmers, above n 9, 86. This has been labelled the 'non-conflict duty'.
13. Dal Pont and Chalmers, above n 9, 86. This has been labelled the 'non-profit duty'.
14. Limitation Act 1950, s 4(9). See generally, Dr Andrew S Butler, above n 11, 964–968.

recision of a transaction in which a breach occurred, equitable damages for loss, or requiring the fiduciary to account for any unauthorised profits) are potentially available for a breach of fiduciary duty.

B THE SIGNIFICANCE OF FIDUCIARY DUTY DOCTRINE FOR MĀORI

The possibility that the Crown owes fiduciary duties to Māori is significant because, unlike the Treaty of Waitangi or unincorporated international law, the duties can be *directly enforced* in the courts.[15] Further, because equitable relief claims are excepted from statutory limitation periods, there is always the possibility of holding the Crown to account for historical breaches of its fiduciary duties.

It is unsurprising that the Crown should be subject to fiduciary duties in its dealings with indigenous peoples. The idea of the Crown protecting indigenous peoples is an old one, even if it is regularly honoured in breach. It is reflected in laws around the globe and in eighteenth- and nineteenth-century colonial policy.[16] Indeed, the assumption that the Crown acquired sovereignty in new territories, and in return owed guardianship duties to indigenous peoples, underlies much of the case law discussed in this chapter. On another note, this paternalistic overtone explains some indigenous peoples' reluctance to utilise fiduciary duty law to seek justice.[17]

III *The FSA and Fiduciary Duties*

The FSA comprehensively defeats any possible fiduciary claim by Māori against the Crown in relation to the foreshore and seabed, whether the claim is based on Māori legal interests in the foreshore and seabed before the enactment of

---

15. As a governmental publication has noted, '[t]he possibility of a claim based on common law fiduciary duty is significant because Treaty rights cannot be directly enforced by the courts unless referred to in legislation, whereas breaches of fiduciary duty can be considered and remedied by a court as part of its normal functions.' Te Puni Kōkiri *He Tirohanga o Kawa ki te Tiriti o Waitangi: A Guide to the Principles of the Treaty of Waitangi as expressed by the Courts and the Waitangi Tribunal* (Te Puni Kōkiri, Wellington, 2000) 66. Lanning writes, 'it is a model that is far less vulnerable to the changing tide of politics, and that has a clarity often lacking in arguments framed in constitutional law. One of the huge potential benefits for Maori, if a fiduciary relationship is established, is a wide array of remedial measures available for breach.' In G Lanning 'The Crown-Maori Relationship: the Spectre of a Fiduciary Relationship' (1997) 8 AULR 445, 446.
16. See Paul McHugh *Aboriginal Societies and the Common Law: A History of Sovereignty, Status and Self-Determination* (Oxford, Oxford University Press, 2005). For example, one of the reasons for the principle of inalienability of aboriginal title except to the Crown is protection of aboriginal peoples. See Kent McNeil 'Self-Government and the Inalienability of Aboriginal Title' [2001] 47 McGill L J 473, 477–481.
17. As discussed in Leonard I Rotman *Parallel Paths: Fiduciary Doctrine and Crown–Native Relations in Canada* (Toronto, University of Toronto Press, 1996).

the FSA, or results from the FSA.

Section 10(1) removes the High Court's pre-FSA jurisdiction to 'hear and determine ... any customary rights claim.' A 'customary rights claim' is defined as:[18]

> Any claim in respect of the public foreshore and seabed, that is based on, or relies on, customary rights, customary title, aboriginal rights, aboriginal title, the fiduciary duty of the Crown, or any rights, titles, or duties of a similar nature, whether arising before, on, or after the commencement of this section and whether or not the claim is based on, or relies on, any 1 or more of the following:
> a. a rule, principle, or practice of the common law or equity;
> b. the Treaty of Waitangi;
> c. the existence of a trust;
> d. an obligation of any kind.

Any possible fiduciary claim arising out of Māori legal interests in the foreshore and seabed before the enactment of the FSA is legislatively extinguished by the removal of the High Court's pre-FSA jurisdiction to hear and determine 'customary rights, customary title, aboriginal rights and aboriginal title' claims. Most fiduciary claims by aboriginal peoples arise out of such rights and titles; if courts cannot hear claims about them, they cannot source fiduciary-duty obligations in them. Potential Māori fiduciary-duty claims are most explicitly defeated by the removal of the High Court's jurisdiction to hear and determine claims based on the 'fiduciary duty of the Crown ... or duties of a similar nature.' To make things even more crystal clear, the FSA goes on remove the High Court's jurisdiction in foreshore- and seabed-related equitable, Treaty, trusts or 'obligation' claims, all of which might have sourced a Māori fiduciary-duty claim before the FSA came into force.

Similarly, the FSA removes the possibility of any fiduciary-duty claims based on Māori interests in the foreshore and seabed that may be recognised under the Māori Land Court's and High Court's 'replacement jurisdiction' under the FSA. As is discussed in other chapters in this book, the pre-FSA jurisdiction of the Māori Land Court and the High Court is replaced by limited jurisdictions to recognise, in specific and confined circumstances, customary rights orders (CROs) and territorial customary rights orders (TCROs). However, the potential that CROs or TCROs might form the basis of Crown fiduciary duties to Māori is legislatively overridden by the extension of section 10(2) to fiduciary-duty claims arising after the commencement of the FSA and section 13(4). Section 13(4) states 'the Crown does not owe any fiduciary obligation, or obligation of a similar nature, to any person in respect of the public foreshore and seabed.'

---

18. Foreshore and Seabed Act 2004 (FSA), s 10 (2).

IV Comparison with Canadian Law

A INTRODUCTION

How does New Zealand's legislative override of any Māori claim based on Crown fiduciary duties in relation to the foreshore and seabed compare to law in Canada? The answer is a resounding one: poorly.

I have chosen Canada as the point of comparison because, despite some significant constitutional differences to New Zealand, most Canadian law relating to Crown fiduciary duties to indigenous peoples does not turn on these. While aboriginal and treaty rights have constitutional protection under the Canadian Constitution Act 1982,[19] unlike in New Zealand, they are not the source of, nor reason behind, Executive fiduciary duties to First Nations.[20] In addition, Canada has been at the forefront of the evolution of law on the Crown fiduciary duties to indigenous peoples, as is illustrated by the important decision of the Supreme Court of Canada in *Haida Nation v British Columbia (Minister of Forests)* (*Haida Nation*).[21] Finally, of overseas jurisprudence, Canadian law on fiduciary duties has been most frequently cited positively in New Zealand case law, as will be discussed in the next part of this chapter.[22]

Obviously, it is important that the comparison between the law on fiduciary duties to indigenous peoples in Canada and New Zealand is fair (that is, it compares oranges with oranges). The FSA *only* extinguishes potential claims based on Crown fiduciary duties to Māori in relation to the foreshore and seabed. It does not extinguish potential claims based on Crown fiduciary duties to Māori in relation to other interests – for example, in other land,

---

19. Constitution Act 1982, s 35.
20. As Kent McNeil writes, 'The fiduciary obligations which arise are not, however, contingent on the constitutional recognition and affirmation of Aboriginal and treaty rights by s 35(1) of the Constitution Act 1982.' See Kent McNeil 'Section 91(24) Powers, the Inherent Right of Self-Government, and Canada's Fiduciary Obligations' (Research paper prepared for the Office of the BC Regional Vice-Chief of the Assembly of First Nations (August 2002)). United States' jurisprudence on fiduciary duties to indigenous peoples, in contrast and while still relevant, stems from nearly centuries-old judicial recognition and enforcement of the guardian–ward relationship between the Federal Government and inherently sovereign Indian tribes. This originates in the famous passage from Marshall CJ's decision in *Cherokee Nation v Georgia* (1831) 30 US (5 Pet) 1, 17:
    > Though the Indians are acknowledged to have an unquestionable, and, heretofore, unquestioned right to the lands they occupy, until that right shall be extinguished by a voluntary cession to our government; yet it may well be doubted whether those tribes which reside within the acknowledged boundaries of the United States can, with strict accuracy, be denominated foreign nations. They may, more correctly be denominated domestic dependent nations. They occupy a territory to which we assert a title independent of their will, which must take effect in point of possession when their right of possession ceases. Meanwhile, they are in a state of pupilage. Their relation to the United States resembles that of a ward to his guardian.
21. *Haida Nation v British Columbia (Minister of Forests)* [2004] 3 SCR 511.
22. See *Te Runanga o Muriwhenua Inc v Attorney-General* [1990] 2 NZLR 641 (CA), *Te Runanga o Wharekauri Rekohu Inc v Attorney-General* [1993] 2 NZLR 301 (CA) and *Te Runanganui o Te Ika Whenua Inc Society v Attorney-General* [1994] 2 NZLR 20 (CA).

activities such as fishing, or the management of Māori funds.²³ The appropriate comparison, then, is to Canadian law on governmental fiduciary duties to First Nations in relation to foreshore and seabed interests only.

Canadian First Nations' interests in the foreshore and seabed have not yet been the exclusive basis of a fiduciary-duty case in Canada. However, there appears to be no reason why Canadian courts would apply different fiduciary standards to Crown dealings with First Nations' foreshore and seabed interests than to First Nations' interests in other geographical areas. Superficially, this may seem to be a bold statement as the issue is complicated by the view, based on the Australian High Court decision in *Yarmirr v Northern Territory* (*Yarmirr*), that the common law cannot recognise full territorial aboriginal title in the foreshore and seabed in the same way it does dry land.²⁴ At first glance, this would appear to affect the application of jurisprudence on Crown fiduciary duties to indigenous peoples in relation to the foreshore and seabed, because aboriginal title is a source of Crown fiduciary duties to indigenous peoples in Canada. However, as we will see, aboriginal title is not the only source of Crown fiduciary duties to indigenous peoples. Crown fiduciary duties arise equally in relation to indigenous peoples' non-territorial aboriginal rights. And, there is no suggestion that the common law cannot recognise non-territorial rights in the foreshore and seabed. Further, it seems highly unlikely that Canadian courts would adopt a similar approach to that of the Australian High Court in *Yarmirr*: common law aboriginal title is markedly different in Australia than it is in Canada;²⁵ and there has been no suggestion by Canadian courts that aboriginal title in the foreshore and seabed would be treated differently from other land cases including claims to the offshore.²⁶

---

23. Notably, though, the potential for claims based on fiduciary duties in relation to other land interests is seriously curtailed by the sad fact that aboriginal title to most dry land in New Zealand has been extinguished.
24. *Commonwealth v Yarmirr* (2001) 184 ALR 184. For example, the New Zealand Government argued, on the basis of that decision, that the foreshore and seabed is a 'special juridical space'. See Waitangi Tribunal *Report on the Crown's Foreshore and Seabed Policy: Wai 1071* (Legislation Direct, Wellington, 2004) 83.
25. See discussion in Shaunnagh Dorsett's chapter in this book, 59–82.
26. As pointed out by Shaunnagh Dorsett in her chapter in this book, 59–82, claims relating to aboriginal title in the off-shore were not considered exceptional in *R v Marshall* (2004) 218 NSR (2d) 78 (NSCA) or *Haida Nation*, above n 21. She similarly points out in a footnote that the Canadian Federal Government's policy relating to the settlement of native claims recognises that negotiations may include offshore areas: Indian and Northern Affairs *Federal Policy for the Settlement of Native Claims* (Indian and Northern Affairs, Ottawa, 1993) 10.

B CANADIAN LAW ON GOVERNMENTAL FIDUCIARY DUTIES TO ABORIGINAL PEOPLES

1. Duties on Executive Government

As mentioned in the introduction, judicial recognition of governmental fiduciary duties to First Nations in specific circumstances is common. Nonetheless, uncertainties remain about the exact source and content of law on governmental fiduciary duties to First Nations in Canada. As Rotman writes, 'in becoming axiomatic, it has obviated judicial perceptions of the need to flesh out the meaning and implications of describing those relations as fiduciary.'[27] Ambiguity is not surprising. It may be explained as inherent in an equitable doctrine applied to evolving circumstances between different polities. It also does not prevent us from isolating the broad contours of the doctrine under Canadian law.

Guerin v The Queen (*Guerin*) is the seminal Canadian decision.[28] With one exception, all Justices found that the Crown owed fiduciary duties to a Band that had surrendered reserve land to the Crown for the Crown to lease on the Band's behalf. Dickson J, delivering what is regarded as the leading judgment, sourced the fiduciary duty in the Band's aboriginal title, the Crown's right of pre-emption over aboriginal title and the Indian Act, under which the surrender was entered into.[29] He also emphasised the sui generis nature of the relationship between First Nations and government, going to some lengths to distinguish fiduciary duties to First Nations from 'public law' duties.[30] Dickson J drew on 'mainstream' fiduciary-duty law to establish the specific duties highlighting, in particular, the significance of Crown undertakings to the Band and the Crown's discretionary power over the Band's interests.[31] Unlike

---

27. Leonard I Rotman '*Wewaykum:* A New Spin on the Crown's Fiduciary Obligations to Aboriginal Peoples' (2004) 37 UBC Law Review 219, 222.
28. *Guerin v The Queen* [1984] 2 SCR 335.
29. *Guerin*, above n 28, 376 Dickson J:
    > The fiduciary relationship between the Crown and Indians has its root in the concept of aboriginal, native or Indian title. The fact that Indian bands have certain interest in lands does not, however, in itself give rise to a fiduciary relationship between the Indians and the Crown. The conclusion that the Crown is a fiduciary depends upon the further proposition that the Indian interest in the land is inalienable except upon the surrender to the Crown.
30. *Guerin,* above n 28, 385 Dickson J:
    > [T]he Crown is not normally viewed as a fiduciary in the exercise of its legislative or administrative function. The mere fact, however, that it is the Crown which is obligated to act on the Indians' behalf does not of itself remove the Crown's obligation from the scope of the fiduciary principle ... the Indians' interest in land is an independent legal interest. It is not a creation of either the legislation or executive branches of government. The Crown's obligation to the Indians with respect to that interest is therefore not public law duty ... Therefore, in this sui generis relationship, it is not improper to regard the Crown as a fiduciary.
31. *Guerin*, above n 28, 384 Dickson J:
    > Where by statute, agreement, or perhaps by unilateral undertaking, one party has an obligation to act for the benefit of another, and that obligation carries with it a discretionary power, the party thus empowered becomes a fiduciary. Equity will then supervise the relationship by holding him to the fiduciary's strict standard of conduct.

Wilson J, who wrote the other significant judgment in *Guerin*, Dickson J did not find that the relationship established a trust,[32] and held that the fiduciary duty arose only on the surrender of the land. The Court found that the Crown breached its fiduciary duty because it entered into a lease much less valuable than the one promised, and substantial damages were awarded.

Shortly after *Guerin*, the Federal Court of Appeal in *R v Kruger* held that Crown fiduciary duties can equally arise where the Crown expropriates First Nations' lands,[33] subsequently confirmed by the Supreme Court of Canada in *R v Sparrow* (*Sparrow*) and more recently in *Osoyoos Indian Band v Oliver (Town of)* (*Osoyoos*).[34] *Sparrow* also extended the reach of fiduciary-duty obligations to cover Crown extinguishment of non-territorial aboriginal rights.

The Crown was held to owe a fiduciary duty to the Blueberry River Indian Band in relation to surrendered mineral rights in the Supreme Court of Canada decision of 1995 in *Blueberry River Indian Band v Canada (Department of Indian Affairs and Northern Development)* (*Blueberry River*).[35] McLachlin J found that, prior to the surrender of Band lands to the Crown, the Crown was under a fiduciary duty to prevent exploitative bargains, that is, it must veto Band decisions to surrender where the terms of the surrender are exploitative.[36] The Federal Court of Appeal followed this reasoning in *Semiahmoo Indian Band v Canada* (*Semiahmoo*).[37] It found that the Crown had breached its fiduciary duty because it did not withhold its consent to the Semiahmoo's decision to surrender its land in circumstances where the surrender was exploitative.[38] In that case, the Court considered the Band vulnerable because its decision to surrender was influenced by knowledge of the Crown's power to expropriate irrespective of the Band's decision to surrender or not. In addition, the Crown, when seeking the surrender, had no specific development plans for the land.[39]

It was implicit in *Blueberry River* that the specific circumstances of the relationship between the Crown and a First Nations Band determine the content

---

32. *Guerin*, above n 28, 376 Dickson J:
    In my view, the nature of Indian title and the framework of the statutory scheme established for disposing of Indian land places upon the Crown an equitable obligation, enforceable by the courts, to deal with land for the benefit of the Indians. The obligation does not amount to a trust in the private law sense. It is rather a fiduciary duty. If, however, the Crown breaches this fiduciary duty it will be liable to Indians in the same way and to the same extent as if such a trust were in effect.
33. *R v Kruger* (1985) 17 DLR (4th) 591 (FCA).
34. *R v Sparrow* [1990] 1 SCR 1075 and *Osoyoos Indian Band v Oliver (Town of)* [2001] 3 SCR 746.
35. *Blueberry River Indian Band v Canada (Department of Indian Affairs and Northern Development)* [1995] 4 SCR 344 (McLachlin J).
36. *Blueberry River*, above n 35, paras 33–35 (McLachlin J).
37. *Semiahmoo Indian Band v Canada* [1998] 1 FC 3 (CA).
38. *Semiahmoo*, above n 37, paras 41–48 Isaac CJ (McDonald JA and Gray DJ concurring).
39. *Semiahmoo*, above n 37, paras 42–43 Isaac CJ (McDonald JA and Gray DJ concurring). See also paragraph 45: 'Even if the land at issue is required for a public purpose, the Crown cannot discharge its fiduciary obligation simply by convincing the Band to accept the surrender, and then using this consent to relieve itself of the responsibility to scrutinize the transaction.'

of the Crown's fiduciary duty to First Nations Bands.[40] In that particular case, the duty of the Crown was described as 'that of a man of ordinary prudence in managing his own affairs' prior to surrender.[41] Further, McLachlin J held that Crown fiduciary duties continue even after they are breached; it is under an obligation to correct that breach if it is able to do so.[42] The Federal Court of Canada described the content of the Crown's fiduciary duty like this in *Fairford First Nation v Canada (Attorney-General)* (*Fairford*): 'A fiduciary must deal with the property he is entrusted to look after as if it was his own. The fiduciary must act with reasonable skill and diligence.'[43]

The *Fairford* Court held that the Crown breached its fiduciary duty to Fairford First Nation when it did not consult with the First Nation about its negotiations with a provincial government in relation to a compensation land agreement for flooding of the First Nation's lands.[44]

The Supreme Court of Canada elaborated on the Crown's fiduciary duties where it expropriates reserve lands for a public purpose in *Osoyoos*.[45] Iacobucci J, delivering the majority judgment, wrote:[46]

> once it has been determined that an expropriation of Indian lands is in the public interest, a fiduciary duty arises on the part of the Crown to expropriate or grant only the minimum interest required in order to fulfil that public purpose, thus ensuring a minimal impairment of the use and enjoyment of Indian lands by the band ... In this way, instead of having the public interest trump the Indian interests, the approach I advocate attempts to reconcile the two interests involved.

The Supreme Court of Canada's decision in *Wewaykum Indian Band v Canada* (*Wewaykum*) is one of its most important on Crown fiduciary duties to First

---

40. As followed by the Federal Court of Appeal in *Semiahmoo* where the Court stated that '[t]he authorities on fiduciary duties establish that courts must assess the specific relationship between the parties in order to determine whether or not it gives rise to a fiduciary duty and, if yes, to determine the nature and scope of that duty.' (*Semiahmoo*, above n 28, para 37 Isaac CJ (McDonald JA and Gray DJ concurring).
41. *Blueberry River*, above n 35, para 104 McLachlin J (citing *Fales v Canada Permanent Trust Co* [1977] 2 SCR 302).
42. *Blueberry River*, above n 35, para 115 McLachlin J.
43. *Fairford First Nation v Canada (Attorney-General)* [1999] 2 FC 48, para 221 (TD) Rothstein J.
44. *Fairford*, above n 43.
45. *Osoyoos*, above n 34.
46. *Osoyoos*, above n 34, para 52 Iacobucci J. He goes on to write at paragraph 53:
    This two-step process minimizes any inconsistency between the Crown's public duty to expropriate lands and its fiduciary duty to Indians whose lands are affected by the expropriation. In the first stage, the Crown acts in the public interest in determining that an expropriation involving Indian lands is required in order to fulfill some public purpose. At this stage, no fiduciary duty exists. However, once the general decision to expropriate has been made, the fiduciary obligations of the Crown arise, requiring the Crown to expropriate an interest that will fulfill the public purpose while preserving the Indian interest in the land to the greatest extent practicable.

Nations since *Guerin*.⁴⁷ The Court broadened the source of fiduciary duties to include the relationship between aboriginal peoples and the Crown more generally rather than, for example, confining it to aboriginal title and the Crown's right of pre-emption, as was indicated in *Guerin*. Instead, the Court refers to the historical reality that 'the degree of economic, social and proprietary control and discretion asserted by the Crown also left aboriginal populations vulnerable to the risks of government misconduct and ineptitude.'⁴⁸ However, Binnie J, writing for the Court, hastens to add that the fiduciary duty is not a source of 'plenary Crown liability covering all aspects of Crown–Indian Band relationship.'⁴⁹ Instead, Crown fiduciary duties exist in relation to specific Indian interests, which include non-territorial interests (as *Sparrow* also held). In each case courts must consider whether the Crown has assumed 'discretionary control' over specific Indian interests.⁵⁰ On the facts at hand, the Court found that a fiduciary duty arose out of the Crown's activities to create a reserve for the Bands in question.

The Court also devoted attention to the content of Crown fiduciary duties to Indian bands, stating that 'the content of the Crown's fiduciary duty towards aboriginal peoples varies with the nature and importance of the interest sought to be protected.'⁵¹ It suggested a sliding scale with greater duties where the Indian interest is strong and lesser duties where the Indian interest is relatively weak, such as a Band's interest in land prior to creation of a reserve. In the latter case, third parties' interests may also be relevant and the duty is 'limited to the basic obligations of loyalty, good faith in the discharge of its mandate, providing full disclosure appropriate to the subject matter, and acting with ordinary prudence with a view to the best interests of the aboriginal beneficiaries.'⁵² However, once a reserve is created 'the content of the Crown's fiduciary duty expands to include the protection and preservation of the band's quasi-proprietary interest in the reserve from exploitation.'⁵³

The recent Supreme Court of Canada's unanimous decision in *Haida Nation* sheds new light on the Crown's obligations to First Nations. It is not strictly a fiduciary-duty decision in the sense the Court ruled that the Crown does *not* owe fiduciary duties to First Nations' Bands in relation to unproven and unspecific aboriginal rights and title, the interests at stake in the case. However,

---

47. Rotman writes, 'the Court engaged in its most substantive discussion of Crown-Native fiduciary relations since it sanctioned the fiduciary nature of Crown–Native interaction in its landmark judgment in *Guerin*.' '*Wewaykum*: A New Spin on the Crown's Fiduciary Obligations to Aboriginal Peoples?', above n 27, 219–220.
48. *Wewaykum Indian Band v Canada* (*Wewaykum*) [2002] 4 SCR 245, para 80 Binnie J for the Court.
49. *Wewaykum*, above n 48, para 81 Binnie J for the Court.
50. *Wewaykum*, above n 48, para 79 Binnie J for the Court.
51. *Wewaykum*, above n 48, above n 53, para 86 Binnie J for the Court.
52. *Wewaykum*, above n 48, para 86 Binnie J for the Court.
53. *Wewaykum*, above n 48, para 86 Binnie J for the Court.

in a relatively progressive move it imposed 'honour of the Crown' duties on the Crown in relation to such interests.[54] The strength of such duties was held to differ according to the strength of a Band's case for aboriginal title and the potentially adverse effect upon the right or title claimed; ranging from relatively weak consultation requirements to accommodation of the Band's interests.[55] The duty arises 'when the Crown has knowledge, real or constructive, of the potential existence of the aboriginal right or title and contemplates conduct that might adversely affect it.'[56]

What was particularly interesting from a fiduciary-duty perspective was that the Court situated the source of Crown fiduciary duties in the broad concept of the honour of the Crown. This seems to be a revision of early cases that sourced the Crown's fiduciary duties in discrete concepts such as aboriginal title and the Crown's right of pre-emption (*Guerin*). On the other hand, it appears to be in line with more recent decisions such as that in *Wewaykum*, which sourced the Crown's fiduciary duties in the more generic relationship between the Crown and First Nations. What this means is that where First Nations have unspecific and unproven aboriginal rights, the honour of the Crown demands consultation and, at the higher end of the scale, accommodation. However, where the First Nations have specific and proven interests (say, where they have proven aboriginal title), the honour of the Crown demands that the Crown is subject to fiduciary duties.[57]

---

54. *Haida Nation*, above n 21, para 27 McLachlin CJ for the Court:
    The Crown, acting honourably, cannot cavalierly run roughshod over Aboriginal interests where claims affecting these interests are being seriously pursued in the process of treaty negotiation and proof. It must respect these potential, but yet unproven, interests. The Crown is not rendered impotent. It may continue to manage the resource in question pending claims resolution. But, depending on the circumstances […] the honour of the Crown may require it to consult with and reasonably accommodate Aboriginal interests pending resolution of the claim. To unilaterally exploit a claimed resource during the process of proving and resolving the Aboriginal claim to that resource, may be to deprive the Aboriginal claimants of some or all of the benefit of that resource. That is not honourable.
55. *Haida Nation*, above n 21, para 39 McLachlin CJ for the Court.
    The content of the duty to consult and accommodate varies with the circumstances. Precisely what duties arise in different situations will be defined as the case law in this emerging area develops. In general terms, however, it may be asserted that the scope of the duty is proportionate to a preliminary assessment of the strength of the cases supporting the existence of the right or title, and the seriousness of the potentially adverse effect upon the right or title claimed.
56. *Haida Nation*, above n 21, para 35 McLachlin CJ for the Court.
57. While the honour of the Crown concept seems to resolve some of the confusion surrounding the origins of the Crown's fiduciary duties to First Nations, its boundaries remain unknown. This is especially true given that the Court sourced the honour of the Crown in 'the Crown's assertion of sovereignty over Aboriginal people and defacto control of land and resources that were formally in the control of that people.' *Haida Nation*, above n 21, para 32 McLachlin CJ for the Court. The Court acknowledges this at paragraph 11, commenting that 'this case is the first of its kind to reach this Court. Our task is the modest one of establishing a general framework for the duty to consult and accommodate, where indicated, before Aboriginal title and rights claims have been decided. As this framework is applied, courts, in the age-old tradition of the common law will be called on to fill on the details of the duty to consult and accommodate.'

2 Duties on the Legislature

The Canadian legislature must also conform to fiduciary standards when enacting laws that infringe upon constitutionally protected aboriginal and treaty rights in Canada. The Supreme Court of Canada held in its pivotal *Sparrow* decision that aboriginal rights, constitutionally protected under section 35 of the Constitution Act 1982, could only be infringed if the Crown can prove that the infringement is pursuant to a valid legislative objective and respects its fiduciary obligations to the First Nations in question.[58] In relation to the valid legislative objective, the Court held that 'public interest' does not in and of itself constitute a valid objective as it is too vague.[59] On the fiduciary-duty limb of the test, the Court required aboriginal rights to be given some priority over others' rights and interests. In addition, factors such as whether there has been as little infringement as possible, fair compensation and consultation would be relevant in an assessment of the Crown's compliance with its fiduciary obligations.[60]

It could be argued that the Court has withdrawn somewhat from the highwater mark it set in *Sparrow* in relation to justifications for infringements of aboriginal and treaty rights.[61] In *R v Gladstone (Gladstone)*, the majority seemed to elevate third-party interests in the assessment of whether the Crown had complied with its fiduciary obligations.[62] However, other cases, such as *R v Adams*, have fortified the *Sparrow* decision by holding that legislative conferral of broad powers to the Executive that do not limit the Executive's power to infringe aboriginal rights fail to satisfy the legislature's fiduciary obligations.[63]

Finally, under *R v Van der Peet*, fiduciary duties were held to necessitate a liberal interpretation of treaties and statutory provisions affecting aboriginal interests in favour of aboriginal peoples.[64]

---

58. *Sparrow*, above n 34.
59. *Sparrow*, above n 34, 1113.
60. *Sparrow*, above n 34, 1119 Dickson CJ and La Forest J for the Court. The Supreme Court elaborated on the consultation requirement in *Delgamuukw v British Columbia* [1997] 3 SCR 1010.
61. See Kent McNeil 'The Vulnerability of Indigenous Rights in Australia and Canada' [2004] 42 Osgoode Hall L J 271, 290.
62. *R v Gladstone* [1996] 2 SCR 723, para 62 Lamer CJ. Lamer CJ for the Majority writes:
    > Where the aboriginal right is one that has no internal limitation then the doctrine of priority does not require that, after conservation goals have been met, the government allocate the fishery so that those holding an aboriginal right to exploit that fishery are given an exclusive right to do so. Instead, the doctrine of priority requires that the government demonstrate that, in allocating the resource, it has taken account of the existence of aboriginal rights and allocated in a manner respectful to the fact that those rights have priority over the exploitation of the fishery over other users.
63. *R v Adams* [1996] 3 SCR 101.
64. *R v Van der Peet* [1996] 2 SCR 507.

C GOVERNMENTAL FIDUCIARY DUTIES TO AMERICAN INDIANS IN THE UNITED STATES AND UNDER INTERNATIONAL LAW

Canadian law on Crown fiduciary duties to indigenous peoples is not unique. Similar jurisprudence exists in the United States and under international law.

1   United States

The source of the United States' trust responsibilities to Indians is in their status as 'domestic dependent nations' as famously declared by Chief Justice Marshall in 1831 in *Cherokee Nation v State of Georgia*.[65] He described Indian tribes as being 'in a state of pupilage; their relation to the United States resembles that of a ward to his guardian.'[66] Initially, this passage was used by the courts in the late nineteenth century to ground Congress' plenary power over Indians in notorious cases such as *United States v Kagama* and *Lone Wolf v Hitchcock*.[67] More recently, it has been used to source limitations on the Executive's power.

While some earlier cases suggest that the Executive's trust duties must be linked to specific treaties, statutes or the like, more recent cases have been more expansive.[68] For example, the United States Supreme Court found the Executive to be subject to duties where it assumes control over Indian monies and properties.[69]

Further, while there is some confusion surrounding the content of fiduciary duties owed by the Executive where they arise, ranging from an 'exacting standard' to lesser duties,[70] they can extend to both Indians not living on reservations and tribes that are not federally recognised.[71] The trust relationship has been the basis for interpreting Indian treaties in favour of Indians.[72] However, trust duties are not imposed on Congress. As Clayton Reid concludes: 'Reading all the cases together, the principle that emerges is that Congress intends

---

65. *Cherokee Nation v Georgia*, above n 20, 17 Marshall CJ.
66. *Cherokee Nation v Georgia*, above n 20, 17 Marshall CJ.
67. The United States Supreme Court held in *Kagama* that '[f]rom [Indian Nations'] weakness and helplessness, so largely due to the course of dealing of the Federal Government with them, and the treaties in which it has been promised, there arises a duty of protection and with that power.' *United States v Kagama* (1886) 118 US 375, 384.
68. See *United States v Creek Nation* (1935) 295 US 103, *Lane v Pueblo of Santa Rosa* (1918) 249 US 110, *Cramer v United States* (1923) 261 US 219, *Pyramid Land Paiute Tribe of Nations v Morton* (1973) 352 F Supp 252, and *Manchester Band of Pomo Indians v United States* (1973) 363 F Supp 1238.
69. In *United States v Mitchell* (1983) 463 US 206 the Court stated that fiduciary obligations exist where:
    [T]he Federal Government takes on or has control or supervision over tribal monies or properties (unless Congress has provided otherwise) even though nothing is said expressly in the authorising or underlying status (or other fundamental document) about a trust fund, or a trust or fiduciary connection.
70. In *Seminole Nation v United States* (1942) 316 US 286, 297 and *Nevada v United States* (1983) 463 US 110.
71. In *Morton v Ruiz* (1974) 415 US 199 and *Joint Tribal Council of Passamaquoddy Tribe v Morton* (1975) 528 F 2d 370 (1st Cir) respectively.
72. *County of Oneida v Oneida Indian Nation* (1985) 470 US 226.

specific adherence to the trust responsibility by executive officials unless it has expressly provided otherwise. Such a formulation preserves the role of Congress as the ultimate umpire of the purposes of the trust relationship while requiring strict executive compliance with the terms of the trust.'[73]

2   Australia

Australian law on Crown fiduciary duties to aboriginal peoples is underdeveloped, but exists in principle. Toohey J in *Mabo v State of Queensland (No 2)* (*Mabo (No 2)*) accepted, based on *Guerin*, that the Crown could be subject to fiduciary duties in relation to aboriginal title interests.[74] The Crown's duties included acting for the advantage of beneficiaries and not in one's own or a third party's interests.[75] They also included the obligation to ensure that traditional title is not impaired or destroyed without consent or otherwise contrary to the interests of the titleholders. Finally, Crown extinguishment or impairment of native title without consent would, Toohey J stated, breach the Crown's fiduciary duty.[76]

3   International Law

Fiduciary-duty jurisprudence in Canada, the United States and Australia is supported by international law. The international principle of guardianship has evolved from early interaction between European colonising states and indigenous peoples.[77] Paul McHugh identifies a common theme in state practice vis-à-vis indigenous peoples and comments that '[t]he theme lies in the dominant colonising power's protestations of its "guardianship" over the colonised indigenous community ... International law specified and continues to define the duties of the guardian and the rights of the indigenous community. In this way, substance is given to the concept of "guardianship".'[78]

These comments are supported by the international legal doctrine of good faith that is applicable to treaties between states and indigenous peoples.[79]

---

73. Clayton Reid 'Judicial Enforcement of the Federal Trust Responsibility to Indians' (1975) 27 Stan L Rev 1213, 1248.
74. *Mabo v State of Queensland (No 2)* (1992) 175 CLR 1, 202–203 Toohey J (HCA).
75. *Mabo (No 2)*, above n 74, 204 Toohey J.
76. *Mabo (No 2)*, above n 74, 204 Toohey J.
77. Paul McHugh *The Maori Magna Carta: New Zealand Law and the Treaty of Waitangi* (Auckland, Oxford University Press, 1991) 189–193.
78. *The Maori Magna Carta: New Zealand Law and the Treaty of Waitangi*, above n 68, 192.
79. See, for example, Benedict Kingsbury 'The Treaty of Waitangi: Some International Law Aspects' in Kawharu (ed) *Waitangi: Maori and Pakeha Perspectives* (Oxford University Press, Auckland, 1989) 121.

D Comparison between Canadian and New Zealand Law on Fiduciary Duties to Indigenous Peoples

In New Zealand the FSA comprehensively statutorily bars possible fiduciary-duty claims in relation to Māori interests in the foreshore and seabed.

In comparison, legislation like the FSA would probably be invalid in Canada for the simple reason that it unjustifiably extinguishes constitutionally protected aboriginal title and aboriginal rights. As we have seen, 'public interest', a rationale behind the Government's enactment of the FSA, is not a valid objective under Canadian law (*Sparrow*). Even if another Government rationale for the FSA – certainty – were considered a valid objective, the FSA falls well short of the Canadian fiduciary-duty-based justificatory requirement that rights-infringing legislation should limit rights to the least degree possible. The Government did not need to extinguish all Māori aboriginal rights in the foreshore and seabed to achieve certainty.

However, more specifically, clauses barring fiduciary duty claims by indigenous peoples could independently fall short of the Canadian Constitution Act's protection of aboriginal and treaty rights. While the Crown's fiduciary-duty obligations are not explicitly protected as aboriginal and treaty rights, the fiduciary duty is inextricably linked to those rights. The Crown must not fall below certain standards when dealing with those exact rights under the fiduciary-duty principles developed by Canadian courts. In this sense, the fiduciary-duty obligations are part and parcel of aboriginal and treaty rights. No doubt, a good argument could also be made that Crown fiduciary duties are inherent in certain treaties between the Canadian Crown and First Nations.

That the FSA – perfectly legal under New Zealand law as an exercise of parliamentary power – would likely be invalid in Canada is a conclusion that rests on fundamental constitutional distinctions between Canada and New Zealand. In contrast, Canadian law on Executive fiduciary duties does not rest on such fundamental differences, as mentioned above.

In Canada, unproven aboriginal title and non-territorial aboriginal rights, like those that Māori groups had before their extinguishment under the FSA, would impose enforceable obligations of consultation and accommodation on the Crown, depending on the strength of the claim and the potential adverse effect of proposed Crown action (*Haida Nation*). Were an aboriginal title or aboriginal right claim proved, the Canadian Crown would be under the obligation to prevent exploitative bargains in relation to that title or right (*Blueberry River* and *Semiahmoo*). Similarly, it would be required to conform to certain standards were it creating a reserve for a Band relating to its proven foreshore and seabed aboriginal rights and title (*Wewaykum*). Were the Crown to expropriate foreshore and seabed subject to proven aboriginal title or rights, or an aboriginal Band to surrender such land to the Crown, the Crown would be subject to more onerous duties (*Guerin* and *Osoyoos*), even if the expropriation or surrender would be in the public interest. In addition, if the Crown breached its duties, it would be required to make good its error (*Blueberry River*). Shed in this light, it is clear that the FSA's provisions on fiduciary duties are inferior to comparable law in Canada.

V What Have Māori Lost Under the FSA in Relation to Crown Fiduciary Duties?

A INTRODUCTION

The purpose of this section is to quantify what Māori have lost as a result of the FSA's statutory prohibition of Māori fiduciary-duty-based claims in relation to the foreshore and seabed. It is a hypothetical assessment. As we have seen, section 13(4) legislatively declares that the Crown does not owe any fiduciary duty in relation to the public foreshore and seabed (the area over which Māori could raise fiduciary-duty claims).

Nonetheless, it is possible to accurately assess the Crown's fiduciary obligations to Māori in relation to the foreshore and seabed immediately before the enactment of the FSA. New Zealand law on Crown fiduciary duties to Māori is known, even if there are uncertainties relating to its application. Māori interests in the foreshore and seabed before the FSA – the source of Crown fiduciary duties – are also known, being unproven aboriginal rights and title.

The assessment of what Māori have lost in relation to fiduciary duties post the enactment of the FSA is more speculative for the simple reason that it is unclear what interests Māori would have been able to prove in the foreshore and seabed if the FSA had not been enacted. In other words, we do not know the nature of the Māori interests that would have sourced and determined the content of a fiduciary claim but for the FSA, that is, had common law aboriginal title and rights and the Māori Land Court's jurisdiction to determine Māori customary title not been replaced by the FSA regime. But it is also important not to exaggerate the degree of uncertainty. We do know that if under the replacement regime the Māori Land Court finds CROs in the foreshore and seabed, or the High Court TCROs, it is highly likely that Māori could have proved more robust territorial and non-territorial rights but for the FSA.[80] The FSA curtails rather than expands previously applicable common law and the

---

80. The FSA restricts the pre-existing common law and Te Ture Whenua Maori Act 1993 tests to establish aboriginal title and rights and customary title respectively.

Māori Land Court's prior jurisdiction.

The Government's argument that Māori would not have been able to establish common law aboriginal title in the foreshore and seabed in any event, based on *Yarmirr* and discussed above, would not have defeated potential Crown fiduciary duties in relation to Māori foreshore and seabed interests. It is a contestable argument in the first place as it assumes Australian jurisprudence would be applied wholesale in New Zealand without reference to the Treaty of Waitangi and irrespective of the unique statutory regime within which Australian native title jurisprudence operates.[81] Regardless, as we have seen in *Sparrow*, and based on a New Zealand case discussed below, non-territorial aboriginal rights can equally source Crown fiduciary duties. The Government has always accepted that Māori could prove non-territorial aboriginal rights in the foreshore and seabed. In fact, many of the FSA's CRO provisions are predicated on that assumption.

Finally, but for sections 10 and 13(4) of the FSA, the Crown could well have been subject to fiduciary duties in its dealings with Māori CROs and TCROs capable of recognition under the High Court's and Māori Land Court's FSA 'replacement' jurisdiction. Again, the content of this duty is perfectly quantifiable as, once the first CROs and TCROs are recognised, the source of the fiduciary duty is known.

There is little point in devoting space to the question whether Parliament can be held to enforceable fiduciary duties to Māori. The New Zealand Parliament is legally unfettered. It suffices to make two points in this regard: as detailed above, the FSA would likely be constitutionally invalid if enacted in Canada; and even though the FSA is perfectly legal in New Zealand, Parliament may still have breached fiduciary duties to Māori by enacting law that unjustifiably extinguishes aboriginal title and rights. Toohey J's comments in *Mabo (No 2)* are apposite here: 'A fiduciary obligation on the Crown does not limit the legislative power of the Queensland Parliament, but legislation will be a breach of that obligation if its effect is adverse to the interests of the titleholders, or if the process it establishes does not take account of those interests.'[82]

This section first examines whether, as a matter of New Zealand law, New Zealand courts would enforce Crown fiduciary duties to Māori in relation to Māori interests as Canadian law has done. As will be illustrated, New Zealand law is not highly developed in this area; a product perhaps of the early loss of so much Māori land and extinguishment of important aboriginal rights, such as fishing interests, which might have sourced more robust fiduciary-duty jurisprudence. However, fiduciary-duty doctrine has been supported in a number of cases by the Court of Appeal and, according to those cases,

---

81. See Shaunnagh Dorsett's chapter in this book, 59–82.
82. *Mabo (No 2)*, above n 74, 205 Toohey J.

would incorporate many of the Canadian principles outlined in Part IV of this chapter. Therefore, there is every reason to suggest that New Zealand law would hold the Crown to fiduciary standards where the facts are such as to give rise to Crown fiduciary duties to Māori. In the light of the examination of New Zealand law, I outline the duties the Crown may have been subject to in relation to Māori interests in the foreshore and seabed but for the FSA.

B *New Zealand Law on Crown Fiduciary Duties to Māori*

1 Application
A number of New Zealand Court of Appeal cases in the early 1990s recognised the applicability of Canadian jurisprudence on Crown fiduciary duties to aboriginal peoples in New Zealand. The statements made, while obiter, strongly suggest that if the right case came before it, the Court of Appeal would hold the Crown to fiduciary standards. In addition, the Court of Appeal suggested that Canadian law would be of major guidance in formulating New Zealand's law. This jurisprudence has also been linked to the principles of the Treaty of Waitangi, as first elaborated in the Court of Appeal's 1987 *New Zealand Maori Council v Attorney-General* (*NZMC (Lands)*) case.[83] Cooke P, as he then was, repeatedly made the point in the early 1990s that the Treaty of Waitangi's principles, which include the concept of partnership, create responsibilities analogous to fiduciary duties and are a major support for the Court's enforcement of Crown fiduciary duties to Māori.

The Court of Appeal in *Te Runanga o Muriwhenua v Attorney-General* (*Muriwhenua*) did not hold the Crown to fiduciary standards. The issues centred on procedural rules, and the status and admissibility of Waitangi Tribunal reports in courts. At heart, though, the case involved Māori fishing rights, which was presumably the impetus behind the statement that:[84]

> More recently in Canada Indian rights have been identified as pre-existing legal rights not created by Royal proclamation, statute or executive order. It has been recognised that, in some circumstances at least, the Crown is under a fiduciary duty to holders of such rights in dealings relating to their extinction.

---

83. *New Zealand Maori Council v Attorney-General* [1987] 1 NZLR 641, 664 Cooke P (CA). Cooke P (for the Court) later summarised that case in *Wharekauri*, above n 22, 304 (CA):

    The present case takes its place in a history. Some of its antecedents should be stated. *New Zealand Maori Council v Attorney-General* [1987] 1 NZLR 641, the lands case, came before this Court under s 9 of the State-Owned Enterprises Act 1986, whereby it is provided that nothing in that Act shall permit the Crown to act in a manner inconsistent with the principles of the Treaty of Waitangi. That provision made it incumbent on the Court to determine what were the principles of the Treaty of 1840 as applied to circumstances a century and a half later. It was held unanimously by a Court of five Judges, each delivering a separate judgment, that the Treaty created an enduring relationship of a fiduciary nature akin to a partnership, each party accepting a positive duty to act in good faith, fairly, reasonably and honourably towards the other. The words of the reasons for the judgment of the five Judges differed only slightly; the foregoing is a summary of their collective tenor.

84. *Muriwhenua*, above n 22, 655 (CA) Cooke P for the Court.

The judgments in *Guerin* ... seem likely to be found of major guidance when such matters come finally to be decided in New Zealand. The approach of this court in the *Maori Council* case to the principles of the Treaty of Waitangi and the partnership and fiduciary analogies there drawn are consistent with them ... There are constitutional differences between Canada and New Zealand, but the *Guerin* judgments do not appear to turn on these. Moreover, in interpreting New Zealand parliamentary and common law it must be right for New Zealand courts to lean against any inference that in this democracy the rights of the Maori people are less respected than the rights of aboriginal peoples in North America.

So, we see that the New Zealand courts would be heavily influenced by Canadian law with regard to indigenous peoples, being conscious that New Zealand law should not protect Māori rights to any lesser extent than Canadian law.

The Court of Appeal made similar comments in *Te Runanga o Wharekauri Rekohu Inc v Attorney-General* (*Wharekauri*).[85] Again, the Court did not hold the Crown to fiduciary-duty standards as the case involved claims relating to legislative process, and the Court held it could not interfere in parliamentary proceedings. However, Cooke P, who delivered the Court's judgment, wrote that New Zealand Court of Appeal judgments such as that in *Muriwhenua* had been strengthened by cases such as *Sparrow* and *Mabo (No 2)*. In his words:[86]

> In these judgments there have been further affirmations that the continuance after British sovereignty and treaties of unextinguished aboriginal title gives rise to fiduciary duty and constructive trust on the part of the Crown: see *R v Sparrow* (1990) 70 DLR (4th) 385, 406, 406-409 per Dickson CJC and La Forest J, delivering the judgment of the court, a passage including the statement 'The sui generis nature of Indian title, and the historic powers and responsibilities assumed by the Crown constituted the source of such a fiduciary obligation'; *Mabo v State of Queensland* (1992) 107 ALR 1, 85-86 per Deane and Gauldron JJ, 157–160 per Toohey J. The other judgments [...] are less definite on the fiduciary question (see Brennan J at pp 43–44) but clearly there is now a substantial body of Commonwealth law pointing to a fiduciary duty.
>
> In New Zealand the Treaty of Waitangi is major support for such a duty. The New Zealand judgments are part of a widespread international recognition that the rights of indigenous peoples are entitled to some effective protection and advancement.

The case concerned the famous Sealords deal settling Māori claims to fishing

---

85. *Wharekauri*, above n 22.
86. *Wharekauri*, above n 22, 306 Cooke P for the Court.

rights. Of the settlement, Cooke P considered that 'a failure to take [the opportunity to purchase an interest for Māori in Sealords] might well have been inconsistent with the constructive performance of the duty of a party in a position akin to a partnership.'[87] The Court of Appeal does not leave the matter there. Cooke P states that the 'constitutional or fiduciary significance' of the Treaty remains.[88] Further, advice to the Crown that the Deed had support from a 'representative and authoritative cross-section' of Māori 'must have a significant bearing on constitutional and fiduciary issues.'[89]

Given that the case arose in relation to fishing rights, it can be inferred that the Court of Appeal made these comments on the basis that non-territorial aboriginal rights can source Crown fiduciary duties.

Perhaps the high water mark in New Zealand jurisprudence on Crown fiduciary duties is *Te Ika Whenua Inc Society v Attorney-General* (*Te Ika Whenua*). Te Ika Whenua brought a judicial review claim seeking an interim declaration that the Minister of Energy refuse to approve a plan to transfer dams on the Rangitaiki and Wheao rivers from the Bay of Plenty Electric Power Board and the Rotorua Electricity Authority to energy companies. Earlier in the year, the Waitangi Tribunal recommended that the power schemes on the rivers and the water rights should be retained in the Board and the Authority, or the Crown, until Te Ika Whenua's substantive claim in relation to the river and water had been determined. In a single judgment delivered by Cooke P, the Court of Appeal considered, and rejected, Te Ika Whenua's claims: 'Neither under the common law doctrine of aboriginal title, nor under the Treaty of Waitangi, nor under any New Zealand statute have Maori ... had preserved or assured to them any right to generate electricity by the use of water power.'[90]

However, the Court of Appeal seemed at pains to confine its decision to Te Ika Whenua's specific claim in relation to electricity generation only, that is, the decision did not affect any Te Ika Whenua aboriginal rights claim to the water: it notes a number of times that the ownership of the dams will not prejudice any Te Ika Whenua claims to water or land; and seems to invite a claim 'if the granting of rights to generate electricity has prejudiced [Te Ika Whenua's] Treaty, customary or fiduciary rights without consent.'[91] The Court of Appeal comments that the decision in *Mabo (No 2)* would require close analysis in such a case. The inference is clear: if Te Ika Whenua could prove customary rights in relation to other interests, Crown fiduciary duties would arise.

Therefore, it is not surprising that the Court of Appeal in *Te Ika Whenua*

---

87. *Wharekauri*, above n 22, 307 Cooke P for the Court.
88. *Wharekauri*, above n 22, 309 Cooke P for the Court.
89. *Wharekauri*, above n 22, 309 Cooke P for the Court.
90. *Te Ika Whenua*, above n 22, 25 Cooke P for the Court.
91. *Te Ika Whenua*, above n 22, 25 Cooke P for the Court.

makes robust statements about the content of both aboriginal title and fiduciary duties, albeit again in obiter statements. It describes the aboriginal title doctrine, states that 'it has been authoritatively said that [aboriginal rights] cannot be extinguished (at least in times of peace) otherwise than by the free consent of the native occupiers, and then only to the Crown in strict compliance with the provisions of any relevant statutes.'[92] In addition, the Court of Appeal held that 'an extinguishment by less than fair conduct or on less than fair terms would be likely to be in breach of the fiduciary duty widely and increasingly recognised as falling on the colonising power.'[93] Compulsory acquisition will require proper compensation. He notes that the Treaty preserves similar rights.[94] The Court of Appeal cites *Muriwhenua*, the cases mentioned in that judgment and the Federal Court of Canada's judgment in *Blueberry River*.[95] Notably, in a word of caution, the judgment reserves to New Zealand courts the jurisdiction to determine the precise contours of aboriginal title and the Crown's fiduciary duties. On the applicability of Australian jurisprudence, the Court notes: '[o]f course nothing said in that case is binding in a New Zealand court. In New Zealand we would have to be guided by our conception of the strength of the competing claims and any others relevant to this country's circumstances.'[96]

On the more generic need to protect indigenous rights, the Court of Appeal notes the increasing recognition of the justiciability of indigenous peoples' claims, citing *Guerin* and *Mabo (No 2)*, among others.[97]

The Court of Appeal elaborated on the fiduciary-duty element of Treaty of Waitangi principles in *Ngai Tahu Maori Trust Board v Director-General of Conservation (Ngai Tahu (Whale Watching))*.[98] It concerned Ngāi Tahu's claim to a right of veto over Ministerial decisions to allocate whale-watching permits off Kaikoura on the basis of Ngāi Tahu's traditional and historical connection to whales in that area. Legislatively incorporated Treaty of Waitangi principles applied. The Court of Appeal held that Ngāi Tahu did not have an aboriginal or treaty right to tourism or whale-watching, as, it found, they were too remote from anything envisaged by the original parties to the Treaty. On that basis, it refused Ngāi Tahu's claim to veto powers. Nonetheless, the Court went on to find that whale-watching was sufficiently linked to taonga such that the Treaty of Waitangi's principles would require Ngāi Tahu to be given a reasonable degree of preference in the allocation of permits. In its analysis of

---

92. *Te Ika Whenua*, above n 22, 24 Cooke P for the Court.
93. *Te Ika Whenua*, above n 22, 24 Cooke P for the Court.
94. *Te Ika Whenua*, above n 22, 24 Cooke P for the Court.
95. *Te Ika Whenua*, above n 22, 24 Cooke P for the Court.
96. *Te Ika Whenua*, above n 22, 25 Cooke P for the Court.
97. *Te Ika Whenua*, above n 22, 27 Cooke P for the Court.
98. *Ngai Tahu Maori Trust Board v Director-General of Conservation* [1993] 3 NZLR 553 (CA).

the Crown's duties under the Treaty of Waitangi principles, the Court cited statements about fiduciary duties in *Wharekauri* and *NZMC (Lands)* positively and expressed the view that the Crown would have fiduciary duties in relation to customary or aboriginal title or treaty rights. The upshot of this is that the Crown, where subject to a legislative Treaty principles, will be required to meet standards like those of a fiduciary.

That the Crown is subject to fiduciary duties when dealing with aboriginal rights and title has been more recently affirmed by the Court of Appeal in *Te Waka Hi Ika o Te Arawa v Treaty of Waitangi Fisheries Commission* (*Te Waka Hi Ika o Te Arawa*),[99] although the Court was not required to address any particular body's fiduciary duties squarely. It cited *Te Ika Whenua* and noted that the Treaty requires compliance with fiduciary standards.[100]

2 Misconception of fiduciary-duty claims

The cases discussed below highlight an unusual development in New Zealand law on Crown fiduciary duties to Māori since the mid-1990s. They suggest that both Māori claimants have advanced, and the courts have conceived of, fiduciary-duty arguments as judicial review claims based on the Treaty of Waitangi. The essence of the arguments, as reported, seems to be that Crown action is amenable to review for compliance with the Treaty of Waitangi principles, even where they are not incorporated into applicable legislation, and that requires the Crown to conform to fiduciary standards. The courts have treated the claims as based on judicial review and have invariably rejected them on the grounds that: the Treaty of Waitangi is not a ground for judcial review of administrative action; the Treaty cannot be directly enforced; or a particular executive decision is not amenable to judicial review because it is not made pursuant to a statute.

It is not surprising that claimants and the courts have grounded their discussion of fiduciary duties in the Treaty. *Ngai Tahu (Whale Watching)*, for example, suggests that is where and how the fiduciary duty arises *at least where the Treaty has been incorporated into legislation*. However, the Treaty principles and judicial review avenue is not, as *Te Ika Whenua* suggests, the only way to pin fiduciary duties on the Crown when it deals with Māori interests. Crown fiduciary duties can arise completely independently as an equitable-law claim where, for example, the Crown takes action in relation to aboriginal rights or title. The courts' failure to view Māori claims based on Crown fiduciary duties under equity, unrelated to the Treaty or Crown public law obligations, obscures New Zealand law on Crown fiduciary duties to Māori. But, it does not undermine it either; the principles that emerged in *Muriwhenua*, *Wharekauri*

---

99. *Te Waka Hi Ika o Te Arawa v Treaty of Waitangi Fisheries Commission* [2000] 1 NZLR 285 (CA).
100. *Te Waka He Ika o Te Arawa*, above n 99, 343 Thomas J.

and *Te Ika Whenua* still apply and remain basically untouched, which, as we have seen, was supported by the Court of Appeal more recently in *Te Waka Hi Ika o Te Arawa*.

The first case that falls into the 'misconceived' fiduciary-duty claim camp is the 1996 *New Zealand Maori Council v Attorney-General (NZMC (Radio Assets))* case about radio assets.[101] The New Zealand Māori Council sought to prevent the Government from selling Radio New Zealand's (RNZ) assets on the grounds that it would make it more difficult for the Government to comply with the Treaty by ensuring adequate airing of te reo Māori. The sale was facilitated by special statutes; the first vested RNZ assets in the Crown and the second removed RNZ from the list of state-owned enterprises in the State Owned Enterprise Act 1986 (SOE Act). At the time of the hearing the second Act had not come into force. The sale was also facilitated, of course, by policy decisions and Crown actions to advance the sale of the radio assets.[102]

The New Zealand Māori Council's fiduciary-duty claim related to the Crown's completion of the sale of the radio assets after the second Act came into force. The New Zealand Māori Council pleaded that the sale would be a breach of the Crown's fiduciary duty to Māori. The majority of the Court concluded simply that the Treaty principles would not apply as the second Act would remove RNZ from the SOE Act, which incorporates the Treaty principles. Instead, the Court stated that the fiduciary-duty-based claim would have to be advanced under administrative grounds on the basis that the Crown failed to comply with Treaty obligations. In turn, the majority suggested that such a claim would have little strength because: the Crown would not be exercising a statutory power in selling the RNZ shares; the Crown would simply be exercising its right as common law owner to sell shares; it was plain that the legislature intended the shares to be sold; and the Crown had considered its Treaty obligations and consulted with Māori.[103]

Unfortunately, the Court did not view the New Zealand Māori Council's claim as a claim in equity per Canadian case law. Conceived of instead as a judicial review claim dependent on the application of the Treaty, it was dismissed.

---

101. *New Zealand Maori Council v Attorney-General* [1996] 3 NZLR 140 (CA).
102. Numerous arguments were raised by New Zealand Māori Council with much being made, of course, of the SOE Act's incorporation of Treaty of Waitangi principles and prohibition on the Crown's sale of its shares in SOEs. A central question was whether those SOE Act provisions applied given the special legislation enacted to facilitate the sale. These arguments were rejected on the grounds that: the Crown's policies are not reviewable; the sale would go ahead in any event, making relief difficult, because its wheels of the sale transaction were legislatively oiled and the Court could not intrude in Parliament; and the Government had considered its Treaty obligations and had consulted with Māori (the suggestion also being that the Government did not need to own the assets to ensure that te reo Māori was aired on radio).
103. *NZMC Radio Assets*, above n 101, 166–7 Richardson P, Gault, Mckay, Henry, Keith and Blanchard JJ.

The case also illustrates that claims based on Crown fiduciary duties to Māori sometimes arise within a statutory framework, as with the legislation that facilitated the sale of the radio assets. But, as we have seen, in Canada the courts have often found a Crown fiduciary duty alongside statutory regimes such as, in Canada, the Indian Act (e.g., *Guerin*). Equitable duties can co-exist with statutory regimes.

Cases involving Māori objections to the auction of management rights in the radio spectrum (the *Radio Spectrum Cases*), based on alleged Crown breach of its fiduciary duties, suffer from the same conceptual problem as *NZMC (Radio Assets)*. In the first High Court decision, Doogue J dismissed the fiduciary argument on the basis that there was no statutory power of decision involved in the auction and it was therefore not reviewable.[104] His decision was upheld in the Court of Appeal on the grounds that the claim was not strong and that these are 'high policy matters [which are] essentially for the government and Maori, not the courts.'[105] In the next related High Court case, Doogue J simply rejected the fiduciary claim on the basis of the earlier Court of Appeal decision.[106] The problem, again, was that the fiduciary-duty claim was conceived of as one for judicial review based on the Treaty.

Ngāi Tahu's claim that the Crown's approval of a particular model for distributing Māori fisheries assets breached the Crown's fiduciary duties failed for similar reasons.[107] It was brought as a judicial review claim pleading non-compliance with the Treaty. McGechan J in the High Court held that the Treaty does not give rise to enforceable obligations.[108] What distinguishes this case, however, is that Ngāi Tahu's fiduciary-duty argument, were it treated as a claim in equity like Canadian cases, could well have been successful. It had all the hallmarks of a sound fiduciary-duty case: Ngāi Tahu's aboriginal fishing rights were at stake; those rights had been surrendered conditionally to the Crown, as in *Guerin*, in return for the fisheries assets; the Crown had power over those fisheries assets, that is, was able to exercise a good deal of discretion over them; and Ngāi Tahu was vulnerable to the exercise of that discretion.

---

104. *Everton v Attorney-General* (5 July 2000) HC WN CP 121–00 Doogue J.
105. *New Zealand Maori Council v Attorney-General* (13 July 2000) CA 134-00, paras 5–7 Gault J for the Court.
106. *New Zealand Maori Council v Attorney-General & Ors* (10 August 2000) HC WN CP 130-00 Doogue J.
107. *Te Runanga o Ngai Tahu v Attorney-General & Ors* (6 November 2003) HC AK CIV 1113 McGechan J (*Ngai Tahu (Fisheries Assets Distribution)*).
108. *Ngai Tahu (Fisheries Assets Distribution)*, above n 107, para 8 McGechan J. More specifically, at paragraph 9 he writes: 'Ngai Tahu alleged obligation including those of a fiduciary character under the Treaty, the Deed of Settlement, the Maori Fisheries Act 1989 and the Settlement Act 1993 and breach by the Crown of those obligations. To avoid misunderstanding I say at the outset that I do not accept either of the Treaty or the Deed of Settlement gives rise in its own right to obligations directly enforceable through the courts.' He then confines his consideration to the statutory obligations under those Acts stating that the Ngāi Tahu claim 'if it is to succeed in court, must be based on the statutory obligations properly interpreted'.

Moreover, the Sealords Deed of Settlement between Māori and the Crown suggests that the Crown has voluntarily assumed a protective role in relation to those fishing rights.

3   Non-interference with political process

A potential difficulty with Māori fiduciary-duty claims in New Zealand is the courts' unwillingness to interfere in political processes, as indicated in *Wharekauri* and in cases where Crown action in Treaty settlement negotiations is criticised. Potentially, as was mentioned earlier, Māori fiduciary claims would often arise in politically charged circumstances.

In *Kai Tohu o Puketapu Hapu Incorporated v Attorney-General and Te Atiawa Iwi Authority* Doogue J held that the Court could not interfere in a political process where there is no evidence of political error.[109] In a similar case about a Treaty settlement process, in which a Crown breach of fiduciary duties was alleged, Goddard J found that the High Court lacked jurisdiction to intervene in the political process leading to a settlement deed.[110] The Court of Appeal has said much the same. In *Milroy v Maori Trust Board & Ors* Tūhoe challenged the proposed settlement of Ngāti Awa's Treaty claims because certain land to be transferred to Ngāti Awa was subject to Tūhoe claims.[111] Gault P, delivering the judgment of a five bench Court of Appeal, said where a claim relates to actions 'undertaken in the course of policy formation preparatory to the introduction to Parliament of legislation, the courts will not intervene.'[112]

It may be that courts would be less reluctant to intervene in cases involving political process and fiduciary-duty-based arguments if they were presented and dealt with as equitable claims rather judicial review proceedings. If the courts were to deny jurisdiction because a legal issue involves political process *only* in judicial review proceedings, the potential for successful Māori fiduciary-duty claims against the Crown under equitable principles remains. In saying that, it seems clear that the closer the political process involved in the case is to legislative process, the more reluctant the courts will be to intervene.

4   Summary

In conclusion, Canadian and Australian jurisprudence on Crown fiduciary duties to aboriginal peoples applies in New Zealand; the Court of Appeal

---

109. Although, he did suggest that the situation might be different if there is an allegation of bad faith, fraud or breach of fiduciary duty. See *Kai Tohu o Puketapu Hapu Incorporated v Attorney-General and Te Atiawa Iwi Authority* (5 February 1999) HC WN CP 344/97 Doogue J.
110. *Watene & Ors v The Minister in Charge of the Treaty of Waitangi* (11 May 2001) HC WN CP 120/01, para 24 Goddard J.
111. *Milroy v Attorney-General* (11 June 2003) CA 197/02 Gault P for the Court.
112. *Milroy v Attorney-General*, above n 111, para 18 Gault P for the Court.

has said as much, and emphatically so (*Muriwhenua, Wharekauri* and *Te Ika Whenua*), although it is likely to be contoured to New Zealand's particular legal landscape (*Te Ika Whenua*). The Treaty is also considered support for Crown fiduciary duties to Māori. The Court of Appeal has indicated that the content of the Crown's fiduciary duties to Māori includes a prohibition on the extinguishment of native title and rights without consent, and requirements that extinguishment conform to relevant statutory provisions and that compensation be paid (*Te Ika Whenua*). Where the Treaty principles are incorporated into applicable legislation, Crown actions will be measured against fiduciary standards (*NZMC (Lands)* and *Ngai Tahu (Whale-watching)*).

Cases in which Crown fiduciary-duty arguments to Māori have been raised have been frequently misconceived in pleadings and court decisions as judicial review claims based on the Treaty of Waitangi. Unsurprisingly, when framed in that way, they have been dismissed on the grounds that: the Treaty is unenforceable; administrative decisions cannot be reviewed for compliance with the Treaty unless the Treaty is incorporated into applicable legislation; or there is no exercise of a statutory decision-making power (*NZMC (Radio Assets), Radio Spectrum Cases* and *Ngai Tahu (Fisheries Assets Distribution)*). The door remains open to a Crown fiduciary duty to Māori claim based on *equitable* principles and sourced in aboriginal title, rights, the historical relationship between Māori and the Crown and the Treaty.

It is unclear whether the courts would be willing to exercise jurisdiction where the facts giving rise to a fiduciary-duty claim based on equitable principles involve political process. It may be that courts would deny jurisdiction on those grounds only in judicial-review-based cases, not in equity-based cases.

C   Quantifying Crown Fiduciary Duties to Māori but for the FSA

As the above suggests, the following analysis proceeds on the basis that Canadian law would be extremely persuasive in filling out New Zealand's relatively underdeveloped law on Crown fiduciary duties to Māori. There is every reason to suggest this is realistic given the reliance placed on Canadian law in decisions such as *Muriwhenua, Wharekauri* and *Te Ika Whenua*. It is also informed by the Court of Appeal's statement that (to quote again) 'in interpreting New Zealand parliamentary and common law it must be right for New Zealand courts to lean against any inference that in this democracy the rights of the Māori people are less respected than the rights of aboriginal peoples in North America.'[113]

---

113. *Muriwhenua*, above n 22, 655 Cooke P for the Court.

1 But for the FSA: Crown duties to Māori in relation to unproven and unspecified aboriginal title and aboriginal rights

Before the FSA was enacted, Māori groups had unproven and unspecified aboriginal title and aboriginal rights in the foreshore and seabed. Post-*Ngati Apa*, Māori groups lodged claims in the Māori Land Court to have these rights recognised.[114] These unproven and unspecified aboriginal title and non-territorial rights are analogous to those held by Haida Nation in the Canadian *Haida Nation* case.

Were it not for the FSA, these Māori unproven titles and rights could well have given rise to Crown duties of consultation and accommodation were *Haida Nation* applied in New Zealand. Of course, applying *Haida Nation*, the Crown's duty would have changed according to the strength of the particular claim and the potential impact of any proposal that would affect those unproven and unspecified rights. The duty would consist of weak consultation rights in cases of weak claims, and accommodation in cases of strong claims. On that note, it is relevant that under the Māori Land Court's pre-FSA jurisdiction, the Māori Land Court had the power to make findings of customary title based on tikanga Māori. A number of groups may have had a strong case to customary title to the foreshore and seabed under that jurisdiction, which would have increased the duties on the Crown. Equally, one can assume that a number of Māori groups had strong common law aboriginal rights claims, which also would have increased the duties on the Crown.

The Crown's duty, applying *Haida Nation*, would have arisen when it had real or constructive knowledge of the potential existence of aboriginal rights or title and contemplated conduct that might adversely affect it. It is unclear when exactly the Government would have had constructive knowledge of potential Māori aboriginal title or rights claims to the foreshore and seabed. However, it is likely to have had that knowledge at least once the Court of Appeal's decision in *Ngati Apa* was handed down in June 2003. It could be argued that it had earlier constructive knowledge; at the latest when the *Ngati Apa* proceedings began, and perhaps earlier given that serious aspersions had been cast on the *In Re Ninety Mile Beach* case on which the Crown's assumption of foreshore and seabed ownership had falsely rested for so many years.[115]

As indicated earlier, the above description of the Crown's duties to Māori in relation to their unproven and unspecified foreshore and seabed interests is conjecture. No court will be able to consider any such related claim unless the

---

114. For example, see Hon Margaret Wilson (30 July 2003) 610 *NZPD* 7434: 'Since 19 June 2003 there have been 16 foreshore and seabed applications in the Māori Land Court. One of these was received in each of the Takitimu, Waiariki, and Tairawhiti registries. Two applications were received in each of the Waikato and Aotea registries, and nine were received in the Te Taitokerau registry.'
115. Richard Boast '*In Re Ninety Mile Beach* Revisited: The Native Land Court and the Foreshore in New Zealand Legal History' (1993) 23 VUWLR 145.

FSA is repealed. Nonetheless, this hypothesis is made soundly. All the elements required for Crown duties to arise were there before the FSA came into force.

Before that date, at least between *Ngati Apa* in June 2003 and the passing of the FSA in November 2004, it is likely that the Crown owed duties of consultation and in some cases accommodation to Māori based on *Haida Nation*. There may even be a sound argument that the Crown breached those duties, in that its development of its foreshore and seabed policies post-*Ngati Apa* did not involve adequate consultation nor accommodation of Māori objections. On the other hand, the courts might have been reluctant to enforce those duties in that context as the breach arguably occurred within the legislative process as in *Wharekauri*.

2   *But for the FSA: Crown fiduciary duties to Māori in relation to proven aboriginal title and rights*
If Māori could have proven aboriginal title and rights in the foreshore and seabed under the Te Ture Whenua Maori Act 1993 (the TTWMA), were the FSA not enacted, the Crown would, adopting Canadian jurisprudence in cases such as *Blueberry River* and *Semiahmoo*, have owed fiduciary duties to Māori to, at the very least, prevent exploitative bargains in relation to those interests. There is every reason to suggest that at least some Māori could have proven aboriginal title and rights in the foreshore and seabed. As discussed above, if Māori can meet the FSA tests to establish TCROs or CROs, they would almost definitely have been able to prove such rights under the common law or under the Māori Land Court's customary-title jurisdiction.

3   *But for the FSA: Crown fiduciary duties to Māori in relation to proven aboriginal title and rights on expropriation or surrender*
Applying both New Zealand and Canadian case law, the Crown would be subject to even stronger fiduciary-duty standards were Māori to have proved aboriginal title and rights, or customary title, and the Crown was involved in their expropriation or surrender. The content of that duty would vary according to the nature and importance of the Māori interest (*Wewaykum*) and, in the case of surrender for Crown lease on behalf of the Māori group, would prohibit the Crown from entering into an agreement less favourable than any discussed with the Māori group holding the aboriginal title or rights (*Guerin*). Were the Crown to have then expropriated Māori aboriginal title or rights in the foreshore and seabed under the auspices of the public interest, it could have only legally done so under statutory powers, with the consent of the relevant Māori group and conforming to principles of fairness (*Te Ika Whenua*). The Crown would have been required to pay compensation (*Te Ika Whenua*). Finally, the Crown would only be permitted to expropriate the minimum

interest required to ensure minimal impairment of Māori use and enjoyment of their lands and rights (*Osoyoos*).

But for the FSA's removal of fiduciary duties in relation to CROs and TCROs Crown fiduciary duties to Māori could have equally been based in CROs or TCROs, judicially cognisable under the High Court's and Māori Land Court's 'replacement jurisdiction' in the FSA. There is no good reason why Māori rights arising out of legislation should not source Crown fiduciary duties, especially where the legislative rights are based on, and "replace", Māori rights under the common law that would have founded Crown fiduciary duties. These duties would have constrained the Crown when dealing with Māori interests in CROs or TCROs including, possibly, in negotiations for redress for Crown breaches of fiduciary duties. Further, on the same rationale and based on *Haida Nation*, unproven CROs and TCROs could have given rise to Crown duties of accommodation and consultation, but for sections 10 and 13(4) of the FSA.

VI *The Possibility of Redress for the Loss of the Potential to Hold the Crown to Fiduciary-Duty Standards in Relation to the Foreshore and Seabed*

Finally, is there any possibility of redress for the taking away of the potential to hold the Crown to fiduciary standards in relation to Māori interests in the foreshore and seabed? The loss of an opportunity to hold the Crown to fiduciary standards could not found an enforceable legal obligation to redress in New Zealand. But a broader perspective of justice would suggest that there is at least a moral obligation on the Crown to do so.

A THE FORESHORE AND SEABED ACT AND REDRESS

If a Māori group can satisfy legislatively imposed, and onerous, TCRO tests, the group can compel the Crown to enter into negotiations for redress. The redress is specifically 'in recognition of' the High Court's TCRO only. As such, the FSA does not envisage redress for the loss of customary title that could have been proved under the TTWMA or aboriginal title that might have been proved under the common law but does not satisfy the strict tests for proving a TCRO.

Under section 38, a Māori group who can prove a TCRO over a particular area is 'not entitled to seek any other form of redress under this Act or any other enactment.'[116] In addition 'no Court has the jurisdiction to consider the

---

116. FSA, s 38(2).

nature or the extent of any matter that the Crown proposes, offers, or gives for the purposes of any redress.'[117]

An alternative to negotiating redress is the option for Māori groups to seek an order to establish a foreshore and seabed reserve. Agreement between the Māori group, the regional council with authority over the specific area of the foreshore and seabed reserve, and representatives of the Crown is required first.[118] A foreshore and seabed reserve is managed by a board as agreed by the parties. Its functions include preparing, approving and reviewing a management plan for the reserve. The reserve is to 'enable that area to be held for the common use and benefit of the people of New Zealand', does not affect Crown ownership, guaranteed public access and the rights of navigation.[119] The management plan for the foreshore and seabed must be prepared in accordance with the Resource Management Act 1991, and must not be inconsistent with the New Zealand Coastal Policy Statement and any relevant national policy statement.[120]

There is no provision for redress for customary rights that Māori might have been able to prove but for the restrictive CRO tests.

B   REDRESS SHOULD TAKE INTO ACCOUNT THE TAKING AWAY OF THE CROWN'S POTENTIAL FIDUCIARY OBLIGATIONS IN RELATION TO THE FORESHORE AND SEABED

Simply because the FSA says 'the Crown does not owe any fiduciary duty', and redress under the FSA relates explicitly *only* to a TCRO, does not mean that as a matter of good policy the Crown should not take into account the legislative override of potential Crown fiduciary duties when providing redress. The Crown could also initiate redress packages outside the FSA framework. This is especially true given that:

- the Crown was so instrumental in preparing and passing a statute, the FSA, that abolishes its potential legal and enforceable duties to Māori;
- if the Crown had attempted to achieve the result of the FSA, namely extinguishment of Māori aboriginal and customary title and restrictions on customary rights, through the exercise of Executive powers it is likely that it would have been prevented from doing so by enforceable fiduciary duties;
- the FSA would be constitutionally invalid in Canada partly because of its legislative override of the Crown's fiduciary duties to Māori;
- the Government has itself indicated that it will be fair in negotiations with

---

117. FSA, s 38(3).
118. FSA, ss 36(1)(b), 40, 41, 42 and, most importantly, 43.
119. FSA, ss 40(1)(b) and 40(3).
120. FSA, s 44(2).

Māori groups that establish TCROs;[121]
- and the Government has legislatively denied Māori the right to go to Court in relation to duties that could well have existed when the FSA came into force (i.e., in relation to Māori unproven aboriginal title and rights under *Haida Nation*).

Most importantly, redress for loss of the potential to hold the Crown to fiduciary standards in relation to fiduciary duties would minimise the massive disjuncture between New Zealand law, on the one hand, and United States, Australian and Canadian law, on the other. The rights of Māori should not be respected any less than the rights of indigenous peoples in North America or Australia.

VI Conclusion

I have attempted to make up for the marked lack of analysis of Crown fiduciary duties to Māori in relation to their interests in the foreshore and seabed in this chapter. It has uncovered that the FSA is comparatively extremely draconian in this area when compared to Canadian law. It has also revealed that, but for the FSA, Māori would have been likely to be able to hold the Crown to fiduciary standards in its dealings with Māori interests in the foreshore and seabed. Finally, it suggests that a fair government, concerned with its international reputation, would provide redress to Māori for the loss of that potential.

---

121. Attorney-General 'Report on the Consistency of Rights Act 1990' (6 May 2004).

The Recognition of Indigenous Peoples' Rights to Traditional Lands: The Evaluation of States by International Treaty Bodies

Andrew Erueti[*]

I Introduction

This chapter considers the difficulties indigenous peoples encounter in seeking state recognition of their rights in traditional lands. The object of this chapter is to place the *Attorney-General v Ngati Apa* (*Ngati Apa*) decision in an international context by examining state methods of recognising indigenous peoples' property rights and the evaluation of those methods by international human rights treaty bodies.[1] This is particularly relevant to New Zealand because of the criticism of the Foreshore and Seabed Act 2004 (FSA) by a United Nations (UN) human rights treaty body. Part II of this chapter reviews state practice to date in the Anglo-Commonwealth states of Australia, Canada and New Zealand by focussing on the restrictive evidential standards forged in domestic aboriginal rights litigation to prove indigenous property rights. In part III, I turn to consider the effectiveness of international human rights treaty bodies in encouraging states to apply less-restrictive evidential standards.

I focus on the treaty bodies that monitor state compliance with the Organisation of American States (OAS) Inter-American human rights instruments – the American Declaration of the Rights and Duties of Man, and the American Convention on Human Rights.[2] I also consider the UN treaties

---

[*] Ngā Ruahinerangi. Senior Lecturer in Law, Victoria University, Wellington.
[1] *Attorney-General v Ngati Apa* [2003] 3 NZLR 643 (CA).
[2] American Declaration of the Rights and Duties of Man (1948) Ninth International Conference of American States, OAS Res XXX, reprinted in *Basic Documents Pertaining to Human Rights in the*

of most relevance to date to indigenous peoples – the International Convention on the Elimination of All Forms of Racial Discrimination (ICERD) and the International Covenant on Civil and Political Rights (ICCPR).[3] Finally, I consider the standards set in relation to proving indigenous property rights by indigenous peoples-specific international instruments – the International Labour Organisation Convention 169 concerning Indigenous and Tribal Peoples in Independent Countries (ILO Convention No. 169),[4] and the UN Declaration on the Rights of Indigenous Peoples (UN Declaration).[5] The focus here is more on the evidential standards established by treaty bodies and the indigenous peoples-specific instruments for the domestic demarcation of land rights, and less on the actual domestic implementation of those principles. Quite plainly, moving from principle to practical implementation will be extremely difficult – not just because of the possibility of domestic rejection of international decisions, but also because of the resources and time required to assess evidence and demarcate land rights on the ground.

The following points are made in this chapter: first, indigenous peoples have used tradition and their distinctiveness vis-à-vis the majority or dominant culture as a justification for rights recognition (domestically and in international fora); second, states have used tradition and indigenous custom to read down the property rights accorded to indigenous peoples or to deny them rights altogether – this approach was adopted in the FSA; third, experience shows that international and regional human rights treaty bodies may serve an important function in monitoring state practice and in particular encouraging states to adopt less-restrictive approaches to the recognition of indigenous peoples' rights in traditional lands; fourth, the previous point illustrates the importance of ensuring indigenous peoples have effective access to treaty bodies. Finally, for those indigenous communities seeking state recognition of their rights in traditional lands, an emerging international standard for demarcation is that states grant rights of ownership in relation to lands 'traditionally occupied and used' by indigenous peoples. This chapter also suggests how that standard might be applied by states.

    Inter-American System OEA/Ser.L/V.II.82, doc. 6 rev. 1 (1992) 17; American Convention on Human Rights (22 November 1969) 32 OAS Treaty Series, 1144 UNTS 123.

3. International Convention on the Elimination of All Forms of Racial Discrimination (4 January 1969) 660 UNTS 195; International Covenant on Civil and Political Rights (19 December 1966) 999 UNTS 171.
4. Convention Concerning Indigenous and Tribal Peoples in Independent Countries, ILO No. 169 (27 June 1989) 172 Official Bull 59.
5. UN Human Rights Council, Declaration on the Rights of Indigenous Peoples, Annex, HRC Res 2006/2 (29 June 2006), available at <http://www.ohchr.org/english/issues/indigenous/docs/declaration.doc>

II State Determination of Rights to Traditional Lands

A THE PROBLEM WITH TRADITION

To obtain distinctive rights domestically and in international law, indigenous peoples and advocates for indigenous peoples' rights have advanced a range of justifications for rights recognition.[6] Indigenous peoples have emphasised their historical self-determination living under a pre-colonial customary legal system; their status as the first, or prior, peoples on the land; the destructive effect of colonisation on their political autonomy and territorial rights and distinctive way of life; and their non-dominant and vulnerable status within a state.[7] Indigenous peoples have also stressed their survival and continued existence as distinctive peoples with a unique culture vis-à-vis the dominant society and other minority groups. Linked to this is the notion that indigenous peoples' rights are inherent in nature in that their rights exist because of their customary laws and not state law.[8]

These justifications have provided a strong foundation for the official recognition of indigenous peoples' rights, and many states have responded by adopting measures to recognise indigenous peoples' customary laws, and traditional land rights, and provide redress for the wrongful taking of lands. International institutions have also sought to protect indigenous peoples' rights, and the UN and OAS Inter-American Human Rights System have prepared detailed declarations of indigenous peoples' rights that seek to maintain and rehabilitate indigenous systems and institutions and protect their relationship with traditional lands.[9]

While all of these justifications have played a role in persuading states and international institutions to recognise indigenous peoples' rights to traditional lands, the focus on tradition and cultural distinctiveness can work against indigenous peoples obtaining due recognition of their rights. The problem is illustrated by the concept that indigenous property rights owe their existence

---

6. On international law's human rights programme and indigenous peoples generally, see S J Anaya *Indigenous Peoples in International Law* (2ed, Oxford University Press, Oxford, 2004).
7. See Jose Martinez Cobo, Chairperson/Rapporteur of the Working Group on Indigenous Populations 'Study of the Problem of Discrimination against Indigenous Populations' (1986) E/CN.4/Sub.2/1986/7/Add.4, paras 379–380.
8. Erica-Irene A Daes, Special Rapporteur, UN Sub-Commission on Prevention of Discrimination and Protection of Minorities 'Indigenous people and their relationship to land: Second progress report on the working paper prepared by Mrs. Erica-Irene A Daes, Special Rapporteur' (3 June 1999) E/CN.4/Sub.2/1999/18.
9. See UN Declaration, above n 5. See also the Proposed American Declaration on the Rights of Indigenous Peoples, Inter-Am. C.H.R., 133d Sess., Art. 18, OEA/Ser L/V/II.95.doc.7, rev. 1997 (1997).

to indigenous customary legal systems.[10] For many it makes sense to speak of indigenous peoples' rights, such as traditional land rights, having their basis in pre-colonial indigenous legal systems. It was this normative system that first created and regulated the use of property and social and political relations. But it can be dangerous to conceive of indigenous rights as having their basis today solely in extant indigenous customary law. It is too easy for states to take the next step and define the nature of modern rights with reference to those laws. The fact is that for many indigenous peoples these customary laws are, after many years of colonisation, difficult to identify. In many states, indigenous peoples have been forced to abandon their distinctive cultural attributes and customary laws. This abandonment has resulted in the loss of much knowledge of the substance of specific customary laws. Additionally, in many cases, indigenous peoples have had to adapt, sometimes radically, their customs and practices just to survive. State and state court inquiries into customary laws may fail to appreciate the capacity for the laws to adapt to the changes wrought by colonisation.[11] Therefore, modern efforts to identify customary laws will in many cases be faced with considerable obstacles. For communities that have suffered the loss of lands, warfare and disease, that task is much harder.

But let me stress that this does not mean that indigenous peoples' customary law should have no role at all in the determination of indigenous land claims. What I wish to emphasise is that relying on evidence of modern customary law *only* to determine the nature of land rights can create substantial evidential difficulties for indigenous peoples. As argued below, it is much easier for indigenous peoples to establish interests in land through the objective standard of how lands are actually used by them. Evidence of customary land tenure laws, if accessible, can assist with this process.

B STATE ENDEAVOURS TO RECOGNISE INDIGENOUS PEOPLES' PROPERTY RIGHTS

1 *Defining Indigenous Peoples' Land Rights with Reference to Indigenous Customary Laws*

The difficulties posed by the focus on indigenous peoples' customary laws are well illustrated by claims to land rights under the common law doctrine

---

10. For the classic judicial pronouncement of this idea, see the judgment of Brennan J in *Mabo v Queensland (No 2)* (1992) 175 CLR 1, 56 (HCA). Brennan J noted that: '[n]ative title has its origin in, and is given its content by, the traditional customs observed by the indigenous inhabitants of a territory.'
11. Generally, see P G McHugh *Aboriginal Societies and the Common Law: A History of Sovereignty, Status, and Self-Determination* (Oxford University Press, Oxford, 2005), commenting on the tendency of historians and courts to view aboriginal histories as a simple tale of communities being overwhelmed by white settlement with little appreciation of their capacity for resistance and adaptation.

of native title in Australia especially, and aboriginal rights in Canada. In Australia, rights to traditional lands (called native title lands) are said to have their juridical basis, or origins, in existing aboriginal custom law.[12] In addition, the Native Title Act 1993 (NTA), enacted to provide a framework for the judicial determination of native title claims, takes the matter a step further by requiring courts to determine 'native title rights and interests' by reference to these customs.[13] This is the unique nature of native title law in Australia. To establish native title rights and interests, aboriginal communities must provide evidence of the customary laws that create and govern the use of aboriginal land practices. It is not enough to provide evidence of the land practices only – there must also be an inquiry into the underlying normative basis for the practice. In addition, the Australian High Court has interpreted the NTA in a very conservative manner, as noted in detail in Dorsett's chapter.[14] The reference to 'native title rights and interests' in the NTA has been read as referring to particular traditional uses of, or interests in, land supported by specific customs – hunting, fishing and so on – and not a broader, overarching 'right to land' arising from an indigenous legal system.[15] The High Court has also ruled that the common law may recognise only those native title rights and interests that have their source ultimately in pre-sovereignty customary laws.[16] There is some room for adaptation of customary laws, but the law of native title cannot give effect to rights and interests that are sourced in new customs established after sovereignty.[17] Besides the complexities raised by the interpretation and translation of indigenous customary law, there is the practical and significant matter of proving the very existence of customary laws. Native title is dependent on customary laws that remain extant at the time of the judicial inquiry (see the comments on continuity, below). This has proven especially difficult for those aboriginal communities subjected to intensive settlement.[18]

---

12. See *Mabo v Queensland (No 2)*, above n 10.
13. NTA, s 223.
14. See Shaunnagh Dorsett's chapter in this book, 59–82.
15. See *Western Australia v Ward* (2002) 191 ALR 1 (HCA) Gleeson CJ, Gaudron, Gummow and Hayne JJ, para 14. See Shaunnagh Dorsett's chapter in this book, 59–82.
16. *Members of the Yorta Yorta Aboriginal Community v Victoria* [2002] HCA 58 (12 December 2002) per Gleeson CJ, Gummow and Hayne JJ, McHugh J and Callinan J, with Kirby J and Gaudron J dissenting.
17. *Members of the Yorta Yorta Aboriginal Community*, above n 16, paras 43-44. The justification for this rule is that after sovereignty indigenous normative systems could not create new rights and interests that are recognised by the new sovereign order as 'there could be no parallel law-making system after the assertion of sovereignty.' Above n 16, para 44.
18. For critiques of this approach see D Lavery 'A Greater Source of Tradition: The Implications of the Normative System Principles in *Yorta Yorta* for Native Title Determinations' (2003) 10(4) E-Law 65 <http://www.murdoch.edu.au/elaw> (last accessed 20 February 2006); and Richard Bartlett 'An

2 Defining Indigenous Peoples' Land Rights with Reference to Indigenous Land Practices

In Canada, the courts have adopted a more flexible approach to proving land rights (called aboriginal rights and title). In order to ground a claim to aboriginal title – which confers a modern right to occupy land exclusively – claimants must establish evidence of exclusive occupation of the land claimed at sovereignty. Such an approach focuses on the objective standard of how lands are actually used by indigenous peoples, rather than on the underlying normative system governing use. This principle was established by Lamer CJ in the leading aboriginal title decision of the Supreme Court in *Delgamuukw v British Columbia* (*Delgamuukw*).[19] The Court in *Delgamuukw* was clearly sensitive to the evidential difficulties that arise from seeking evidence of specific customary laws.

What amounts to occupation, however, can be contentious. In *Delgamuukw* the state (British Columbia and Canada) had argued that occupation must be the physical occupation of the land in question at sovereignty as determined by the common law. On the face of it, that implied the need for evidence of regular and intensive use of the lands by the aboriginal title claimants. The aboriginal claimants (the Gitxsan nation), however, argued that aboriginal title may be established, at least in part, by reference to aboriginal customary law.[20] The reason for this argument plainly was that aboriginal land tenure systems at sovereignty did not always strictly conform to the types of occupation and use that would ordinarily qualify as occupation under the common law. The claimants, therefore, sought to have the common law test of occupation adjusted to accommodate indigenous forms of land tenure.

Lamer CJ decided that both common law and aboriginal perspectives must be taken into account given that aboriginal title involved reconciling aboriginal rights with the Crown's assertion of sovereignty.[21] According to Lamer CJ, the aboriginal perspective could be gleaned in part, but not exclusively, from aboriginal systems of law (including a land tenure system or laws governing land use).[22] In relation to the common law test, Lamer CJ noted that physical occupation may be established in a variety of ways:[23]

> ranging from the construction of dwellings through cultivation and enclosure of fields to regular use of definite tracts of land for hunting, fishing or otherwise exploiting its resources. In considering whether occupation sufficient to ground

---

Obsession with Traditional Laws and Customs Creates Difficulty Establishing Native Title Claims in the South: *Yorta Yorta*' (2003) 31 UWALR 35.
19. *Delgamuukw v British Columbia* [1997] 3 SCR 1010.
20. *Delgamuukw*, above n 19, para 146 Lamer CJ.
21. *Delgamuukw*, above n 19, para 148 Lamer CJ.
22. *Delgamuukw*, above n 19, paras 147–148 Lamer CJ.
23. *Delgamuukw*, above n 19, para 149 Lamer CJ.

title is established, one must take into account the group's size, manner of life, material resources, and technological abilities, and the character of the lands claimed.

According to the common law, occupation is thus a relative matter that depends upon the nature of the land and the uses to which it can practically be put. The meaning of 'manner of life' referred to by Lamer CJ was elaborated by La Forest J, who stated that:[24]

> when dealing with a claim of 'aboriginal title', the court will focus on the occupation and use of the land as part of the aboriginal society's *traditional way of life*. In pragmatic terms, this means looking at the manner in which the society used the land *to live*, namely to establish villages, to work, to get to work, to hunt, to travel to hunting grounds, to fish, to get to fishing pools, to conduct religious rites, etc.

As noted, there must be evidence that the occupation at sovereignty was exclusive. But again, Lamer CJ noted that the determination of exclusivity must consider both common law and aboriginal perspectives, placing equal weight on each:[25]

> [E]xclusive occupation can be demonstrated even if other aboriginal groups were present, or frequented the claimed lands. Under those circumstances, exclusivity would be demonstrated by the intention and capacity to retain exclusive control … Thus, an act of trespass, if isolated, would not undermine a general finding of exclusivity, if aboriginal groups intended to and attempted to enforce their exclusive occupation.

In sum, the meaning of 'occupation' and 'exclusivity' in aboriginal title claims must take account of aboriginal perspectives. That will require consideration of the way the land is actually used by the community in terms of the physical practices conducted on the land, such as the construction of habitations and the use of particular gardens and hunting sites, and also their customary laws and spiritual and sociopolitical attachment to the land. The aboriginal perspective would prove useful in those cases where the state has adopted a narrow approach to the question of occupation, requiring aboriginal peoples to prove that the land claimed has been occupied in a regular and intensive manner. The aboriginal perspective allows aboriginal peoples to argue that while land may not have been occupied on a permanent basis – for example, it was used seasonally or cyclically – in their eyes the land was occupied by them.

---

24. *Delgamuukw*, above n 19, para 194 La Forest J (emphasis in the original).
25. *Delgamuukw*, above n 19, para 149 Lamer CJ.

Nevertheless, the recent companion decisions of the Canadian Supreme Court in *R v Marshall* and *R v Bernard* illustrate how difficult it remains for aboriginal peoples with a semi-nomadic history to meet the standards required for an aboriginal title claim.[26] *Marshall* and *Bernard* concerned two separate appeals from criminal convictions for the logging of timber on state lands without authorisation in the adjacent eastern seaboard provinces of Nova Scotia and New Brunswick.[27] In each case, the defendants were Mi'kmaq Indians who claimed a logging right on the specific tracts of lands for commercial purposes pursuant to aboriginal title.[28] In the *Marshall* case, the evidence at trial showed that the Mi'kmaq, at the date of sovereignty, consisted of small communities living in most of mainland Nova Scotia and there was no other aboriginal group there at that time.[29] The Mi'kmaq were described as 'moderately nomadic' peoples who did not have permanent settlements and 'moved with the seasons and circumstances to follow their resources.'[30] Nonetheless, the trial judge found that the Mi'kmaq were familiar with their territory and considered all of Nova Scotia to be their territory.[31] In the *Bernard* case, the trial evidence disclosed a similar nomadic existence for Mi'kmaq residing within New Brunswick.[32]

The central questions were whether the Mi'kmaq had satisfied the *Delgamuukw* tests of occupation in relation to the specific cutting sites and whether that occupation was exclusive. The trial courts in each case concluded that exclusive occupation required proof of intensive, regular use of the cutting sites and that had not been established in evidence.[33] On appeal, both the Nova Scotia and New Brunswick Courts of Appeal ruled that these standards were too strict and that there was no need for the appellants to prove regular use of the cutting sites to establish aboriginal title.[34] In *Marshall* the appellate court ruled that it was sufficient to prove occasional entry and acts on the logging sites.[35] The appellate court in *Bernard* similarly concluded that it was only necessary to show that the Mi'kmaq had occupied an area near the cutting site.[36]

---

26. *R v Marshall* and *R v Bernard* [2005] 2 SCR 220.
27. *R v Bernard* [2000] 3 CNLR 184; *R v Marshall* [2001] 191 NSR(2d) 323.
28. *R v Marshall* and *R v Bernard*, above n 26. The defendants also raised a treaty right to harvest timber as a defence based on friendship treaties (not involving the cession of aboriginal lands) that recognised a right to trade in items traditionally traded in 1760–61. This argument also failed in the Supreme Court.
29. *R v Marshall* and *R v Bernard*, above n 26, para 79 (citing *R v Marshall*, above n 27, para 142).
30. *R v Marshall* and *R v Bernard*, above n 26, para 79.
31. *R v Marshall*, above n 27 para 135.
32. *R v Marshall* and *R v Bernard*, above n 26, para 81 (citing *R v Bernard*, above n 27 paras 107–08, 110).
33. *R v Bernard*, above n 27, para 107; *R v Marshall*, above n 27 paras 139–42.
34. *R v Marshall* [2003] 218 NSR(2d) 78, para 136; *R v Bernard* [2003] 262 NBR(2d) 1, para 119.
35. *R v Marshall*, above n 34.
36. *R v Bernard*, above n 34.

In the Supreme Court, McLachlin CJ, delivering the majority judgment, rejected the more expansive approach adopted by the appellate courts. According to McLachlin CJ, the courts' central task is to determine whether the pre-sovereignty aboriginal practice comported with the modern legal right claimed.[37] If the claim related to aboriginal title – conferring a modern right to exclusive use and occupation of land – then it was essential that the pre-sovereignty practice demonstrate some correlation with that right.[38] This did not require 'absolute congruity,' provided 'the practices engage the core idea of the modern right.'[39] The aboriginal perspective, according to McLachlin CJ, would assist the Court in its assessment of the true nature of the pre-sovereignty right or practice.[40] Based on these propositions, the judge concluded that both trial decisions had correctly ruled that the Mi'kmaq had not occupied the logging sites in question on a regular and exclusive basis and therefore could not claim an aboriginal title to the lands claimed.[41]

The *Marshall* and *Bernard* decisions would seem to represent a retreat from the principles established in *Delgamuukw* by Lamer CJ. The aboriginal perspective is not employed to temper the common law standards of occupation and exclusivity – as was intended by Lamer CJ – but rather as a mere interpretative tool to determine whether a pre-sovereignty practice corresponds with the rights embodied in aboriginal title.[42] If those aboriginal practices do not indicate possession similar to that associated with title at common law then there can be aboriginal title.

However, failing to adjust the common law standards to accord with aboriginal forms of land tenure has the effect of penalising aboriginal peoples for normative divergence. After *Bernard* and *Marshall* it appears that only those aboriginal peoples with a relatively settled and agrarian history will have some opportunity of obtaining aboriginal title.[43]

3   *The Requirement of Continuity of Indigenous Peoples' Rights in Lands*
The doctrine of native title in Australia is directed at the recognition and enforceability of *extant* traditional property rights, being those rights that are

---

37. *R v Marshall* and *R v Bernard*, above n 26, para 48 McLachlin CJ.
38. *R v Marshall* and *R v Bernard*, above n 26, paras 48, 51 McLachlin CJ.
39. *R v Marshall* and *R v Bernard*, above n 26, paras 48, 51 McLachlin CJ.
40. *R v Marshall* and *R v Bernard*, above n 26, paras 48–50 McLachlin CJ.
41. *R v Marshall* and *R v Bernard*, above n 26, paras 70, 72 McLachlin CJ.
42. *R v Marshall* and *R v Bernard*, above n 26, paras 48–50 McLachlin CJ.
43. See the minority decision of LeBel J (with Fish J concurring) in *R v Marshall* and *R v Bernard*, above n 26. LeBel J notes that the majority approach places too much emphasis on the common law notion of occupation. Instead LeBel and Fish JJ, argue that 'aboriginal conceptions of territoriality, land-use and property should be used to modify and adapt the traditional common law concepts of property in order to develop an occupancy standard that incorporates both the aboriginal and common law approaches.'

in existence at the date of the judicial inquiry. In addition, aboriginal claimants in Australia must produce evidence of a continuous traditional association with their native title lands from the date of the judicial inquiry back to the time of sovereignty through customary law. This requirement of continuity of native title has its origins in the judgment of Brennan J in *Mabo v Queensland (No 2)* (*Mabo (No 2)*):[44]

> [W]hen the tide of history has washed away any real acknowledgment of traditional law and any real observance of traditional customs, the foundation of native title has disappeared. A native title which has ceased with the abandoning of laws and customs based on tradition cannot be revived for contemporary recognition.

That creates significant evidential obstacles for Australian aboriginal peoples, especially those who have felt the full effects of western settlement and expansion.[45]

In Canada, as noted by McNeil in his chapter, continuity is not used in the Australian sense so that an aboriginal title expires through the claimant group's lack of a continuing association with aboriginal title lands.[46] Rather, McNeil's analysis of the Canadian case law illustrates that the need to establish continuity only arises where there is no evidence of exclusive occupation of aboriginal title lands at sovereignty. In such cases, aboriginal title claimants are able to rely on present occupation as evidence of occupation at sovereignty if they show the substantial maintenance of a connection with the land from the present back to the time of sovereignty.[47] As McNeil puts it, the use of continuity is intended to 'help overcome the onerous burden faced by aboriginal claimants in proving rights based on ... occupation of land a long time in the past.'[48] The Canadian approach to continuity, then, is fundamentally different to the Australian. But, that said, even though aboriginal title claimants may rely on their present occupation of lands, they are still required to provide evidence of their connection to the land back to the time of sovereignty. That is a very long time and in Canada, as with Australia, there is a well-known history of state oppression of aboriginal peoples and tribal displacement.

---

44. See *Mabo (No 2)*, above n 10, 59–60 Brennan J.
45. See Shaunnagh Dorsett's chapter in this book, 59–82.
46. See Kent McNeil's chapter in this book, 83–118.
47. *Delgamuukw*, above n 19, para 153.
48. See Kent McNeil's chapter in this book, 115. In addition to this, aboriginal claimants must also show that the group claiming rights today is connected with the group that held the land at the time of sovereignty; and claimants of aboriginal rights – that is, right to engage in specific traditional activities – must show that the present activity claimed fits within the scope of the activity exercised in pre-colonial times.

4   The Impact of Litigation

It must be emphasised that an indigenous peoples' claim to traditional lands in Australia and Canada is an adversarial process and as a result is intensely political. Claims to traditional lands are highly contentious matters and courts are acutely sensitive to the political nature of their decisions. Judges, as one would expect in such circumstances, tend to err on the side of conservatism. Many judges, aware of the limits of litigation, have expressed their preference for indigenous claims to lands to be addressed through negotiation or a system of arbitration. For example, McHugh J, noting the few gains made in native title litigation in the High Court decision of *Western Australia v Ward*, suggested instead that the state consider implementing an arbitral system that accords rights on the basis of merit and justice:[49]

> The dispossession of the Aboriginal peoples from their lands was a great wrong ... But it is becoming increasingly clear – to me, at all events – that redress cannot be achieved by a system that depends on evaluating the competing legal rights of landholders and native-title holders. The deck is stacked against the native-title holders whose fragile rights must give way to the superior rights of the landholders whenever the two classes of rights conflict. And it is a system that is costly and time-consuming. At present the chief beneficiaries of the system are the legal representatives of the parties. It may be that the time has come to think of abandoning the present system, a system that simply seeks to declare and enforce the legal rights of the parties, irrespective of their merits. A better system may be an arbitral system that declares what the rights of the parties *ought to be* according to the justice and circumstances of the individual case.

This illustrates the importance of states establishing mechanisms for recognition that are not weighed down by strict legal criteria and are sympathetic to the effect of colonisation on indigenous communities.

---

49. See *Western Australia v Ward*, above n 15, para 561 McHugh J (emphasis in the original). See also the comments of Callinan J in *Western Australia v Ward*, above n 15, para 970: 'I do not disparage the importance to the Aboriginal people of their native title rights, including those that have symbolic significance. I fear, however, that in many cases because of the chasm between the common law and native title rights, the latter, when recognised, will amount to little more than symbols. It might have been better to redress the wrongs of dispossession by a true and unqualified settlement of lands or money than by an ultimately futile or unsatisfactory, in my respectful opinion, attempt to fold native title rights into the common law.' In relation to Canada, see the comments of Lamer J in *Delgamuukw*, above n 19, para 186: 'Ultimately, it is through negotiated settlements, with good faith and give and take on all sides, reinforced by the judgments of this Court, that we will achieve what I stated in *Van der Peet* to be a basic purpose of s. 35(1) – "the reconciliation of the pre-existence of aboriginal societies with the sovereignty of the Crown."'

5   Importing the Common Law Jurisprudence to New Zealand

It seems clear, even from the *Ngati Apa* decision, that the Māori Land Court's post-*Ngati Apa* jurisdiction would have been coloured by the standards of proof established in Australian native title and Canadian aboriginal rights litigation. While not required to determine the rights claimed in the *Ngati Apa* decision, Elias CJ indicated that the rights available, after determination by the Māori Land Court, could be limited to specific and discrete areas such as shellfish banks and closely held harbours.[50] Further, Gault J considered that the creation of a Māori freehold title was unlikely unless the customary title rights and incidents were comparable to the ownership interests that come with a freehold title.[51] In other words, to acquire such a freehold title, tribes would need to prove that the land was occupied exclusively in the common law sense. The Waitangi Tribunal, when considering the possible trajectory of the jurisdiction of the Māori Land Court post-*Ngati Apa*, implicitly concluded that rights could expire over time through lack of association with the foreshore, resulting in the loss of customary interests altogether.[52] It is clear, too, that the Australian continuity test greatly influenced the New Zealand Government's formulation of the standards of proof outlined in the FSA. Before the enactment of the FSA, the Deputy Prime Minister counselled New Zealanders concerned about the possible impact of the *Ngati Apa* decision on their rights of access to the coast:[53]

> Non-Maori New Zealanders need not fear a wholesale limitation on their rights of access to their favourite portions of the coast. The weight of legal precedent indicates that customary rights are recognised and protected only where they have been exercised more or less continuously. It is hard to argue that a practice is in fact a 'custom' if it has fallen into abeyance over many years. In this instance, past history must be corroborated by recent practice … What this means is that a relatively small proportion of the foreshore and seabed is likely to be the subject of customary use. It is certainly not envisaged that on large stretches of the coast long dormant practices might be resuscitated and granted status as customary rights.

The Australian continuity test has been incorporated into the FSA.[54] The FSA provides for the recognition by the High Court of a right akin to Canadian aboriginal title, called a territorial customary right order (TCRO).

---

50. *Ngati Apa*, above n 1, para 9 Elias CJ.
51. *Ngati Apa*, above n 1, para 106 Gault P.
52. See Waitangi Tribunal *Report on the Crown's Foreshore and Seabed Policy: Wai 1071* (Legislation Direct, Wellington, 2004) para 3.7.2.
53. Hon Dr Michael Cullen 'Address to Waipukurau Rotary Club' (Waipukurau Rotary Club, 15 March 2004) Official Website of the New Zealand Government <http://www.beehive.govt.nz> (last accessed 17 March 2006).
54. See chapters in this book by Kent McNeil (83–118) and Shaunnagh Dorsett (59–82).

To obtain such an order, Māori tribes must prove that the foreshore land in question has been continually occupied and exclusively so, without substantial interruption, from 1840 to the commencement of the FSA.[55] (If such a right is proved, the TCRO holders are not entitled to occupy the lands, rather the holders are entitled to either enter into negotiations with government officials to discuss redress or establish a reserve for the co-management of the land with the Government.) To obtain a customary rights order (CRO) – which confers the right to engage in traditional activities – tribes must prove that the activity is integral to tribal custom (tikanga Māori) and has been practised in a substantially uninterrupted manner from 1840 to the commencement of the FSA.[56] It can be seen too, that CROs entail a judicial inquiry into the substance of tribal customary law and that with claims to TCROs, there is no express requirement that occupation and exclusivity be determined with reference to Māori tribal perspectives.

6 *Summary*

While Australia, Canada and now New Zealand have taken steps to recognise indigenous peoples' rights in traditional lands, states tend to use tradition to deny or read-down rights to traditional lands. There is no need for courts to adopt a strictly linear approach to continuity of association with lands, and land rights do not have to be defined by reference solely to indigenous peoples' custom law. Further, indigenous peoples should not be penalised because their land tenure patterns do not meet common law standards of occupation and exclusivity. Many of these problems result from the use of custom and tradition to rationalise aboriginal rights claims, but it is also due to the legal formalism that is inherent in native title and aboriginal rights litigation, and especially the highly political nature of litigation. The approach towards recognising traditional lands is all-important. If states fail to meet indigenous peoples' expectations, often the only alternative, if the avenue is available to them, is to have their claims contested before international human rights treaty bodies. This chapter now turns to consider the role that these treaty bodies have had in monitoring the methods by which states recognise indigenous land rights.

III *International and Regional Human Rights Treaties and Indigenous Peoples' Traditional Lands*

Different types of international human rights treaties have been appealed to by indigenous peoples to advance their claims to rights within states. The

---

55. FSA, s 32.
56. FSA, s 50(1)(b).

treaties may have either a regional or international scope, but they only apply to states that have ratified the treaty. These include international treaties like the International Covenant on Civil and Political Rights (the ICCPR), and the International Convention on the Elimination of All Forms of Racial Discrimination (the ICERD) – which have both been widely ratified[57] – and regional treaties such as the American Convention on Human Rights.[58]

Most of these human rights treaties establish judicial-like bodies, or treaty bodies, to monitor state compliance with the treaty by reviewing periodic reports from states on their performance. In addition, states may consent to a complaint mechanism under the treaty, whereby individuals within the state may lodge a complaint, called a communication, to the treaty body alleging the infringement of specific rights in the treaty. In most cases, communications may be lodged only after all domestic remedies have been exhausted. The actual hearing of the communication and a decision from the treaty body can be slow in coming. Recognition of this has prompted the ICERD Committee to establish a new early warning procedure whereby a complaint may be promptly addressed by the Committee where there is particular cause for concern that some proposed state action may result in violation of the ICERD.[59] Through all of these processes human rights treaty bodies are often required to evaluate the methods by which states recognise indigenous land rights.[60]

It is often said that these treaties are not ideal for indigenous peoples in that they are based on the notion of protecting the rights of the individual as against the state and as such do not fully accommodate indigenous peoples' collective rights.[61] For example, protection of the right to property does not appear, on its face, to accommodate indigenous forms of property because the property is held collectively. Nevertheless, indigenous peoples have had some success in co-opting these norms by expanding the ordinary meaning of human rights within treaties so they may include indigenous peoples' rights.

---

57. ICCPR and ICERD, above n 3. In 2007 the ICCPR was ratified by 160 states and the ICERD by 173 states: Office of the High Commissioner for Human Rights *Status of Ratifications of the Principal International Human Rights Treaties* (9 June 2004) Office of the High Commissioner for Human Rights <http://www.ohchr.org/english> (last accessed 20 February 2007).
58. See American Convention on Human Rights, above n 2.
59. The ICERD Committee's criteria for invoking its early warning procedure are not closed but include matters such as the lack of an adequate legislative basis for defining and criminalising all forms of racial discrimination, and inadequate implementation of enforcement mechanisms – including the lack of recourse procedures. This makes the early warning procedure of special interest to indigenous peoples in states that lack sufficiently robust constitutional constraints in relation to the enactment of legislation affecting their land rights. See the discussion in Claire Charters and Andrew Erueti 'Report From The Inside: The CERD Committee's Review of the Foreshore and Seabed Act 2004' (2005) 36 VUWLR 257.
60. See S J Anaya, above n 6, 248–271.
61. See Claire Charters 'Developments in Indigenous Peoples Rights Under International Law and their Domestic Implications' (2005) 21 NZULR 511.

The OAS Inter-American Human Rights System, as noted below, accepted the argument from the indigenous peoples' advocates that the right to property in the treaty under consideration included collective property rights to land based on traditional patterns of use and occupation.[62]

A   THE ORGANISATION OF AMERICAN STATES INTER-AMERICAN HUMAN RIGHTS SYSTEM

The most progressive and comprehensive decisions from treaty bodies on traditional lands have come from the Inter-American system of human rights established by the Organisation of American States (OAS).[63] The OAS has for several decades been keenly conscious of the struggle of indigenous peoples in the Americas, and in particular within those regions subject to civil war and severe human rights abuse.[64] The human rights system has two treaty bodies charged with monitoring compliance with OAS human rights treaties.[65] The Inter-American Commission on Human Rights (Inter-American Commission) hears complaints, or petitions, from individuals or groups who claim the violation of any right under the American Convention on Human Rights (American Convention),[66] where OAS member states have ratified that treaty, and the American Declaration of the Rights and Duties of Man (American Declaration),[67] which extends to all OAS member states.

The Inter-American Commission may only start an investigation if all domestic remedies have been exhausted. While the Inter-American Commission's decisions are recommendatory, if states fail to respond appeals can be made to the Inter-American Court of Human Rights (Inter-American Court), a judicial body which may issue binding decisions, if the state concerned is a party to the American Convention and has consented to the Court's jurisdiction. Appeals to the Inter-American Court can be lodged by the Inter-American Commission or states. Recent decisions of the Inter-American Commission and Court exemplify the utility of human rights treaty bodies in protecting indigenous peoples' rights to traditional lands and illustrate alternatives to the evidential standards seen in Australia, Canada and New Zealand.

The *Mayagna (Sumo) Awas Tingni Community v Nicaragua* (*Awas Tingni*)

---

62. See the decision of the Inter-American Court of Human Rights in *Mayagna (Sumo) Awas Tingni Community v Nicaragua* (31 August 2001) Inter-Am Court H R (Ser C) No 79, paras 138, 164. See also the Inter-American Commission of Human Rights decision in *Maya Indigenous Communities of the Toledo District v Belize* (12 October 2004) Inter-Am Comm H R Case 12.053 Report No 40/04, paras 20–21.
63. See generally, S J Anaya, above n 6.
64. See S J Anaya, above n 6.
65. See S J Anaya, above n 6, 258–271.
66. American Convention on Human Rights, above n 2.
67. American Declaration of the Rights and Duties of Man, above n 2.

decision[68] and *Maya Indigenous Communities of the Toledo District v Belize* (*Maya*) decision[69] – of the Inter-American Court and Commission, respectively – both concerned efforts by indigenous communities to obtain formal legal recognition of their traditional lands. The Awas Tingni petition was concerned with Miskito, Mayagna (Sumo) and Rama Indians of the Atlantic coast of Nicaragua, while the Maya petition was concerned with Maya communities of the Toledo district of southern Belize.[70] In each case, the communities occupied their traditional lands, but they had been unable to obtain formal recognition of their titles from the state. In the meantime, the states had simply treated the lands as state lands and granted concessions to third parties for resource exploitation over the lands. The Awas Tingni petition was brought before the Inter-American Court in June 1998 by the Inter-American Commission on behalf of the indigenous communities after Nicaragua had failed to comply with a direction from the Commission to demarcate and officially recognise their lands. The Maya communities, being unable to obtain relief domestically, lodged a petition in August 1998 with the Inter-American Commission under the American Declaration. In each case, the communities alleged violation of the right to property, among other rights.[71] With regard to the right to property, it was argued that 'property' should be interpreted to encompass not only Western property rights recognised by the state, but also the property interests that arise from indigenous systems of land tenure.

1 The Requirement of Continuity of Indigenous Peoples' Rights in Lands

In response to the Maya and Awas Tingni petitions, both Nicaragua and Belize argued that while the communities inhabited the traditional lands claimed, they were not the ancestral occupants of the lands – that is, the land claimed was not occupied by them in pre-colonial times. In relation to the *Awas Tingni* case, Nicaragua argued that the community was a recent migrating group, with a nomadic lifestyle, that had travelled to the land in question after splitting from an original community in the mid-twentieth century. Their claims were

---

68. *Mayagna (Sumo) Awas Tingni Community v Nicaragua* (31 August 2001) Inter-Am Court H R (Ser C) No 79 (also published in (2002) 19 Ariz J Int'l & Comp L 395). For a description of the proceedings leading to the decision, see S J Anaya and C Grossman 'The Case of *Awas Tingni v Nicaragua*: A New Step in the International Law of Indigenous Peoples' (2002) 19 Arizona J Int'l and Comp L 1.
69. *Maya Indigenous Communities of the Toledo District v Belize* (12 October 2004) Inter-Am Comm H R Case 12.053 Report No 40/04.
70. The petition was lodged by the Indian Law Resource Center and the Toledo Maya Cultural Council on behalf of the Mopan and Ke'kchi Maya People of the Toledo District of Southern Belize.
71. Article 21 of the American Convention on Human Rights provides: 'Everyone has the right to the use and enjoyment of his property.' Similarly, article XXIII of the American Declaration of the Rights and Duties of Man affirms the right of every person 'to own such private property as meets the essential needs of decent living and helps to maintain the dignity of the individual and the home.'

not, therefore, ancestral as their ancestral lands were elsewhere. The same issue arose in the *Maya* case. Belize argued that as it was once an English colony, the common law jurisprudence of aboriginal rights – which would be either binding or of significant persuasive influence on the Belize courts – would apply to the Maya communities. According to those principles, it was not clear that the Maya could establish an aboriginal title right to occupy the lands exclusively.[72] In particular, Belize asserted that four criteria are necessary for the establishment of aboriginal title:[73]

1. that the applicants and their ancestors were members of an organized society;
2. that the organized society occupied the specific territory over which they assert the aboriginal title;
3. that the occupation was to the exclusion of other organized societies; and
4. that the occupation was an established fact at the time sovereignty was asserted.

Belize claimed that most of the villages and lands claimed were established in the late 1900s, some as late as 1992, and that this illustrated 'a significant break in the continuity of occupation of the area over which title is asserted',[74] and in the absence of continuous exclusive occupation, the claim could not be established. The Awas Tingni and Maya communities, in response to the states' arguments, had argued that there was a clear historical continuity between them and pre-colonial peoples, and that they had occupied and used the land in question for a long duration in accordance with their traditional land tenure. Because of the passage of time and the effects of colonisation, these communities could not be expected to have continuously resided within fixed ancestral territories from pre-colonial times.

The Inter-American Court, in relation to the *Awas Tingni* decision, and the Inter-American Commission, in relation to the *Maya* decision, accepted that on the evidence, there was a communal property right to the lands inhabited by their communities and that this property was protected by the right to property in the relevant OAS human rights treaties. This property right was based on their 'traditional, ancestral patterns of use and occupation.'[75] The Commission and Court clearly rejected the claim that there must be evidence of a continuous connection to the lands claimed from the time of sovereignty. There was a clear historical continuity between the communities and pre-

---

72. It is clear that the reference to 'aboriginal title' was the type of title recognised in *Delgamuukw*, above n 19; that is, it conferred on the title-holders the right to occupy aboriginal title lands exclusively.
73. *Maya* decision, above n 69, para 71.
74. *Maya* decision, above n 69, para 72.
75. *Maya* decision, above n 69, para 20-21. *Awas Tingni* decision, above n 68, para 138, 164.

colonial peoples, and the communities had occupied and used the land in question for a long duration.[76]

2   Guiding Principles for the Demarcation of Lands

While the Awas Tingni had argued before the Inter-American Court that their traditional land tenure system generated a body of customary laws, they did not claim that demarcation and titling of their lands should occur with reference only to their customary laws. Rather, Awas Tingni had argued that their communal property rights to lands and natural resources were 'based on traditional patterns of use and occupation of ancestral territory.'[77] This would suggest that the identification and demarcation of Awas Tingni lands should occur with reference to their physical occupation and use of lands under their land tenure system. However, the Inter-American Court in its decision did not provide clear guidance about how the Awas Tingni lands should be demarcated. The Court did note that '[a]s a result of customary practices, possession of the land should suffice for indigenous communities lacking real title to property of the land to obtain official recognition of that property.'[78] But the reference to 'possession of the land' simply begs the question of what might constitute 'possession'. The Court's reference to 'customary practices' might suggest that the Awas Tingni possesses those lands that are physically occupied and used by the community. But the matter is far from clear as the Court's final direction to Nicaragua is that it identify and demarcate the Awas Tingni lands 'in accordance with their customary law, values, customs and mores.'

The *Maya* decision, decided by the Inter-American Commission after the *Awas Tingni* decision, provides much clearer guidance on this point. The Inter-American Commission concluded that the Maya communal property right to their lands was based on their 'long standing use and occupancy of the territory.'[79] The Commission then recommended that Belize 'provide the Maya people with an effective remedy, which includes recognising their communal property right to the lands that they have traditionally occupied and used, without detriment to other indigenous communities, and to delimit, demarcate and title the territory in which this communal property right exists, in accordance with the customary land use practices of the Maya people.'[80]

It is clear, then, that in the *Maya* decision the Commission does not direct Belize to demarcate the Maya lands solely in accordance with customary law.

---

76. *Maya* decision, above n 69, para 127–30.
77. *Awas Tingni* decision, above n 68, para 140(a).
78. *Awas Tingni* decision, above n 68, para 151.
79. *Maya* decision, above n 69, paras 127–30.
80. *Maya* decision, above n 69, para 6.

Rather it is the current and long-standing physical occupation and use of the land that is all-important. The Maya community has the property right to those lands that they have traditionally occupied and used. In addition, the reference to 'traditional' occupation and use, and the Commission's direction to demarcate lands in accordance with the customary land use practices of the Maya people, illustrates that demarcation must be consistent with Maya perspectives on their use and occupation of lands. The meaning of 'occupation and use' must therefore be determined with regard to Maya land tenure practices, their customary laws (if accessible), and their spiritual and sociopolitical connection with the land. This would counter any argument that the right of occupation is limited to only those lands that are occupied on a regular and intensive basis.[81] The principles of demarcation, therefore, closely resemble those principles applied to determine aboriginal title claims in Canada, although in the *Maya* decision only the indigenous perspective was relevant.

3   Summary

The inquiry embarked upon by the Inter-American Court and Commission is like that of an arbitral system that declares what the rights of the parties ought to be according to the justice and circumstances of the individual case and thus resonates with the comments made by McHugh J in *Western Australia v Ward*. The decisions are sympathetic to the experience and specific needs of the Awas Tingni and Maya communities and thus reject strict rules of continuity. While the *Awas Tingni* decision contains some ambiguous directions about the manner in which demarcation should proceed, the *Maya* decision indicates that lands should not be demarcated on the basis of specific customary laws only, but rather on the basis of the Maya community's traditional occupation of lands. The general principle in these decisions will no doubt apply to similar cases throughout the Americas and should provide guidance to all states subject to indigenous peoples' claims to traditional lands. In addition, the approach of the Inter-American Commission and Court to these evidential questions may serve as a guide to other human rights treaty bodies that are required to address similar complaints in relation to indigenous peoples' traditional lands.

---

81. In 2005, the Inter-American Court of Human Rights reached similar conclusions in relation to a claim from the N'djuka community to traditional lands from which they were expelled by force. The traditional lands claimed included their village sites and traditional hunting, farming, and fishing territory, which extended for tens of kilometres into the forest outside of these villages. The Court ruled that 'their traditional occupancy of Moiwana Village and its surrounding lands – which has been recognized and respected by neighboring N'djuka clans and indigenous communities over the years – should suffice to obtain State recognition of their ownership.' See *Moiwana Village v. Suriname* (June 15, 2005) Inter-Am Court H R (ser. C) No 125, para 133.

B ICERD AND THE ICERD COMMITTEE

The ICERD Committee, the treaty body tasked with monitoring compliance with the ICERD, has also issued important statements and decisions in relation to indigenous peoples' traditional lands, especially in the last decade. ICERD's focus, as its name suggests, is on the abolition of all forms of racial discrimination. The ICERD, like the other UN human rights treaties, is directed at the protection of individual rights, although it is clear that the ICERD Committee considers that the ICERD protects indigenous peoples and their collective rights. The ICERD Committee, in a special statement on indigenous peoples issued in 1997, emphasised that the situation of indigenous peoples has always been a matter of close attention and concern, especially in its examination of state reports. The ICERD Committee noted that in many regions of the world indigenous peoples have been, and are still being, discriminated against, especially with regard to the loss of their traditional lands, and that it is therefore vital that states recognise and respect indigenous peoples' distinct culture and identity. On the subject of traditional lands, the special statement requests states to 'recognise and protect the rights of indigenous peoples to own, develop, control and use their communal lands, territories and resources and, where they have been deprived of their lands and territories traditionally owned or otherwise inhabited or used without their free and informed consent, to take steps to return those lands and territories.'[82]

More specifically, the ICERD expressly prohibits discrimination in relation to the right to own property alone as well as in association with others.[83] The ICERD Committee's resolve to assist indigenous peoples has been illustrated in relation to land disputes that have arisen recently in Australia and New Zealand. In each case, the ICERD Committee has, through its early warning procedure, been required to assess the fairness of statutory codes established by states to recognise indigenous land rights and, in particular, whether those codes were discriminatory.

The ICERD Committee first considered Australia's statutory code, the Native Title Act 1993 (NTA), in 1994 when examining Australia's periodic state report to the Committee. Initially, the NTA's focus on defining native title rights with reference to custom law received little attention. The negative effect of that approach would not be fully appreciated for another ten years as appeals worked their way through to the High Court. However, the ICERD Committee did express its concern with the NTA's necessity for claimants to prove that they have maintained their connection with the land and that their

---

82. UN Committee on the Elimination of Racial Discrimination, *General Recommendation No. 23: Indigenous Peoples*, Annex V, U.N. Doc. A/52/18/Annex (18 August 1997).
83. ICERD, above n 3, art 5(e)(iv).

title has not been extinguished.[84]

The ICERD Committee invoked its early warning procedure in relation to Australia in 1998 (the NTA decision). The inquiry was focussed on the legislative amendments to the NTA, which rendered native title more susceptible to legal extinguishment where native title rights conflicted with non-indigenous rights. The ICERD Committee's decision, as is typical of the ICERD Committee's early warning comments, was very brief but addressed the core issue of extinguishment raised by the amendments. The ICERD Committee noted that 'while the original Native Title Act recognises and seeks to protect indigenous title, provisions that extinguish or impair the exercise of indigenous title rights and interests pervade the amended Act ... [The amended NTA] appeared to create legal certainty for governments and third parties at the expense of indigenous titles.'[85]

The ICERD Committee then requested that Australia address these concerns as a matter of utmost urgency. It urged that the 1998 amendments be suspended and discussions be reopened with aboriginal representatives with a view to finding solutions acceptable to the indigenous peoples and consistent with ICERD. Australia's response was to reject the ICERD Committee's advice. But the ICERD Committee, primarily through its state-reporting process, has continued to apply pressure on Australia.[86]

In relation to New Zealand's early warning hearing before the ICERD Committee, the arguments made by tribes focussed directly on the discriminatory effect of the FSA (the FSA decision).[87] One of the central arguments made by Māori tribes was that, while the FSA allowed tribes to claim customary interests in the foreshore – that is, through CROs and TCROs – the tests for establishing CROs and TCROs were an inelegant amalgam of the worst aspects of the tests applied in Canadian aboriginal rights and Australian native title law.[88] The question of evidential criteria was raised and argued in detailed written and oral submissions by both New Zealand and tribal advocates. However, in its decision, the ICERD Committee did not comment directly upon the FSA's evidential standards. Rather, the ICERD Committee expressed its concern 'at the apparent haste with which the

---

84. UN Committee on the Elimination of Racial Discrimination 'Concluding observations on Australia' (19 September 1994) CERD A/49/18, para 544.
85. See UN Committee on the Elimination of Racial Discrimination 'Decision 2(54) on Australia' (18 March 1999) CERD A/54/18.
86. UN Committee on the Elimination of Racial Discrimination, 'Concluding Observations of the Committee on the Elimination of Racial Discrimination: Australia' (March 2005) CERD/C/AUS/10/15, para 16.
87. See the discussion in A Erueti and C Charters, 'Report From The Inside: The CERD Committee's Review of the Foreshore and Seabed Act 2004', above n 59.
88. See the chapters in this book by Shaunnagh Dorsett (59–82) and Kent McNeil (83–118).

legislation was enacted'[89] and noted that 'insufficient consideration may have been given to alternative responses to the *Ngati Apa* decision, which might have accommodated Māori rights within a framework more acceptable to both the Māori and all other New Zealanders.'[90] In terms of discrimination, the ICERD Committee honed in on the most obnoxious aspect of the FSA, that is, the removal of the right of Māori to claim a customary title in the foreshore and the failure to provide a guaranteed right of redress for the non-recognition of TCROs. The ICERD Committee then recommended that 'the New Zealand Government enter into a dialogue with Māori to seek ways of mitigating the FSA's discriminatory effects, including through legislative amendment, where necessary.'[91] New Zealand rejected the decision of the ICERD Committee, describing the Committee as a body at the 'outer edges of the UN system.'

The ICERD Committee, then, has played an important function in promoting indigenous peoples' rights. In particular, it has sent a clear signal to states that it is prepared to invoke the early warning procedure when it considers indigenous peoples' land rights are being diminished. If it finds evidence of discrimination, the ICERD Committee has effectively sent states back to the drawing board to discuss with indigenous peoples rules for recognition that are fair and comply with principles of equality. While New Zealand and Australia have largely dismissed the ICERD Committee's decisions, the decisions have focussed international attention on the issues and prompted vigorous discussion within those states on the discriminatory effect of the NTA and the FSA. Moreover, the ICERD Committee will continue to apply pressure on both states through the reporting process. In relation to the FSA decision, it is unfortunate that the ICERD Committee did not comment in more detail on the evidential standards in the FSA. The ICERD Committee may have hoped that those matters would be addressed through the dialogue it suggested between Māori and the New Zealand Government, although it also appears that the ICERD Committee's broad findings and recommendations reflect a reluctance to intervene too closely in domestic affairs. In addition, the urgent nature of the procedure leaves the ICERD Committee with little time to offer more detailed and reasoned decisions. There remains, however, the potential for the ICERD Committee to offer more detailed comment on evidential matters, as the ICERD Committee continues to monitor New Zealand's conduct through its state-reporting process.

---

89. UN Committee on the Elimination of All Forms of Racial Discrimination 'Decision 1(66): New Zealand Foreshore and Seabed Act 2004' (11 March 2005) CERD/C/66/NZL/Dec.1.
90. 'Decision 1(66): New Zealand Foreshore and Seabed Act 2004', above n 89.
91. Interview with Rt Hon Helen Clark, Prime Minister (John Dunne, Breakfast Show TRN 3ZB, 14 March 2005). Transcript provided by Newztel News Agency Ltd (Wellington).

C   The ICCPR and the Human Rights Committee

The Human Rights Committee (HRC) is the treaty body charged with monitoring state compliance with the ICCPR. The HRC examines reports from states which have ratified the ICCPR and may hear communications, once domestic remedies have been exhausted, from individuals in states which have also ratified the first Optional Protocol to the ICCPR.

The HRC has proven to be amenable to the unique communications received from indigenous peoples despite the fact that the ICCPR is focused on the protection of individual rights. For example, in *Hopu and Bessert v France*, the petitioners sought to invoke articles 17 and 23 of the ICCPR – which require states to protect the right to family – to prevent the development of lands that contained the remains of their ancestors.[92] While the petitioners could not establish a direct kinship link with these ancestors, the HRC accepted that their relationship was sufficient to constitute a family relationship. The HRC observed that 'the objectives of the Covenant require that the term "family" be given a broad interpretation so as to include all those comprising the family as understood in the society in question.'[93]

Many of the HRC's decisions on indigenous peoples relate to communications in relation to article 27 of the ICCPR – which affirms the right of individual members of minorities to enjoy their right to culture. Individual members of indigenous communities have invoked this provision in communications to the HRC to protect their right to membership of a traditional tribe,[94] and to engage in specific traditional activities.[95] However, to date there has been no communication addressed by the HRC that relates simply to claims to indigenous peoples' traditional lands. That is no doubt influenced by the absence of a right to property guarantee in the ICCPR and the apparent limited scope of article 27. The language of article 27 would, on its face, appear to be limited to protecting rights to engage in traditional activities (like hunting, fishing and religious practices)[96] and to only encompass broader claims to traditional lands obliquely in those cases where traditional land was considered central to the conduct of particular activities.[97]

---

92. *Hopu and Bessert v France* (29 July 1997) Comm No 549/1993 CCPR/C/60/D/549/1993.
93. *Hopu and Bessert v France*, above n 92, para 10.3.
94. *Sandra Lovelace v Canada* (30 July 1981) Comm No 24/1977 CCPR/C/OP/1 37 (1984).
95. See *Apirana Mahuika et al v New Zealand* (15 November 2000) Comm No 547/1993 CCPR/C/70/D/547/1993; Office of the Commissioner for Human Rights 'Report of the Human Rights Committee' (7 November 2001) A/56/40 Vol II.
96. It is clear, however, that a traditional activity can be practised in a modern form and that there is a right to development attached to the right. For example, see *Apirana Mahuika et al v New Zealand* (15 November 2000) above n 95, where it was accepted that the cultural right of Māori to traditional fisheries could be manifested in Māori participation in a modern commercial fishing operation.
97. See, for example, *Bernard Ominayak, Chief of the Lubicon Lake Band v Canada* (10 May 1990) Comm No 167/1984 CCPR/C/38/D/167/1984; Office of the Commissioner for Human Rights 'Report

However, the HRC, in comments on state reports, has indicated that article 27 may encompass broader territorial rights to traditional lands. In response to Canada's state report, the HRC cited article 27 and expressed its concern at the state's practice of extinguishing aboriginal title in modern treaties.[98] In addition, through the state-reporting process, the HRC has joined the ICERD Committee in criticising Australia in relation to the 1998 NTA amendments, citing article 27 and calling upon Australia to amend the NTA and restore and protect indigenous titles.[99]

D   THE STANDARDS SET BY INDIGENOUS-SPECIFIC INTERNATIONAL INSTRUMENTS

This chapter now turns to consider the standards for proving indigenous property rights contained in the international instruments that are directed solely at indigenous peoples and their rights. They are the ILO Convention on Indigenous and Tribal Peoples, No. 169 of 1989 (Convention No. 169),[100] and the United Nations Declaration on the Rights of Indigenous Peoples (UN Declaration).[101]

1   *The ILO Convention on Indigenous and Tribal Peoples, No. 169 of 1989*

The Convention No. 169 represents for now the most binding international instrument for the protection of the rights of indigenous peoples and tribal peoples, and it has served as an important point of reference in the formulation of the rights contained in the UN Declaration.[102] The central significance of traditional lands to indigenous peoples is emphasised by article 13(1) of Convention No. 169, which states:

> In applying the provisions of this Part of the Convention governments shall respect the special importance for the cultures and spiritual values of the peoples

---

of the Human Rights Committee' (1990) A/45/40 Vol II, in which the HRC found that 'the failure to assure to the Lubicon Lake Band a reservation to which it had a strong claim and the effect on the Band of certain recent developments including oil and timber concessions threaten the way of life and culture of the Lubicon Lake Band, and constitute a violation of article 27 so long as they continue.'

98. UN Human Rights Committee 'Concluding observations of the Human Rights Committee: Canada' (2 November 2005) CCPR/C/CAN/CO/5.
99. UN Human Rights Committee 'Concluding observations of the Human Rights Committee: Australia' (24 July 2000) A/55/40, paras 498–528.
100. Convention No. 169, above n 4. Convention No. 169 is a partial revision of the Convention concerning the Protection and Integration of Indigenous Populations and Other Tribal and Semi-Tribal Populations in the Independent Countries (2 June 1959) 107 ILO 1957 (ILO Convention No. 107). ILO Convention No. 107 contained strong protections for indigenous lands but was widely criticised as pursuing assimilationist goals.
101. UN Declaration, above n 5.
102. See also the Proposed American Declaration on the Rights of Indigenous Peoples, above n 9.

concerned of their relationship with the lands or territories, or both as applicable, which they occupy or otherwise use, and in particular the collective aspects of this relationship.

Article 14 provides for the legal recognition of traditional lands and the creation of mechanisms to address claims of dispossession:

1. The rights of ownership and possession of the peoples concerned over the lands, which they traditionally occupy shall be recognised. In addition, measures shall be taken in appropriate cases to safeguard the right of the peoples concerned to use lands not exclusively occupied by them, but to which they have traditionally had access for their subsistence and traditional activities. Particular attention shall be paid to the situation of nomadic peoples and shifting cultivators in this respect.
2. Governments shall take steps as necessary to identify the lands, which the peoples concerned traditionally occupy, and to guarantee effective protection of their rights of ownership and possession.
3. Adequate procedures shall be established within the national legal system to resolve land claims by the peoples concerned.

Article 14(2) requires states to establish mechanisms that will identify indigenous peoples' rights to their traditional lands. In terms of evidential standards, article 14 directs states to identify and recognise rights of ownership in lands that are currently occupied by indigenous peoples. That is, it would appear to be directed to those cases, like the *Maya* and *Awas Tingni* decisions, where indigenous peoples inhabit lands and have done so for long continuous periods, yet have not received legal recognition of their land rights from the state. There is no suggestion in article 14 that indigenous peoples must have continuously occupied the land in question from pre-colonial times.

Article 14(1) indicates that the occupation of traditional lands must be exclusive. It draws a distinction between traditional lands and lands not occupied exclusively yet used for traditional purposes. However, the reference to 'traditionally occupy' would clearly suggest that the factual inquiry into whether there is occupation, and exclusive occupation, must consider the traditional land-tenure practices of the community concerned. In my view, in light of the principle established in the *Maya* decision, that would require states to determine occupation and exclusivity from the perspective of indigenous peoples themselves with reference to their land-tenure practices and their customary laws and spiritual and sociopolitical attachment to the lands. This will prove especially important to those indigenous communities who occupy certain lands on a seasonal or cyclical basis.[103]

Article 14's focus on present occupation of lands might appear to rule out claims for the legal recognition of traditional lands lost because of forced removal, confiscation or other state action. And article 14(3) requires states to implement procedures to resolve claims of dispossession. However, Anaya has argued that Convention No. 169's reference to the cultural and spiritual importance of traditional lands to indigenous peoples in article 13(1) of the Convention would suggest that 'a sufficient present connection with lost lands may be established by a continuing cultural attachment to them, particularly if dispossession occurred recently.'[104] Anaya also notes that in cases of dispossession, indigenous peoples may rely upon the remedial provisions in article 14(3) of the ILO Convention No. 169, which requires states to create adequate procedures to resolve land claims by the peoples concerned.[105] Anaya notes that there is no temporal limitation imposed by this provision, meaning that it extends to historical forms of dispossession.[106] For the purposes of assessing restitution or compensation in relation to historical forms of dispossession, the extent of territory lost – in terms of the lands once traditionally occupied – ought to be determined from the perspective of the affected indigenous community.[107]

While the Convention No. 169 contains significant protections for indigenous peoples, only eighteen states have ratified it.[108] Indigenous peoples, it must be said, have not swung behind Convention No. 169, in large part because of the lack of meaningful input by indigenous peoples into its design and the fact that it lacks a strong statement on an indigenous right to self-determination.[109]

---

103. Article 14(1) indicates that in other areas, where indigenous peoples' interests intersect with the interests of other indigenous communities or non-indigenous interests (for example National Parks owned by the State and arguably private lands), indigenous peoples are guaranteed a right of access for the purpose of subsistence and traditional activities.
104. S J Anaya, above n 6, 144.
105. S J Anaya, above n 6, at 144.
106. S J Anaya, above n 6, at 144.
107. See ILO Convention 169, above n 4, art. 16. Similarly, the ILO Convention No. 169 addresses state endeavors to relocate indigenous communities. Where (in 'exceptional cases and under prescribed conditions') indigenous peoples are to be relocated from their lands, article 16 of the ILO Convention No. 169 provides indigenous peoples with the right to return to those lands as soon as the grounds for relocation cease to exist. Above n 4, art 16. Where the lands are unable to be returned to indigenous peoples, they are entitled to new lands of 'quality and legal status at least equal to that of the lands previously occupied by them' or, if they so decide, compensation. Above n 4, art 16(4). In addition, the reference to 'relocation' instead of removal implies that where indigenous peoples are relocated they must be given new lands. For the purposes of assessing compensation or the provision of new lands, the extent of territory lost, in relation to lands traditionally occupied, should be determined from the perspective of the affected indigenous community.
108. The states that have ratified ILO Convention 169 include: Argentina, Bolivia, Brazil, Colombia, Costa Rica, Denmark, Dominica, Ecuador, Fiji, Guatemala, Honduras, Mexico, Netherlands, Norway, Paraguay, Peru, Spain and Venezuela. ILO Convention 169, above n 4.
109. S J Anaya, above n 6, 58–59.

That is unfortunate since for now, Convention No. 169 is the only formally enforceable indigenous-specific instrument – it is a treaty and not merely a declaration of rights – and as noted it contains strong guarantees in relation to indigenous peoples' traditional lands. Additionally, Convention No. 169 contains complaint mechanisms, which means that indigenous peoples have access to an independent arbiter to evaluate state practice and compliance with Convention No. 169.

2 United Nations Declaration on the Rights of Indigenous Peoples

The most significant instrument in relation to indigenous peoples' rights (including land rights) is the UN Declaration, drafted with considerable input from indigenous peoples and intended as a declaration of universal application in all states once it is adopted by the UN General Assembly.[110] The UN Declaration is the most progressive and comprehensive instrument dealing with indigenous rights. While technically not legally binding on states, it requires that 'states in consultation and cooperation with indigenous peoples ... take the appropriate measures, including legislative measures, to achieve the ends of the Declaration.'[111] The original version of the UN Declaration was promulgated by the UN Working Group on Indigenous Populations in 1993, after almost a decade of discussions in which both states and indigenous peoples from throughout the world participated. That original version was then submitted to a further UN Working Group for elaboration and again, both states and representatives of indigenous peoples participated in vigorous discussions on the specific wording and policy underpinning the rights in the Declaration. The final version was adopted by the UN Human Rights Council at its first meeting in June 2006.[112]

Article 25 of the UN Declaration emphasises the intergenerational and spiritual dimensions of indigenous land ownership:[113]

> Indigenous peoples have the right to maintain and strengthen their distinctive spiritual relationship with their traditionally owned or otherwise occupied and used lands, territories, waters and coastal seas and other resources and to uphold their responsibilities to future generations in this regard.

Article 26 of the UN Declaration addresses indigenous peoples' rights in their traditional lands:[114]

> 1. Indigenous peoples have the right to the lands, territories and resources which

---

110. UN Declaration, above n 5, at preamble.
111. UN Declaration, above n 5, art 38.
112. See UN Declaration, above n 5.
113. See UN Declaration, above n 5.
114. See UN Declaration, above n 5.

they have traditionally owned, occupied or otherwise used or acquired.
2. Indigenous peoples have the right to own, use, develop and control the lands, territories and resources that they possess by reason of traditional ownership or other traditional occupation or use, as well as those which they have otherwise acquired.
3. States shall give legal recognition and protection to these lands, territories and resources. Such recognition shall be conducted with due respect to the customs, traditions and land tenure systems of the indigenous peoples concerned.
4. States shall establish and implement, in conjunction with indigenous peoples concerned, a fair, independent, impartial, open and transparent process, giving due recognition to indigenous peoples' laws, traditions, customs and land tenure systems, to recognize and adjudicate the rights of indigenous peoples pertaining to their lands, territories and resources, including those which were traditionally owned or otherwise occupied or used. Indigenous peoples shall have the right to participate in this process.

According to article 26, the right of ownership, use, development and control of traditional lands occurs in those cases mentioned in the second paragraph where indigenous peoples currently possess lands because of traditional ownership or other traditional occupation or use. That is, the evidential standard for recognising traditional lands is essentially the same as that provided for in article 14 of Convention No. 169 – the present possession of lands that are traditionally owned or occupied and used. As with article 14 of Convention No. 169, there is no suggestion that indigenous peoples must have occupied the land in question from pre-colonial times. Again the use of the adjective 'traditional' in 'traditional lands' suggests that the question of ownership, occupation and use is to be determined from the perspective of indigenous peoples (and that is explicitly confirmed by the third paragraph). Article 26 establishes detailed standards for the implementation of a transparent mechanism to give recognition to these rights. What is curious, though, is that article 26 also contains a right to lands traditionally owned and occupied (in paragraph one), and a right to pursue that through mechanisms established by the state (in paragraph four), but does not describe what that right might be. Presumably, it relates to a right to legal ownership of lands formerly occupied by indigenous peoples but that have not been 'confiscated, taken, occupied, used or damaged.'[115]

Again, the focus on the legal recognition of indigenous peoples' rights to lands currently occupied (as with article 14 of Convention No. 169) raises the question of the status of those lands that are not currently occupied by indigenous peoples. The argument raised by Anaya in relation to article 14 of

---

115. See UN Declaration, above n 5, art 28.

Convention No. 169 would extend to article 26 so that indigenous peoples, especially those dispossessed recently, could claim a sufficient present connection with lost lands through their continuing cultural attachment to them. This would be supported by the reference in article 25 of the UN Declaration to the spiritual importance of lands to indigenous peoples.[116]

In cases of clear dispossession of lands, however, article 28 addresses remedial measures for traditional lands that have been lost through confiscation, occupation or damage:[117]

1. Indigenous peoples have the right to redress, by means that can include restitution or, when this is not possible, of a just, fair and equitable compensation, for the lands, territories and resources which they have traditionally owned or otherwise occupied or used, and which have been confiscated, taken, occupied, used or damaged without their free, prior and informed consent.
2. Unless otherwise freely agreed upon by the peoples concerned, compensation shall take the form of lands, territories and resources equal in quality, size and legal status or of monetary compensation or other appropriate redress.

In those cases where indigenous peoples have been deprived of their lands, whether this occurred recently or many years ago, indigenous peoples are entitled to redress. This may involve the return of the lands actually taken (i.e., restitution) or other lands equal in quality, size, and legal status to those taken. Like the ILO Convention No. 169, it is clear that for the purposes of assessing redress, the extent of territory lost must be determined from the perspective of the affected indigenous community. This is clear because redress is provided for the loss of those 'lands, territories and resources which they have traditionally owned or otherwise occupied or used.'[118]

IV *Conclusion*

In conclusion, indigenous peoples around the globe struggle to acquire meaningful rights in their traditional lands. In the common law jurisdictions, over the last ten years especially, domestic courts have developed strict legal criteria for the determination of land rights. In many cases, courts define land rights with reference to indigenous peoples' custom laws only and they

---

116. See UN Declaration, above n 5, art 25.
117. See UN Declaration, above n 5, art 28.
118. See UN Declaration, above n 5, art 28(1). In addition, the UN Declaration strictly prohibits relocation of indigenous peoples from their lands without their 'free, prior and informed consent' and only 'after agreement on fair and just compensation ... with the option of return.' Above n 5, art 10. In these cases too, the extent of territory lost (those lands traditionally occupied) for the purposes of compensation would need to be assessed from the perspective of indigenous peoples.

require evidence of a continuing association with traditional lands from pre-colonial times. Additionally, courts may penalise indigenous peoples for their normative differences by subjecting them to common law standards of occupation and exclusivity. These present significant evidential barriers to rights recognition. Indigenous peoples in Central-American states have also faced similar evidential problems in their efforts to obtain official recognition of their rights to land.

International and regional human rights treaty bodies may serve an important function in monitoring state endeavours to recognise indigenous lands. The *Maya* and *Awas Tingni* decisions, in particular, demonstrate how treaty bodies may prompt states to adopt less-restrictive approaches to recognising indigenous peoples' land rights. The decisions have recognised indigenous land rights in situations where indigenous peoples have occupied and used their lands for a long duration (but not necessarily since pre-colonial times). On the subject of demarcation the *Maya* decision, while treating custom law as a juridical basis of indigenous peoples' property rights, did not direct Belize to define the nature and extent of Maya property rights solely with reference to their customary laws. Rather, the physical fact of occupation and use of the land provides the factual standard. In addition, the decision indicates that occupation and use must be determined from the perspective of the Maya community and not from state conceptions of what amounts to occupation. The indigenous perspective may include accounts of customary law, but it is clearly not limited to that.

The *Awas Tingni* and *Maya* decisions will also be of value for the interpretation of the indigenous land rights provisions in the Convention No. 169 and the UN Declaration. Both instruments contain articles emphasising the importance of lands to indigenous peoples and requiring states to give formal recognition to traditional lands. Both the Convention No. 169 and the UN Declaration direct states to grant indigenous peoples ownership of their lands on the basis of their current traditional occupation and use of lands. The reference in both instruments to *traditional* occupation indicates, consistently with the *Maya* and *Awas Tingni* decisions, that the determination of matters such as occupation, use and exclusivity is to be determined in accordance with the relevant indigenous peoples' perspective. Also, neither instrument expressly requires indigenous peoples to establish evidence of continuous, exclusive occupation of the lands since pre-colonial times. Furthermore, both instruments provide for redress for the loss of traditional lands.

More generally, the *Awas Tingni* and *Maya* decisions and the standards set by the Convention No. 169 and UN Declaration add weight to the idea of searching for alternative models to domestic common law based aboriginal rights litigation - models that adopt a more merit-based approach to recognising indigenous peoples' traditional lands.

The ICERD Committee has handed down important decisions criticising legislative mechanisms in New Zealand and Australia for recognising land rights. The NTA and FSA decisions stress the inequality present in those mechanisms, favouring non-indigenous property rights over the property rights of indigenous peoples. The early warning procedure has provided New Zealand and Australian indigenous peoples with prompt access to the ICERD Committee, and the decisions have called upon the states to re-enter discussions with indigenous peoples to establish procedures that recognise indigenous land rights on fair terms.

The Human Rights Committee has upheld complaints from indigenous peoples relating to their right to enjoy traditional activities under the article 27 'right to culture' provision, and has questioned various states about their approach to land rights recognition through its state-reporting process. But to date there has been no communication and decision from the Committee directly addressing indigenous claims to traditional lands. It would seem that the lack of a guarantee of property rights and the apparent limited scope of the 'right to culture' guarantee would account for this.

The decisions from the Inter-American Court and Commission and ICERD Committee especially demonstrate the importance of ensuring that indigenous peoples have effective access to treaty bodies through early warning and communication procedures so that they may have an independent arbiter, with expertise in human rights, to evaluate state practice and encourage states to adopt less rigid approaches to the recognition of indigenous rights. If domestically there is no, or little, political will to recognise indigenous peoples' rights then international treaty bodies might provide the impetus needed to shift domestic policy.

Contributors

RICHARD BOAST is an Associate Professor of Law at Victoria University of Wellington and currently teaches property law, legal history and energy and resources law. Richard also practises in the area of Māori and Treaty litigation and represents several iwi groups in inquiries currently being heard by the Waitangi Tribunal. He was lead counsel in the Waitangi Seabed and Foreshore Inquiry, and Counsel for Ngāti Toa in the Privy Council appeal from the Court of Appeal foreshore and seabed decision.

CLAIRE CHARTERS, Ngāti Whakaue, is a Senior Lecturer at Victoria University of Wellington specialising in indigenous peoples' rights in international law and in comparative jurisdictions. She is currently writing her PhD at the University of Cambridge.

DR SHAUNNAGH DORSETT is an Associate Professor at Victoria University of Wellington. She writes primarily at the intersection of aboriginal rights, legal history and property. Her recent work has been focused on the Foreshore and Seabed Act 2004, and she is currently examining regimes of customary ownership of foreshore and seabed in the South Pacific.

ANDREW ERUETI, Ngā Ruahinerangi/Ngāti Ruanui/Te Āti Haunui-a-Pāpārangi, is a Senior Lecturer at Victoria University of Wellington teaching, researching and writing on comparative indigenous peoples' rights, property law, Māori land law and Māori customary law. He is currently writing his SJD at the University of Toronto.

CATHERINE IORNS MAGALLANES is a Senior Lecturer at Victoria University of Wellington teaching, researching and writing on indigenous peoples' rights law (domestic, international and comparative), plus environmental law and statutory interpretation. She has published primarily on indigenous rights, her most cited piece being 'Indigenous Peoples and Self Determination: Challenging State Sovereignty' 24(2) CWRJIL 199.

KENT MCNEIL is a Professor at Osgoode Hall Law School in Toronto, where he has taught since 1987. He is the author of many works on the rights of indigenous peoples in Canada, Australia and the United States, including two books: *Common Law Aboriginal Title* (1989) and *Emerging Justice? Essays on Indigenous Rights in Canada and Australia* (2001). His work has been cited and relied upon in influential decisions on indigenous rights in Canada and Australia, most notably in *Delgamuukw v British Columbia* (Supreme Court of Canada 1997) and *Mabo v Queensland* (High Court of Australia, 1992).

DR DAVID V WILLIAMS has degrees in history, law and theology from Victoria University of Wellington and the University of Oxford, where he was a Rhodes Scholar. He was a full-time law teacher at the University of Dar es Salaam and the University of Auckland before taking up independent research and barristerial work specialising in legal history relevant to Treaty of Waitangi claims. In 2001 he returned to fulltime law teaching at the University of Auckland, and was promoted to Professor (personal chair) in 2005. In addition to many journal articles and book chapters, he produced the Maori Land Legislation Manual and authored *'Te Kooti tango whenua': The Native Land Court 1864–1909*. In 2001 the Waitangi Tribunal chose two of his research reports for publication: *Crown Policy Affecting Maori Knowledge Systems and Cultural Practices*, and *Matauranga Maori and Taonga*. He is joint editor and contributor to *Waitangi Revisited: Perspectives*.

Index

Ahipara 25
Alaska 66, 86n19
American Convention on Human Rights 175, 188, 189, 190n71
American Declaration of the Rights and Duties of Man (American Declaration) 175, 189, 190
August Policy 2, 3, 128–9
Awapuni Lagoon 24
Awas Tingni 190–3
Bay of Plenty Electric Power Board 163
Belize 190–2, 204
Blueberry River Indian Band 151
Brash, Don 5n14, 52–4, 130–1, 132
British Columbia 63, 180
CERD Committee *see* United Nations Committee on the Elimination of Racial Discrimination
Clark, Helen 117n152, 126, 196
Colonial Office 33, 34, 49
Couch, Ben 45
CRO *see* customary rights order
Crown Law Office 15–17, 20, 24, 28
Cullen, Michael 47, 56
customary rights order 3, 5, 29, 59, 74, 77–8, 92–3, 97, 103, 136–8, 141, 147, 159–60, 171, 172–3, 187, 195
December Policy 129–30, 131
Delaware Bay 128n43
Department of Conservation 120
Edward II 51
European Community 55
Fairford First Nation 152
FitzRoy, Governor 35
Fox–Vogel Government 14
Gitxsan 180
Golden Bay 123
Green Party 58n97, 132
Grey, Earl 34–36
Grey, George 34, 35
Haida Gwaii (Queen Charlotte Islands) 62, 63
Haida Nation 62, 170
Heiltsuk Nation 108–9
Hīkoi: of Hope 54; Māori Land March, 1975 54; ki Waitangi 54

Hobson, Governor 50, 53
Hohepa, P 33
Hokianga harbour 24
hui: fiscal envelope 1995 54; Hīrangi, 1995 54; national, at Tūrangawaewae 54
Human Rights Committee (HRC) 197–8, 205
ICERD *see* International Convention on the Elimination of All Forms of Racial Discrimination
Inter-American Commission on Human Rights (Inter- American Commission) 189–91, 192, 193
International Convention on the Elimination of All Forms of Racial Discrimination (ICERD) 96, 176, 178, 188, 194–5; CERD Committee 188, 194–6, 198, 205
International Covenant on Civil and Political Rights (ICCPR) 176, 188, 197
International Labour Organisation Convention 169 concerning Indigenous and Tribal Peoples in Independent Countries (ILO Convention No. 169) 176, 198–201, 202–3, 204
Kidd, Douglas 46
Labour Government 53, 54, 125
Lake Rotorua 16, 18, 40
Lake Taupō 16, 17, 18, 20
Lake Wairarapa 16
Land-protest occupations: Bastion Point/ Takaparawhau 54; Moutoa Gardens/ Pākaitore 54; Raglan/Whaingaroa 54
Lane, Barbara 108–9
Mackenzie, Alexander 108–9
Mahuta, Nanaia 143n2
Māori language petition to Parliament 54
Māori Party 2, 4, 52, 58n97
Marlborough District Council 123, 124, 125nn
Marlborough Sounds 43, 84, 117, 122, 123, 124, 125, 127, 128
mātaitai reserves 127n40, 128n43
Mayagna (Sumo) Indians 190
McLean, Donald 14
Meredith, Vincent 24, 25
Meriam people 95, 96
Mètis 88n30, 100, 114n138

Mi'kmaq Indians 111, 182–3
Minister of Conservation 130n55, 138, 141
Minister of Energy 163
Minister of Fisheries 122
Minister of Māori Affairs 45, 46, 81, 91, 130n55
Minister of Native Affairs (Native Minister) 14, 41
Miskito Indians 190
Napier lagoon *see* Te Whanganui-a-Orotū
National Government Cabinet 125
National Party 53n82, 54
New Brunswick 182
New Zealand Centre for Public Law 32
New Zealand Coastal Policy Statement 128, 134, 137, 173
New Zealand Māori Council 45, 166
New Zealand Parliament 3, 38, 39, 48, 54, 55, 56, 57, 59, 80, 96n58, 97, 116–17, 131, 160, 166n102, 168
Ngā Puhi 19
Ngāi Tahu 164, 167
Ngakororo mudflats 24
Ngata, Apirana 39, 41, 57
Ngāti Apa Ki Te Waipounamu Trust 124
Ngāti Awa 168
Ngāti Koata 128n43
Ngāti Porou 29
Ngāti Tama ki te Tau Ihu 123, 125n27, 128n43
Ngāti Toa 15, 37
Ngāti Tūwharetoa 20
Nicaragua 190, 192
Ninety-Mile Beach 28
Normanby Instructions 1839 34
Northern Territory 67, 70
Nova Scotia 111, 182
Organisation of American States (OAS) 175, 189, 191; OAS Inter-American Human Rights System 177, 189–93
Queen Charlotte Islands *see* Haida Gwaii
Radio New Zealand 166
Rama Indians 190
Rangitaiki River 163
Rotorua Electricity Authority 163
Rotorua lakes 16, 17, 20
Royal Instructions 1846 34, 35
Russell Instructions 1840 34
Salmond, John 16, 17, 18, 20, 24, 38, 39, 40, 45, 46, 57
Scottish Parliament 55
Sealord Marine Farms 124n22; Sealords settlement 46, 162–3, 168
taiāpure 127n40, 128n43
Tasman Bay 123
TCRO *see* territorial customary rights order
Te Arawa 40

Te Arawa Māori Trust Board 20
Te Ātiawa Manawhenua ki te Tau Ihu Trust 123
Te Aupouri 26
Te Aute College Old Boys' Association 41
Te Ika Whenua 163
Te Rarawa 25, 26
Te Whānau-a-Apanui 29
Te Whanganui-a-Orotū 23
territorial customary rights order 2–3, 29, 147, 159–60, 171–2, 187, 195-6
Tolmie, William 108–9
Torres Strait Islands 95
Totaranui Ltd 123
Treaty of Waitangi 19, 26, 27, 28, 39, 45, 50, 126, 146, 163, 165; breaches 3, 131, 143; Crown pre-emption and 13; compared with Australian situation 80, 160; consent authorities and 120; Don Brash and 5n14, 53–4; environmental principles and 6; impact on NZ legal culture 80; 'injudicious proceedings' 35; judicial review claims 165, 166, 167, 169; Native Land Court 19; partnership 119, 136, 141, 142; principles of 23, 42, 49, 120, 124n24, 130, 161, 162, 164–5, 166n102; rights 85, 86, 121, 147; as 'simple nullity 37
Tūhoe 168
Turia, Tariana 4, 52
United Kingdom Parliament 55
United Nations Committee on the Elimination of Racial Discrimination (CERD) 1, 1n3; 2n4; 3, 44, 95, 96, 97, 195nn, 196
United Nations Declaration on the Rights of Indigenous Peoples (UN Declaration) 176, 198, 201–3, 204
United Nations Human Rights Council 201
United Nations Special Rapporteur on the Situation of Human Rights and Fundamental Freedoms of Indigenous People 3
United States Congress 16, 156, 157
Waikato River 20n51, 22
Welsh Assembly 55
Western Australia, Government 59
Whanganui River 22, 27, 28, 30
Wheao River 163
Yorta Yorta 76, 104, 105, 109, 110
Young Maori Party 41